Romantic Weekend Getaways

Romantic Weekend Getaways

The Mid-Atlantic States

Larry Fox
Barbara Radin-Fox

WILEY

John Wiley & Sons, Inc.
New York • Chichester • Brisbane • Toronto • Singapore

Copyright © 1990 by Larry Fox and Barbara Radin-Fox

Published by John Wiley & Sons, Inc.

Library of Congress Cataloging-in-Publication Data

Fox, Larry, 1945–
    Romantic weekend getaways : the Mid-Atlantic / Larry Fox, Barbara Radin-Fox.
        p. cm.
    Includes bibliographical references.
    ISBN 0-471-50995-7
    1. Hotels, taverns, etc.—Middle Atlantic States—Guide-books.
    2. Middle Atlantic States—Description and travel—Guide-books.
    I. Radin-Fox, Barbara. II. Title.
    TX907.3.M53F68 1990
    647.947501—dc20   89-22682
                                                                    CIP

Printed in the United States of America

90 91 10 9 8 7 6 5 4 3 2 1

Dedicated to the ones we love,
especially Jonathan and Clayton,
and to everyone everywhere who is in love.

❦

Preface

❦ AWAY FOR THE WEEKEND

"Can you help us find a romantic place to go for the weekend?"

It is a simple question, one we are often asked. The answer, however, is more complicated. What makes a romantic weekend getaway for one couple may be a boring trek for another.

There are some elements common to any weekend of romance: a small, elegant inn or hotel; an intimate restaurant with superb food; interesting activities and beautiful settings that enhance warm feelings.

Romantic Weekend Getaways guides you on trips centered around specific themes—art, antiques, sports, big cities, wine, the bay and ocean, the grand resorts, the mountains, and retreats to nature. At the end of each chapter we list intimate inns, fine restaurants, annual festivals and helpful telephone numbers for the area.

The places we describe were selected because we found them exceptional in beauty, quality, location, or atmosphere. This means we have left out some familiar places—big hotels, unimaginative restaurants, ordinary museums—because they aren't romantic.

Our getaways are within the Mid-Atlantic, a region that covers all of Maryland, Virginia, Delaware, and the District of Columbia, and portions of North Carolina, Pennsylvania, New Jersey, and West Virginia. Most of the trips we outline are within a half-day's drive of the residents in this region.

Travelers will find the Mid-Atlantic rich in natural beauty, with magnificent mountains, mighty rivers, and glorious beaches providing a backdrop for the many attractive towns and cities in the region.

Before you go, though, here is some advice we hope you take along:

❦ Be flexible; don't plan every moment of a trip. Leave enough time for just relaxing with each other.

❦ Don't be afraid to explore inviting country lanes, even if you don't know where they lead. We have discovered some wonderful surprises—antique shops, local festivals, quaint towns, and beautiful scenery—when we got away from our planned route.

❦ Stay off the interstate highway system. It is fast, but it bypasses many interesting sights. The old U.S. routes will take you to your destination almost as quickly and, as a bonus, lead you to some small towns with their own treasures. Whenever possible, go through a small town rather than taking the bypass around it.

❦ Once upon a time inns were quaint, cheap alternatives to the standard chain motels. Today, inn prices are comparable to their better known competitors, but the inns offer atmosphere, elegance, and an opportunity to socialize with the innkeepers and other guests.

❦ Staying at an inn requires some compromises. Few inns have television, air conditioning, or huge, modern bathrooms. Always ask the innkeeper whether you have a private bath or must share. If you smoke, ask whether that is permitted.

❦ We have wasted a lot of time trying to find a "nice place to dance" on out-of-town trips. Except in a few instances, the local entertainment was not worth the time or effort. The places we do mention in this book, though, are very special and have live entertainment most weekends.

We sought to make this guide as current as possible, but realize that new inns and restaurants are opened every weekend. If you find an inn or restaurant that is exceptional, please write us in care of our publisher, John Wiley & Sons, 605 Third Ave., New York, NY 10158-0012.

The places we have selected for this book have warmed our hearts. Before you go, remember that romance is not a destination; it is that indefinable something that you have in your heart long before you begin to plan and pack for a trip. The trips offered here, however, can help both of you unlock that mystery and wonder.

LARRY FOX
BARBARA RADIN-FOX

Kensington, Maryland
January 1990

We gratefully thank Betty Ross for believing in us,
Roger Piantadosi for his constant encouragement,
and Rochelle Jaffe for helping us make a dream reality.

Contents

1 ❦ The Beauty of the Mid-Atlantic   1

Maryland   2

Frederick County   2

Pennsylvania   3

Delaware River Valley   3
Brandywine Valley   5
Amish Country   8

Virginia   10

The Hunt Country   10
Jefferson's Country   10
Young Washington's Hometown   12

North Carolina   13

Land of the Mountains   13

For More Information 14

Important Times and Numbers 15
Annual Events 17

Inns and Restaurants 19

Maryland 19
Pennsylvania and Delaware 21
Virginia 27
North Carolina 31

2 ❦ The Magnificent Bay 33

Annapolis 34

Chestertown, Maryland 36

St. Michaels, Maryland 37

Oxford, Maryland 39

Easton, Maryland 40

Taking the Tour 41

Sailing Schools 41
Cruise Lines 41
Annapolis Festivals 42
Tours 42
Museums 42
Useful Numbers 43

Inns and Restaurants 43

Annapolis 43
Chestertown, Maryland 46
St. Michaels, Maryland 48
Oxford, Maryland 49
Easton, Maryland 49

3 🐛 *The Atlantic Shore*   51

Cape May, New Jersey   52

Rehoboth Beach, Delaware   54

Chincoteague, Virginia   55

The Outer Banks, North Carolina   57

Useful Numbers   59

Festivals   59

Museums   60

Parks   61

Inns and Restaurants   61

Cape May, New Jersey   62
Rehoboth Beach, Delaware   65
Chincoteague, Virginia   67
The Outer Banks, North Carolina   68

4 🐛 *Murder, Music, and More*   71

Murder, Anyone?   72

Victoriana   75

Christmas   77

Drama   78

Health and Fitness   78

Gardens   79

Sports   80

On the Water   82

Food and Wine   83

Music   84

Arts, Crafts, and Antiques   85

History 86

Inn-Keeping 87

Miscellaneous 87

The Resorts 88

5 ❦ **The Grand Resorts** 89

The Top Three 90

The Greenbrier 90
The Homestead 92
The Williamsburg Inn 95

A Half-Dozen Delights 96

The Boar's Head Inn 97
Grove Park Inn 97
Hotel Hershey 98
Hidden Valley 99
The Tides Inn 100
Wintergreen 101
How We Rate Them 103

6 ❦ **Wine Country** 104

Virginia 105

Maryland 108

Pennsylvania 109

Taking the Tour 110

Virginia 111
Maryland 111
Pennsylvania 112

Inns and Restaurants 112

Virginia 112
Maryland 115
Pennsylvania 117

7 ❦ *A Tale of Four Cities* 121

Baltimore 122

Philadelphia 124

Richmond 127

Washington, DC 130

For More Information 135

Important Times and Numbers 135
Annual Events 138

Hotels and Restaurants 139

Baltimore 140
Philadelphia 141
Richmond 143
Washington, DC 144

8 ❦ *A Change of Pace* 148

The Colonial Life 148

Taking the Tour 154
Inns and Restaurants 155
Sidetrip 158

Peaceful Island 158

Getting There 159
Inns and Restaurants 159

An Old Fashioned Fourth 159

Inns and Restaurants 161

Back on the Farm 161

Maryland 162
Pennsylvania 162
Virginia 164
West Virginia 166

9 ❦ Mountain Manors 167

Grove Park Inn 167
Hound Ears Club 168
Mountain Lake Hotel 169
Wintergreen 170

Mountain Inns and Restaurants 171

Maryland 172
North Carolina 173
Pennsylvania 174
Virginia 177
West Virginia 181

10 ❦ Adventure and Sports 183

Ballooning 184

Hang Gliding 185

Soaring 185

Rafting 186

Canoeing and Kayaking 187

Horseback Riding 188

Sailing 188

Golf and Tennis Resorts   189

Skiing   190

11 ❦ A Wealth of Festivals   191

Delaware   191

Maryland   192

New Jersey   194

North Carolina   195

Pennsylvania   195

Virginia   197

Washington, DC   199

West Virginia   199

12 ❦ Travel Tips   201

Index   205

Romantic Weekend Getaways

Chapter One

The Beauty of the Mid-Atlantic

The stage is set for romance: gentle mountains, quaint villages, historic inns, grand resorts, intimate restaurants, lavish mansions, colorful gardens, eclectic antique shops, and museums filled with incredible masterpieces.

Only the two of you are missing.

The attractions in the Mid-Atlantic region seem endless, a bountiful feast for the eye as well as the heart. For couples seeking a weekend full of beauty, there are eight areas where the works of man compete with the wonders of nature.

Bucks County, for one, mixes antiques, art, and museums with 200-year-old homes, covered bridges, and a picturesque canal perfect for leisurely strolls. The Brandywine Valley of Delaware and Pennsylvania, for a second, celebrates the works of two dynasties—the Du Ponts and the Wyeths—amid an abundance of natural beauty. Other areas in Maryland, Virginia, and North Carolina feature the works of the past while showcasing the attractions of the present.

In this chapter we will guide you through these areas, telling you about the museums, gardens, antique shops, arts and crafts galleries, scenic views, and other beautiful sights. At the end of this chapter, as in all the chapters in this book, we list the important telephone numbers you need, the best of the annual festivals, and our favorite inns and restaurants.

❦ MARYLAND

Frederick County

Frederick is a gem of a town in the foothills of central Maryland. Founded in 1745, it has a history that predates this nation. Frederick's citizens repudiated the infamous Stamp Act eight years before the tax rebellion in Boston got all the headlines. During the Civil War, residents raised a $200,000 ransom to keep Confederate General Jubal Early from torching the town. The payoff was both immediate and long-reaching. The town was saved, and today numerous eighteenth- and nineteenth-century homes line its tree-shaded streets.

The **Visitor Information Center** (19 Church St.) offers free maps and brochures and, for a small fee, guides who take you on walking tours of the historic district.

The historic homes open for tours include the **Barbara Fritchie House** (154 West Patrick St.), the two-centuries-old home of the Civil War heroine immortalized in Whittier's poem; the federal mansion and formal gardens that are the home of the **Historic Society of Frederick** (24 East Church St.); and the oldest building in town, the **Schifferstadt Architectural Museum** (1110 Rosemont Ave.), a German farmhouse built in 1756. All the homes are open for tours on weekends and most weekdays.

With all this history, it isn't surprising that Frederick is also a center of crafts and antiques. The **Frederick Crafts Fair** draws more than 500 artisans to its show every May, while the antique sales go on year-round in town and in nearby villages.

In town, the All Saints Antiques Arcade (41 East All Saints St.) and Warehouse Antiques (47 East All Saints St.) offer nineteenth- and twentieth-century antiques, including some unusual collectibles. Around the corner, Cannon Hill Place (111 South Carroll St.) houses thirty dealers offering a variety of antiques in two buildings, one of which is a stone granary that dates back to the Revolutionary War era.

Two larger antique centers are the Antiques Emporium at Creekside (112 East Patrick St.), with 80 dealers, and the Antique Station (194 Thomas Johnson Dr.), with scores of vendors.

Everedy Square and **Shab Row**, two renovated industrial buildings, have shops featuring fine clothes, gifts, toys, and crafts.

These shops and the antique centers are open weekends and most weekdays.

Three day-trips offer even more antiques. **New Market**, a quaint village west of Frederick, has more than forty shops. Take I-70 west from Frederick to Route 75 north, then follow signs to town. The shops are on the only main road in town, and are usually open only on weekends. **Emmitsburg**, twenty minutes north on U.S. 15, has more than 100 dealers selling a variety of antiques at the Emmitsburg Antique Mall (1 Chesapeake Ave.).

In **Brunswick**, a small town on the Potomac River, the Brunswick Museum (40 West Potomac Street) displays antique furnishings, memorabilia and model trains. The Brunswick Antique Mall and Gunther's Auction Gallery (both at 24 South Virginia Ave.) showcase numerous antiques. Auctions are held at Gunther's most Sundays and major holidays. Take Route 340 west to the Route 17 exit to Brunswick.

If these man-made works need tempering with the beauty of nature, head for the mountains. **Catoctin Mountain Park** and **Cunningham Falls State Park**, 15 miles north on U.S. 15, have waterfalls, a lake for swimming, and shaded glades. The mountain scenery is splendid enough to attract presidents, who have been coming to Camp David, the presidential retreat here, since the days of FDR.

The best scenic view is at **Sugar Loaf Mountain**. Take I-270 south to the Route 109 exit and drive to the mountain, a massive rounded peak that juts up from the valley floor. A road to the top offers some stunning views of the surrounding countryside.

Finally, don't miss the three lovely **covered bridges** in Frederick County. They are hard to find, but the Visitor Information Center has maps that will guide you.

🍎 PENNSYLVANIA

Delaware River Valley

Bucks County north of Philadelphia mixes wonderful antiques and art with elegant inns, stunning restaurants and the natural beauty of the rugged Delaware River Valley.

The center of attractions in this county is **New Hope**, a lively town on the banks of the Delaware River just north of where George Washington and his Colonial forces crossed the river on Christmas night and defeated the Hessians encamped at Trenton.

New Hope is a mecca for day-trippers, a situation that often leads to parking problems on weekends when the weather is good. The best way to find a parking place is to drive west of Route 32, across the lovely canal that flows through town, and then park and walk back to Route 32, the main shopping area.

The streets of New Hope are lined with boutiques selling everything from antiques to art, from avant garde accessories to vintage clothing more costly than some new designer dresses.

Antique-lovers should try Three Cranes Gallery (18 Mechanic St.) for antiques, original art, and wearable art for both men and women. Europine II (186 Old York Rd.) showcases country pine antiques from England and Scotland; David M. Mancuso Antiques (Route 202 and Upper Mountain Rd.) features country antiques and folk art. Katy Kane, Inc. (34 West Ferry St.) displays stunning (and expensive) antique clothing and fine linens.

Arts and crafts fans will like A. Mano (128 South Main St.), where kaleidoscopes, rugs, willow furniture, and other artworks are displayed, and Harvey Galleries (102 South Main St.), where metal sculpture is displayed.

Another famous landmark is the **Bucks County Playhouse** (70 South Main St.), a river-front theater that hosts star actors and actresses in its productions.

Across the river, in **Lambertville**, N.J., the **Porkyard** (8½ Coryell St.) is a colorful complex on the canal with whimsical shops. The Coryell Gallery at the Porkyard sells fine oil paintings and watercolors. The Corners Gallery (12 Church St.) displays Native American, Haitian, and contemporary art, and Bridge Street Antiques (15 Bridge St.) houses fourteen dealers of art, china, furniture, and primitives.

The biggest concentration of antique and crafts galleries is found along Route 202 from New Hope west to the Bucks County line. **Peddler's Village** in Lahaska is a new complex of boutiques, restaurants, and galleries selling everything from ice cream and crafts to clothing and antiques. A giant flea market is held almost every weekend across the street from the Village.

Further west on Route 202 is **Doylestown**, where a blend of Victorian, Federal, and contemporary homes line the streets. The most famous attractions in town were created by Henry Chapman Mercer, an archeologist, writer, ceramist, and eccentric.

Mercer built **Fonthill**, a medieval-style castle made of stressed concrete, near the site of his **Moravian Pottery and Tile Works**. Both the castle and the tile works are on Swamp Road north of Route 202, and visitors can tour either. The other Mercer attraction is the **Mercer Museum** (Pine and East Ashland streets), another concrete fortress where tools, antique vehicles and other items used by tradesmen in the nineteenth century are displayed. It is a strange museum, very different from most we have visited, but we found it fascinating.

Other Doylestown attractions include the new **James A. Michener Arts Center** (138 South Pine St.) across from the Mercer Museum and the antique- and art-filled home of author Pearl Buck (eight miles northwest of town on Route 611). While in Doylestown, visit the **Bucks County Tourist Commission** (152 Swamp Rd.) for maps, brochures, and schedules of attractions.

Another historic home that you should visit is **Pennsbury Manor** in Morrisville (400 Pennsbury Memorial Lane), the restored home of William Penn, founder of Pennsylvania Colony.

Southeast of Doylestown on Route 413 is the three-centuries-old village of **Newtown**, another charming center of antiques, crafts, and more than 225 homes on the National Register of Historic Places. For antiques, visit Ren's Antiques (14 South State St.), Witch Hill American Country (17 South State St.), or the Village Smithy (149 North State St.)

Bucks County is full of beautiful drives. Route 32 along the river takes you past some stunning homes and natural vistas. It is difficult to get lost in Bucks County, so dare to experiment and explore inviting country lanes. Sooner or later they bring you back to main roads, but not until they have taken you past wineries, 200-year-old stone barns and farmhouses still in use, and a dozen covered bridges.

The most romantic attraction we found in the county was the old **Delaware Canal** that runs parallel to the river. The path that runs alongside it is a peaceful walk, one that takes you past covered bridges, ducks and geese, old homes, and wonders of nature. If you'd rather ride, a mule-pulled barge will take you on a voyage up the canal. The barge ride starts on New Street on the south end of New Hope.

There is no best time to visit Bucks County on the weekend. New Hope, Doylestown, and the other attractions are busy year-round. If there is a slow season, it is winter, when you can take part in a scene that recalls Currier & Ives prints.

In the winter the canal freezes over, making it a perfect rink for ice skating. If you have the stamina, you can skate from inn to inn on the canal, stopping along the way for hot drinks and good cheer.

Brandywine Valley

The Brandywine River is a small stream whose mild appearance belies the fact that it helped spawn two dynasties whose legacies are part of our lives today.

The Brandywine Valley, an area in southeast Pennsylvania and northern Delaware, is where the Du Ponts made their fortunes in gunpowder and chemicals, and where three generations of Wyeth artists have created the art that has moved, amused, and intrigued us.

Today visitors can tour mansions and gardens created by the Du Ponts, view the works of the Wyeths, and tour small villages studded with galleries, boutiques, and antique shops.

A tour of the region starts on Route 52. As this road leaves Wilmington, Delaware, the crowded buildings give way to spacious farms and elegant stone greathouses.

Just outside of the city is **Nemours Mansion and Gardens** (25 Rockland Rd.), a 77-room modified-Louis XVI French chateau displaying antiques, works of art, and personal items collected by Alfred I. Du Pont. Visitors during the May-to-November touring season get a glass of juice, a flower from the garden, a brief lecture on the history of the chateau, and a guided walk through the mansion.

Further out Route 52 is another Du Pont mansion, **Winterthur**. This elegant mansion displays in period settings thousands of antique and decorative arts used in America between 1650 and 1850. Not all 196 rooms are open at all times, but three tours with different themes are offered frequently each day. Take time to visit the 200 acres of beautifully landscaped gardens and virgin woods.

The Du Pont dynasty traces back to **Eleutherian Mills**, the first Du Pont estate. The house and the **Hagley Museum**, the first Du Pont powderworks (on Route 141, a half mile north of Route 52), offer tours of house and garden and demonstrations of eighteenth-century crafts.

If you continue out Route 52 into Pennsylvania, the small villages of Centerville, Fairville, and Mendenhall offer interesting antique, craft, and gift shops.

At U.S. 1, turn south toward **Longwood Gardens**, a 350-acre formal garden with six acres of conservatories. Its lakeside gazebo is pictured on the cover of this book. Longwood offers numerous attractions other than flowers, shrubs, and trees. Concerts, colorful fountain displays, and fireworks are held on selected evenings during the summer. The Visitor's Center can provide a schedule.

The most striking display we've seen at Longwood is the chrysanthemum festival in November. The show is wonderful during the day, but far more interesting at night. After dark, the incandescent lights are turned off and black lights are turned on, causing the blossoms to fluoresce. Another colorful festival takes place when the Christmas decorations go up in December.

Back on U.S. 1 head north to **Chadds Ford**, passing antique shops, a winery, and wonderful homes along the way. In Chadds Ford is the **Brandywine River Museum**, a renovated century-old mill that houses some of the works of illustrator N.C. Wyeth, his son Andrew, and grandson Jamie. The works of Howard Pyle and other American artists are also displayed. This museum is next to the gentle Brandywine River. The riverside walk takes you past some whimsical sculptures of a cow and other animals.

Across from the museum are the Chadds Ford Barn Shops, a complex of delightful antique and gift shops; the Chadds Ford Gallery offers Wyeth reproductions.

History isn't forgotten in the Brandywine. North of Chadds Ford on U.S. 1 is the **Brandywine Battlefield Park**, where Washington and Lafayette met. Other historical sites include the **John Chad House** (a quarter-mile north of U.S. 1 on Route 100), a living museum of eighteenth-century history; and the **Barns-Brinton House** (on U.S. 1 in Chadds Ford), where costumed guides help you tour the restored eighteenth-century brick tavern.

Side trips in the Brandywine Valley should include **St. Peter's Village** (take Route 100 north of U.S. 1 to Route 23, turn west and watch for the signs), a fairytale village of Victorian houses. It was once a resort attracting travelers to the cooling air and waters of the falls of French Creek. The tourists have gone, but the old Victorian homes remain, renovated now into restaurants and shops.

Swiss Pines Park (Charles Road near Phoenixville) is an eleven acre bamboo garden with a Japanese teahouse. **Hopewell Village** (Route 345 six miles south of Birdsboro) is a restored ironmaking village with costumed guides recreating the life and work of the early 1800s.

Three other cities deserve a close look. **West Chester** is a small university town with a wealth of lovely, tree-shaded neighborhoods and antique shops. Our favorites are Old Goat's Antiques (Echo Valley Farm on Valley Road) and Baldwin's Book Barn (Route 100 outside of town), a marvelous stone structure with five floors of books, maps, prints, letters, and other paper items. **The Chester County Historical Society** (225 North High St.) displays a collection of more than 50,000 examples of textiles, furniture, decorations, and pottery that reflect the history of the area.

Wilmington has the **Delaware Art Museum** (2301 Kentmore Pkwy.), featuring Wyeths, Pyles, and a collection of English pre Raphaelites; and **Rockwood Museum** (610 Shipley Rd.), where English, American, and European decorative arts are displayed in the manor house, conservatory, and other buildings.

New Castle, Delaware, a small town on Route 9 south of Wilmington, once had a busy harbor and was important enough to be the home of three signers of the Declaration of Independence. Life centers around **The Green** (3rd and Delaware), the park on which are located the Old Court House, the Old Dutch House, and other grand homes. The attractions include some fine shops, elegant homes, the wonderful David Finney Inn, and a view of the river.

In the autumn, one of the favorite attractions is the fall foliage tour by steam train on the **Wilmington and Western Railroad**. The depot is on Route 41 four miles west of Wilmington. Rides are offered weekend and holiday afternoons, May through October. Call 302/998-1930 for details.

We usually end our visits to the Brandywine Valley with a quiet visit to the river-front park on Delaware Street in New Castle, where the view of the giant ships heading upriver to Philadelphia is a sharp contrast to the grand eighteenth- and nineteenth-century homes and gardens on the river front.

Amish Country

Amish Country has traditionally meant Lancaster County, a fertile farming region where the Amish have maintained their simple lifestyle despite the pressures of modern life.

This definition, however, would seriously limit the attractions you would see in southeastern Pennsylvania. Lancaster County is full of interesting diversions, but all around the region are countless antique and craft shops, historic parks, magnificent inns, and vistas of rolling farmlands ripe with produce.

Before you start your auto tour of the area, stop by the **Pennsylvania Dutch Convention & Visitor's Bureau** on Route 30 east of Lancaster. There you can pick up maps guiding you to the attractions. You will need them, for the attractions in Lancaster County are often hidden by the blaring commercialism that screams at you on Route 30.

Off the main roads, though, the real delights of Amish Country become visible: narrow black horse-drawn buggies roll along carrying a family of The Folk; the front yard of a substantial farmhouse becomes a playground for young Amish lads dressed in black and white; along the road walk young Amish ladies, their hair covered in white bonnets and their dresses simple but somehow stylish frocks.

A visitor can never really experience the Amish lifestyle, but there are a few places where you can increase your knowledge of their ways: the **Amish Farm and House** (Route 30 east of Lancaster); the **Amish Homestead**, a real working farm (2034 Lincoln Highway East, Lancaster); and the **Central Market** (King and North Queen streets, Lancaster), where Mennonite women sell the produce of the farms on Tuesdays and Fridays.

Out of Lancaster are wonderful towns with attractions that would make them a standout in any area. Antique lovers will like **Adamstown** (Route 272 northeast of the Pennsylvania Turnpike), where more than 1,000 antique dealers can be found on weekends. The biggest complexes are the Black Angus Antiques Mall (160 dealers and 50 crafts vendors), Renninger's (450 dealers), The Adamstown Antique Emporium (5,000 square feet), Hummer's Antiques and Collectibles (spacious inside, 150 dealers outside), and the Lancaster County Antique and Collectible Market (28 dealers). Shupp's Grove is touted on billboards along the way, but we have found this outdoor flea market lacking in both quantity and quality of dealers.

More antique shops can be found just about anywhere there is a crossroad. The best are in Strasburg, Ephrata and Lititz. In Ephrata, you'll also find the **Ephrata Cloister** (632 West Main St.), a restored community of eighteenth-century religious recluses. The wood frame buildings and the grounds are peaceful and worth a visit between antique shops.

East of Lancaster, Route 30 is a tacky commercial corridor. West of Lancaster, Route 30 takes you to some wonderful towns filled with inns, antiques, and lovely old homes. The best are York, Abbottstown, East Berlin (a few miles north of Route 30 on Route 194), New Oxford and Gettysburg, where commercialism tends to overwhelm the austere beauty of the Civil War battlefield park.

If you like festivals, the most famous of the lot is the **Kutztown Antique and Collectors Outdoor Extravaganza**, held each June and early fall in Kutztown, midway between Allentown and Reading, on Noble Street one mile south of town. More than 1,200 dealers are expected at each show, offering everything any collector could ever want.

Whether you are coming to see the Amish or the antiques, take the time to slow down and wander the countryside. The farms, the Amish people, the covered bridges, and other scenic delights await those who look for them.

❦ VIRGINIA

The Hunt Country

The gently rolling hills of the horse country in the northern Virginia countryside west of Washington, D.C., are part of a serene landscape dotted with grand houses, rustic stables, and small towns catering to the wealthy estate owners.

The center of this area is **Middleburg**, a quaint, wealthy village of stone houses and the unofficial capital of Hunt Country. Middleburg's main street is lined with restaurants, inns, and antique and gift shops whose main decorative theme appears to be horses and hounds.

Not to be overlooked during a tour of the Hunt Country are other towns and historic houses in the area. **Leesburg** is the biggest town in the area, but after you pass by the new shopping centers and subdivisions you'll find a city center filled with historic old buildings, fine antique and craft shops, and interesting restaurants. The entire town of **Waterford** (Route 622 north of Leesburg) is listed on the National Register of Historic Places. This eighteenth-century Quaker village is a great place to visit any time, but particularly on the first weekend in October, when the popular Homes Tour and Craft Exhibit is held.

Aldie (Route 50 east of Middleburg), **Hillsboro** (Route 9 west of Leesburg), and **Upperville** (Route 50 west of Middleburg) are beautiful towns with grand homes, antique shops and art galleries. **Lincoln** (off Route 690 south of Purcellville) is a simple village, one settled by Quakers in the eighteenth century and still the center of activity for the group.

The estates that make this part of Virginia Hunt Country are off-limits except during late May, when the Trinity Episcopal Church in Upperville sponsors the **Hunt Country Stables Tour** of about a dozen estates in the area.

The Oatlands, a fine Greek Revival mansion built around 1805, hosts numerous festivals every year, including a British Isles celebration in May and the Loudoun Spring Point-to-Point races. The Oatlands (U.S. 15 six miles south of Leesburg) is open daily. **Morven Park** (Old Waterford Rd. one mile north of Leesburg) is a 1,200-acre estate with a magnificent mansion, gardens, and nature walks. The estate is the site of the Fall National Hunt Steeplechase. It is open weekends May through October, daily except Mondays during the summer.

Jefferson's Country

Once upon a time, the heart of Jefferson's Country—**Charlottesville**—must have been a wonderful town to visit. It still is, but only after you struggle through the suburban sprawl that has clogged its approaches, desecrated its gentle hills and raised the pancake house to a new art form.

Charlottesville's real inner beauty is found at the **University of Virginia**, one of the more attractive campuses in the nation. Majestic red brick buildings, broad lawns, wonderful views, and huge old shade trees make the university planned by Thomas Jefferson a romantic place to roam.

Other attractions that make Jefferson's Country a marvelous place to visit are found outside of Charlottesville. South of town are Jefferson's home, **Monticello** (three miles southeast on Route 53) and the home of President James Monroe, **Ash Lawn–Highland** (1.5 miles beyond Monticello on Route 53).

The mountain-top Monticello is far more elegant than the simple farmhouse owned by Monroe. Both estates are marvelous places to visit, particularly during the summer when Monticello frequently has afternoon concerts on weekends and Ash Lawn–Highland has a seven-week festival of music, opera, and crafts. The performances at Ash Lawn–Highland are particularly striking, for they are held in the massive boxwood gardens near Monroe's house. The wandering peacocks have been known to make appearances during the operatic productions.

Montpelier, the home of President James Madison (off Route 20 four miles west of Orange), is now open to the public, as is its cemetery with the graves of James and Dolley Madison.

For antique enthusiasts, the Charlottesville Antique Center (Route 29 north of the city limits), Consignment House Unlimited (121 West Main St. on the Mall), South Street Antiques (100 South St.), and the Eternal Attic (Route 250 west of town) offer antiques of all sorts.

The largest collection of shops, though, is fifteen miles north of Charlottesville at **Ruckersville**, the crossroads of routes 29 and 33. The shops here have proved our undoing in the past. The best of the lot are the thirty-four Greene House Shops; Pace's Antiques; and Joseph, Joseph, and Joseph Antiques.

Charlottesville and its surrounding countryside have attracted fine artists for many years. The best display their art at the annual **Crozet Arts and Crafts Festival** (take Route 250 west to Route 240 to Crozet) in early May. It features some of the best artists in the Mid-Atlantic, the same ones you would encounter at bigger and better-publicized shows elsewhere. This festival is small, but the quality is very, very high.

If you want to see some of the artists at work, visit the **McGuffey Art Center** (201 Second St. NW), where about forty have studios.

Young Washington's Hometown

Fredericksburg is where all those stories started. You know, the one where George Washington is said to have chopped down a cherry tree and declined to lie about it, and where it was said he threw a dollar across the river.

In those days, Fredericksburg was a busy port for ships from abroad that sailed up the Chesapeake Bay and into the Rappahannock River, which flows through town. The Civil War was brutal to Fredericksburg, with four major battles being fought nearby. Control of the town changed hands seven times by one count, threatening the many grand homes in the city.

We're thankful that enough of these homes survived to make this town a great getaway.

A visit to Fredericksburg should start at the **Visitor's Center** (706 Caroline), where you can pick up brochures guiding you to antique shops, restaurants, and historic homes. You can also get a sticker that allows you to ignore the two-hour parking restriction in the downtown area.

Once you have parked, you'll find Fredericksburg is small enough that you can walk to all the attractions. Start with the historic sites.

Washington Avenue is the grand boulevard of Fredericksburg. Mary Washington, George's mother, lived in this neighborhood; her house (1200 Charles St.) can be visited today. **Kenmore** (1201 Washington Ave.) was home of Col. Fielding Lewis, brother-in-law of Washington, and remains today a magnificent mansion whose molded plaster ceilings are works of art. At the other end of the avenue is the **obelisk** raised on the site where Mary Washington is said to have come to pray.

Other historic sites include the **Hugh Mercer Apothecary Shop** (1020 Caroline St.); the **Rising Sun Tavern** (1306 Caroline St.); and the **Old Slave Block**, a circular stone from which slaves were sold (William and Charles streets).

The main street in town is **Caroline**, a wonderful restored area of antique shops, art galleries, and restaurants. The best antique shops are Cross Creek for American and primitive antiques (602 Caroline), Upstairs-Downstairs (701 Caroline), Moreland House Antiques for exceptional furniture and silver (716 Caroline), and Anrapo Antique Imports for European furniture (1027 Caroline). The Antique Court of Shoppes (910 Caroline), Antique Court of Shoppes II (1001 Caroline), and Victoria Mall (1023 Caroline) house many vendors selling a variety of antiques and collectibles. Don't miss **Sophia Street**, the riverfront road one block off Caroline. It is lined with old warehouses now filled with antiques.

Antiques are not the only delights on Caroline. Staley's (710) offers Civil War books, costumes, and other memorabilia. Three Rabbits (809) sells children's clothing and gifts, and Redfern & Sons (822) is jammed with country crafts.

For fun, step into Goolrick's Pharmacy (901 Caroline), which seems to have stopped changing sometime around the end of World War II. The soda fountain serves a light lunch and a heavy plate of memories.

Before you leave Fredericksburg, take a tea break at the Windsor Tea Room (724 Caroline), where you can relax over a pot of tea and nibble away on finger sandwiches and cakes.

❦ NORTH CAROLINA

Land of the Mountains

Western North Carolina is a region of scenic mountain chains whose names ring in the ears: Great Smoky, Blue Ridge, The Black. These mountains, whose peaks often top a mile in elevation, have attracted travelers for generations, giving birth to one city that is a center of mountain arts and folk culture and several Victorian villages that are now golfing and skiing resorts.

Asheville is the center of this region, and the jewel in its crown is **Biltmore**, the lavish 255-room chateau that sits on 10,000 acres and is surrounded by thirty-five acres of gardens. Biltmore was created by George W. Vanderbilt in the 1890s. His wife established the Biltmore Homespun Shops, a school that taught the dying arts of weaving, spinning, and other crafts.

The interest in crafts continues. The **Folk Art Center** (Milepost 382 on the Blue Ridge Parkway) has craft exhibitions, demonstrations, and other programs. The Southern Highland Handicraft Guild sponsors an annual crafts fair in August. It has a shop at 930 Tunnel Road. Two other crafts schools—the Joseph Campbell Folk School in Brasstown and Penland near Spruce Pines—offer arts classes and other programs.

The region's culture is also celebrated in two festivals, the **World Gee Haw Whimmy Diddle Competition** in May and the **Mountain Dance and Folk Festival** in early August.

The **Asheville Art Museum** (152 Pearson Dr.) has some worthy exhibits, and the **Colburn Mineral Museum** (170 Coxe Ave.) displays 1,000 fossils and minerals.

Asheville's favorite son was author Thomas Wolfe, whose boarding house (48 Spruce St.) is kept as a shrine.

Northeast of town, off the wonderfully scenic mountain road called the Blue Ridge Parkway, the towns of **Blowing Rock, Banner Elk**, and **Boone** encompass a golf and ski resort area known for its fine inns and majestic vistas.

🐛 FOR MORE INFORMATION

In Maryland

🐛 Tourism Council of Frederick, 19 East Church Street, Frederick, MD 21701. 301/663-8703.

In Pennsylvania

🐛 Bucks County Tourist Commission, 152 Swamp Rd., Doylestown, PA 18901. 215/345-4552.

🐛 Pennsylvania Dutch Convention and Visitor's Bureau, 501 Greenfield Road, Lancaster, PA 17601. 717/299-8901.

In Delaware

🐛 Greater Wilmington Convention and Visitor's Bureau, 1300 Market Street, Wilmington, DE 19801. 302/652-4088 (also 800/441-8846 outside Delaware, 800/282-8667 in Delaware).

🐛 Delaware County Convention and Tourist Bureau, 602 E. Baltimore Pike, Media, PA 19062. 215/565-3679.

In Virginia

🐛 Thomas Jefferson Visitor's Bureau, P.O. Box 161, Charlottesville, VA 22902. 804/293-6789.

🐛 Fredericksburg Visitor's Center, 706 Caroline Street, Fredericksburg, VA 22401. 703/373-1776.

🐛 Leesburg Visitor's Center, 108 South Street SE, Leesburg, VA 22075. 703/777-0519.

In North Carolina

🐛 Asheville Area Chamber of Commerce, 151 Haywood Street, Box 1011, Asheville, NC 28802. 704/258-5200.

Important Times and Numbers

In Frederick County, Maryland

❦ Barbara Fritchie House, 154 West Patrick Street, Frederick. Open 10–4 Monday–Saturday, 1–4 Sunday. 301/663-3833.

❦ Brunswick Museum, 40 West Potomac Street, Brunswick. Open 10–4 Saturday, 1–4 Sunday. 301/834-7100.

❦ Historic Society of Frederick, 24 East Church Street. Open daily. 301/663-1188.

❦ Schifferstadt Architectural Museum, 1110 Rosemont Avenue, Frederick. Open daily. 301/663-6225.

In Bucks County, Pennsylvania

❦ Fonthill Museum, Swamp Road, Doylestown. Open 10–5 daily, last tour leaves at 4. 215/348-9461.

❦ James A. Michener Arts Center, 138 South Pine Street, Doylestown. Open 10–4 Tuesday–Friday, 1–4:30 weekends. 215/340-9800.

❦ Moravian Pottery and Tile Works, Swamp Road, Doylestown. Open 10–5 daily, last tour leaves at 4. 215/345-6722.

❦ Mercer Museum, Pine and East Ashland streets, Doylestown. Open 10–5 Monday–Saturday, 1–5 Sunday. 215/345-0210.

❦ Pennsbury Manor, 400 Pennsbury Memorial Lane, Morrisville. Open 9–5 Tuesday–Saturday, noon–5 Sunday. 215/946-0400.

❦ Pearl S. Buck's home, Green Hills Farm, Perkasie. Tours daily at 10:30 and 2. 800/242-BUCK.

❦ Washington Crossing Historic Park, Routes 32 and 532. Open 9–5 Monday–Saturday, noon–5 Sunday. 215/493-4076.

In the Brandywine Valley, Pennsylvania and Delaware

❦ Barns-Brinton House, One and a half miles south of Chadds Ford, PA, on U.S. 1. Open weekends in summer, other times by appointment. 215/388-7376.

❦ Brandywine River Museum, U.S. 1 and Route 100, Chadds Ford, PA. Open 9:30–4:30 daily. 215/388-7601.

❦ Delaware Art Museum, 2301 Kentmore Parkway, Wilmington, DE. Open 10–5 Monday–Saturday, 1–5 Sunday. 302/571-9590.

❦ Hagley Museum and Eleutherian Mills, On Route 141 a half-mile north of Route 52 in Delaware. Open daily 9:30–4:30. 302/658-2400.

❦ John Chad House, Quarter-mile north of U.S. 1 in Chadds Ford, PA. Open weekends in summer, other times by appointment. 215/388-1132.

❦ Longwood Gardens, U.S. 1 and Route 52, Kennett Square, PA. Open 9–6 daily. 215/388-6741.

❦ Nemours, 25 Rockland Road, Wilmington, DE. Open May to early November, with tours offered several times daily except Mondays. Reservations strongly suggested. 302/651-6912.

❦ Rockwood Museum, 610 Shipley Road, Wilmington, DE. Open 11–3 Tuesday–Saturday. 302/571-7776.

❦ Winterthur, Route 52, Wilmington, DE. Open 10–4 Tuesday–Saturday, noon–4 Sunday. Three different tours offered. Reservations suggested. 302/654-1548.

In Amish Country, Pennsylvania

❦ Amish Farm and House, 2395 Route 30. East of Lancaster, PA. Open daily. 717/394-6185.

❦ Amish Homestead, 2034 Lincoln Highway East. Three miles east of Lancaster off Route 462. Open daily. 717/392-0832.

❦ Central Market, Penn Square in Lancaster. Near the intersection of King Street (U.S. 30) and North Queen Street (U.S. 222). Open Tuesday and Friday.

❦ Ephrata Cloister, 623 West Main Street, Ephrata, PA. Open daily. 717/733-6600

❦ Gettysburg National Military Park, Battlefield Park on U.S. 15 south of Gettysburg. Open daily. 717/334-1124.

In the Middleburg area of Virginia

❦ Morven Park, Old Waterford Road, Leesburg. Open 10–5 Tuesday–Saturday, 1–5 Sunday during the summer, weekends only in May and from Labor Day to early October. 703/777-2414.

❦ Oatlands. On U.S. 15 six miles south of Leesburg. Open 10–5 Monday–Saturday, 1–5 Sunday. 703/777-3174.

In the Charlottesville area of Virginia

❦ Ash Lawn–Highland, Route 53. Four and a half miles south of the city. Open 9–6 daily March through October, 10–5 rest of the year. 804/293-9539.

❦ Monticello, Route 53. Three miles south of the city. Open 8–5 daily March through October, 9–4:30 rest of the year. 804/295-8181.

❦ Montpelier. Off Route 20 four miles west of Orange. Open 10–4 daily. 703/672-1162.

❦ University of Virginia, west end of Main Street, Charlottesville. Daily tours start at the Rotunda. 804/924-1019.

In Fredericksburg, Virginia

❦ Kenmore, 1201 Washington Ave. Open daily 9–5 March through November, 10–4 rest of the year. 703/373-3381.

❦ Hugh Mercer Apothecary Shop, 1020 Caroline Street. Open daily 9–5 April through October; 9–4 November, December, and March. Closed January and February. 703/373-1569.

❦ Rising Sun Tavern, 1306 Caroline Street. Open daily 9–5 April through October; 10–4 November, December, and March. Closed January and February. 703/373-1569.

❦ Mary Washington House, 1200 Charles Street. Open daily 9–5 April through October; 9–5 November, December, and March. Closed January and February. 703/373-1569.

In Asheville, North Carolina

❦ Ashville Art Museum, 152 Pearson Drive. Closed Mondays and holidays. 704/253-3227.

❦ Biltmore Estate. On U.S. 25 three blocks north of I-40. Open daily except Thanksgiving, Christmas, and New Year's Day. 704/274-1776.

❦ Colburn Memorial Mineral Museum, 170 Coxe Avenue. Open daily. 704/254-7162.

❦ Folk Art Center, Milepost 382, Blue Ridge Parkway. Open daily. 704/298-7903.

❦ Thomas Wolfe Memorial, 48 Spruce Street. Open daily April–Oct, daily except Monday November–March. 704/253-8304

Annual Events

For more information and the exact dates, contact the local tourist agencies.

In Frederick County, Maryland

❦ Frederick Craft Fair. May.

❦ New Market Days. Eighteenth-century festival with music and other entertainment. September.

In Bucks County, Pennsylvania

❦ Mercer Folk Festival, Mercer Museum, Doylestown. Mid-May.

❦ Bucks County Antiques Dealers Association Show; the Tinicum Civic Association Antique Show, Buckingham Antiques Show. June.

❦ State Craft Festival, Newtown. September.

❦ Bucks County Artists' Show, Pearl Buck's Home. October.

❦ House Tours; Christmas Festivals. December.

In Brandywine Valley, Pennsylvania and Delaware

❦ Wilmington Garden Day. May.

❦ Brandywine Arts Festival. September.

In Amish Country, Pennsylvania

❦ Craft Days, Pennsylvania Farm Museum in Landis. June; Harvest Days, Pennsylvania Farm Museum. October.

In Middleburg/Leesburg, Virginia

❦ Virginia Foxhound Show. April.

❦ Homes and Gardens Tour. April.

❦ Hunt Country Stable Tour. Visit the barns of the rich and famous. May.

❦ Christmas at Oatlands. December.

In Charlottesville, Virginia

❦ Garden Week. Late April.

❦ Ash Lawn–Highland Summer Festival. Opera, music, crafts. June–August.

In Fredericksburg, Virginia

❦ Historic Garden Week. April.

❦ Christmas in Fredericksburg. Many special events commemorate the season. December.

In Asheville, North Carolina

❦ Southern Highland Handicraft Guild Fair. More than 100 artisans and entertainers gather for a festival. Third weekend July and October.

❦ World Gee Haw Whimmy Diddle Competition. Mid-May

❦ Mountain Dance and Folk Festival. Early August.

❦ INNS AND RESTAURANTS

Here are our favorites, but first an explanation of how we break down our cost categories:

One night in an inn for two (often but not always including breakfast):

Inexpensive Under $75
Moderate $75 to $125
Expensive More than $125

For dinner for two (wine and drinks not included):

Inexpensive Less than $25
Moderate $25 to $60
Expensive More than $60

Maryland

Bed and Board at Tran Crossing In the heart of Frederick's restored area of Federal and colonial homes is this very small B&B in a three-story Victorian townhouse. The public rooms are furnished with antiques while the two guest rooms, which share a bath, have more modern furniture. This inn is close to the historic homes and antique shops of Frederick as well as the wine country to the east. Moderate. 121 East Patrick Street, Frederick, MD 21701. 301/663-8449.

The Inn at Buckeystown This inn is in a century-old Victorian mansion with an adjacent cottage in a former church. The nine guest rooms and cottage are furnished with Victorian antiques. Lovers swear by the suggestive decor of the "Love Room" and the made-for-snuggling "Fireplace Room." At the cottage, beautiful stained glass windows, a private hot tub and a cozy loft bed await. Expensive, but rates include breakfast and a five-course dinner. 3521 Buckeystown Pike (Route 85), Buckeystown, MD 21717. 301/874-5755.

The Strawberry Inn This small inn began life as a farmhouse in the mid nineteenth-century. Today the two-story white frame house anchors the small downtown of New Market, a city filled with antique and craft shops. The five rooms, all with private baths, are furnished with Victorian pieces. Inexpensive. 17 Main Street, New Market, MD 21774. 301/865-3318.

The Summer House This two-room cabin sets on a 60-acre farm near the two-century-old main house outside Westminster, in the center of Maryland's wine country. Downstairs in the cabin is an antique-filled living room and a fireplace; the upstairs bedroom offers a four-poster bed and a full bathroom. The adjacent pond and weeping willows make for peaceful surroundings. Moderate. Write The Traveler in Maryland, P.O. Box 2277, Annapolis, MD 21404. 301/269-6232.

The Turning Point Inn This large Edwardian home is both a popular restaurant and a five-room inn furnished with country antiques and crafts. All the rooms have private baths, and visitors should sample the dining room's offerings. Moderate. 3406 Urbana Pike (Route 355, in the center of the village of Urbana), Frederick, MD 21701. 301/874-2421.

Fine dining in central Maryland requires a bit more searching:

The Inn at Buckeystown serves five-course dinners featuring game and fish served in a creative manner. Adding to the meal are the Victorian china and silver. Inn guests get preference here, but call anyway for reservations. Expensive. 3521 Buckeystown Pike (Route 85), Buckeystown. 301/874-5755.

The Turning Point Inn features some outstanding seafood dishes, with an airy room and deck overlooking Frederick County farmland and Sugar Loaf Mountain. Moderate. 3406 Urbana Pike (Route 355 in the center of Urbana), Frederick. 301/874-2421.

Bushwaller's in downtown Frederick serves American cuisine in the dark-wood atmosphere of the new American saloon. Inexpensive/moderate. 209 N. Market Street. 301/694-5697.

Di Francesco's serves classic Italian dishes. Moderate. 26 N. Market Street, Frederick. 301/695-5499.

Voilà serves French cuisine with an emphasis on seafood that is winning acclaim. Moderate. 611 N. Market Street, Frederick. 301/663-0009.

For other options, we suggest strolling the low-numbered blocks of North Market Street in downtown Frederick, where you will find a large selection of restaurants, none of which are really outstanding, but most of which are fine.

Pennsylvania and Delaware

Brandywine Valley

Buttonwood Farm This 185-year-old stone farmhouse has three antique-filled guest rooms. Guests can roam the farm or play a set on the clay tennis court. The hosts will prepare a French-style dinner on request. Inexpensive. 231 Pemberton Road, Kennett Square, PA 19348. 215/444-0278.

Cornerstone The large stone farmhouse just outside Philadelphia is a treasure: eighteenth- and nineteenth-century antiques, six fireplaces, original woodwork. There are four guest rooms and two antique-filled suites with complete kitchen facilities. Moderate. For relaxation, try the hot tub and pool. Write c/o Guesthouses, RD 9, West Chester, PA 19380. 215/692-4575.

David Finney Inn This stylish inn sits across from The Green in lovely New Castle. The twenty rooms are nice, but not outstanding. Moderate. 216 Delaware Street, New Castle, DE 19720. 302/322-6367.

Fairville Inn Located on a gentle slope about ten miles from Chadds Ford between Longwood Gardens and Winterthur, this inn offers fifteen rooms in the main house and the new, country-rustic annexes. The rooms are comfortable, all with private baths and five with fireplaces. Moderate. The inn is in Fairville, on Route 52 near the village of Mendenhall. P.O. Box 219, Mendenhall, PA 19357. 215/388-5900.

Hamorton House This magnificent stone manor house in Glen Mills was built a decade before the Civil War and is on the National Register of Historic Places. The main rooms are filled with antiques, and the six guest rooms with family pieces. Moderate. Write c/o Guesthouses, RD 9, West Chester, PA 19380. 215/692-4575.

Hotel Du Pont This stately hotel doesn't look like much outside, but inside it is a glorious treasure, with gilded mirrors, elegantly decorated ceilings and dining rooms, and 266 guest rooms filled with antique reproductions. Moderate if you get a weekend package. P.O. Box 991, Wilmington, DE 19899. 800/441-9019.

The Log House at Battle Hill The twenty acres of meadows surrounding this restored eighteenth-century, two-room log cabin make this a special spot in Chadds Ford. There are two lakes, a pool surrounded by hedges for your private enjoyment, and evening walks through the lantern-illuminated lawn. Expensive. Write Guesthouses Bed & Breakfast, R.D. 9, West Chester, PA 19380. 215/692-4575.

Pickering Bend This 200-year-old farmhouse in Malvern offers one suite with a woodstove, private patio, and quiet, wildflower-filled fields.

Moderate. Write c/o Bed and Breakfast of Philadelphia, P.O. Box 630, Chester Spring, PA 19425. 215/827-9650.

For fine dining:

The Country House at Kimberton serves an American menu in a colonial setting, accented with antiques, fireplaces, millhouse, and a duck pond. The specialties are seafood, particularly crabmeat au gratin and salmon. Moderate. Route 113, Phoenixville, PA. 215/933-8148.

David Finney Inn has an American menu that matches the tastefully colonial decor of its dining room. The sole and rack of lamb are spectacular, but save this place for a lunch on a nice day—the garden behind the inn is a pleasant place to dawdle. Moderate. 216 Delaware Street, New Castle, DE. 302/322-6367.

Hotel Du Pont has two outstanding dining rooms. The Green Room, serving a French menu, looks like the dining room at Versailles. A harpist plays during dinner on a tiny balcony overlooking the tables. The Brandywine Room is a club-like room with dark wood walls and an American menu. If you can, skip dinner and hit the High Tea served in an intimate area off the hotel lobby. The experience is wonderful; the sandwiches, pastries, jams, and teas are filled with calories. Try it anyway. The dining rooms are expensive, the tea is moderate. Eleventh and Market streets, Wilmington, DE. 302/594-3156.

Inn at Historic Yellow Springs is devilishly hard to find, but after we found it we discovered the French gourmet fare was worth the trouble. Expensive. Art School Road, Chester Springs, PA. Call 215/827-7477 for directions.

Silk Purse is a very chic restaurant, one that tries the latest styles. Thankfully, they pull it off. Stick to seafood and veal. Expensive. 1307 North Scott Street, Wilmington, DE. 302/654-7666.

Towne Hall really is a former town hall from the turn of the century. Now decorated with Victorian antiques, it features an American menu. Try the pheasant sauteed in brandy and fruit sauces. Moderate. 15 South High Street, West Chester, PA. 215/692-6200.

Bucks County

Black Bass Hotel This antique-filled inn has a river view and seven beautiful rooms. Moderate. Route 32, Lumberville, PA 18933. 215/297-5815.

Evermay-on-the-Delaware This riverfront mansion has a carriage house, twenty-five acres of gardens, and sixteen rooms or suites filled with Victorian antiques. Moderate. River Road, Erwinna, PA 18920. 215/294-9100.

Golden Pheasant Inn The four guest rooms in this small country inn are furnished with American and European antiques. Moderate/expensive. River Road, Erwinna, PA 18920. 215/294-9595.

Indian Rock Inn Eight large and nicely decorated rooms make this inn on 300 acres on the canal a wonderful retreat. Moderate. Upper Black Eddy, PA 18972. 215/982-5300.

Joseph Ambler Inn There are twenty-eight guest rooms in this inn, all decorated with antiques or reproductions. Moderate. 1005 Horsham Road, North Wales, PA 19454. 215/362-7500.

Hollileif The guest rooms in this bed and breakfast are in a 290-year-old farmhouse. The furnishings are country. Moderate. 677 Durham Road, Wrightstown, PA 18940. 215/598-3100.

The Inn at Phillips Mill This is a small inn, only five rooms in a stone building that is more than two centuries old. All five rooms are cozy and tastefully furnished with country furniture and accessories. Moderate. North River Road (Route 32), New Hope, PA 18938. 215/862-2984.

Pineapple Hill This inn is located in a farmhouse built around 1800. The five rooms and two suites are furnished with country furniture and antiques, while the common rooms serve as showplaces for many country arts and crafts. Inexpensive/moderate. 1324 River Road, New Hope, PA 18938. 215/862-9608.

The Logan Established in 1727, this inn has sixteen antique-filled rooms. Moderate/expensive. 10 West Ferry Street, New Hope, PA 18936. 215/862-2300.

Tattersall Inn The six rooms in this two-century-old, lilac-colored mansion are furnished with antiques. Moderate. Cafferty and River roads, Box 569, Point Pleasant, PA 18950. 215/297-8233.

Widow Brown's Inn There are fourteen elegant rooms furnished with country antiques in this inn. Moderate. P.O. Box 40, Route 611 and Stump Road, Plumsteadville, PA 18949. 215/766-7500.

For fine dining:

Centre Bridge Inn is a resurrected inn. The original 1706 inn burned down and was rebuilt in the 1950s, but this inn on the canal serves a wide variety of meats and seafood, all very well-prepared. Expensive. Routes 32 and 263, New Hope, PA. 215/862-9139, 215/862-2048.

Golden Pheasant Inn specializes in venison, pheasant, and other game dishes. Expensive. River Road, Erwinna, PA. 215/294-9595.

The Inn at Phillips Mill serves excellent French cuisine, with special dishes for vegetarians. Outdoor dining in the summer. Moderate. North River Road, New Hope, PA. 215/862-9919.

The Sign of the Sorrel Horse serves some stunning continental dishes, from magnificently creative appetizers through desserts. Our dinner wrecked our diets. The dining room is in a building built in 1749. In the summer, you can dine on the veranda overlooking the forest, a flower garden, and a pool with a fountain. Expensive. R.D. 3, Old Bethlehem Road, Quakertown, PA. (We urge you to call 215/536-4651 for directions.)

Upper Black Eddy Inn offers superior country dining in a colonial atmosphere. Moderate. River Road, Upper Black Eddy, PA. 215/982-5554.

Vicker's Tavern is a nineteenth-century farmhouse that now serves creative continental cuisine. Try the quail with chestnut stuffing. Expensive. Gordon Drive and Welsh Pool Road, Lionville, PA. 215/363-7998.

The Walking Treaty Inn serves fine continental fare, with entertainment on Fridays and Saturdays. Moderate. River Road, Point Pleasant, PA. 215/297-5354.

Amish Country

Cameron Estate Inn Only a few minutes from the Mt. Hope Winery, this spacious eighteen-room inn is surrounded by farmland laced with trout streams and hiking trails. All but two of the rooms have private baths; all are filled with antiques and reproductions. The dining room's menu of American and continental cuisine has won acclaim. Inexpensive/moderate. RD #1, Box 305, Mount Joy, PA 17552. 717/653-1773.

Donegal Mills Plantation There are seventeen rooms in this eighteenth-century mansion, all furnished with period antiques. Adjacent to the inn is a restaurant in an old mill and a semi-restored village that is a tourist attraction. Moderate. Trout Run Road, P.O. Box 204, Mount Joy, PA 17552. 717/653-2168.

General Sutter Inn This twelve-room inn is on the square in Lititz, a picture-perfect community with a chocolate factory, pretzelmaker, and a surprising number of eighteenth-century houses. The inn is a quaint place, something you might find as the setting for a Victorian novel; the lobby is filled with exotic birds in cages and the main decorating theme in the rooms is wicker. Still, it is a fine place, with a nice dining room and garden plaza. Inexpensive. 14 East Main Street, Lititz, PA 17543. 717/626-2115.

Mercersburg Inn This is a contender for the finest inn in the Mid-Atlantic. The mansion is stunning, the fifteen guest rooms spacious, some with bathrooms large enough to hold a cocktail party. The location

❧ The Mercersburg Inn, a mansion on the western fringe of Amish country that offers elegant accommodations and superb food.
Photo by Barbara Radin-Fox.

is in Mercersburg, a historic town on the western fringe of Amish country. Moderate. 405 South Main Street, Mercersburg, PA 17236. 717/328-5231.

The Mill House This 1766 stone house, furnished with early American antiques, is set near a mill stream and a humpbacked bridge. There are three rooms, all tastefully furnished with period pieces. Outside, you may bump into some of the peacocks strolling the grounds. Inexpensive. 313 Osceola Mill Road, Gordonville, PA 17529. 717/768-3758.

Roundtop This very secluded stone house overlooks the Susquehanna River valley. The five rooms are furnished with a mixture of antiques and contemporary pieces. Moderate. RD 2, Box 258, Wrightsville, PA 17368. 717/252-3169. Call for directions.

Witmer's Tavern The early American tavern has seven rooms decorated in Victorian or country. Inexpensive. 2014 Old Philadelphia Pike, Lancaster, PA 17602. 717/299-5305.

For fine dining:

Accomac Inn features classic French dishes in a formal riverfront setting. Moderate. In Wrightsville. 717/252-1521.

The Cameron Estate Inn is operated by Betty Groff, whose Amish fare at Groff's Farm is famous in the region. At the estate, the menu is continental and still noteworthy. The Sunday brunch is exceptional. Moderate. Donegal Springs Road, Mount Joy, PA. 717/653-1773.

General Sutter Inn serves surprisingly good American fare, but take time, if weather permits, to have a cocktail on the garden patio that overlooks the town square. Moderate. 14 E. Main Street, Lititz, PA. 717/626-2115.

Groff's Farm is a restaurant in an old stone farmhouse that serves authentic Pennsylvania Dutch fare that includes some of Betty Groff's own creations, such as Chicken Stoltzfus (chunks of chicken in a cream sauce on a bed of light pastry) and black raspberry tarts. Reservations required for dinner. Moderate. Pinkerton Road, Mount Joy, PA. 717/653-2048.

Inn at Oley serves up some creative dishes featuring steak and seafood. Moderate. Friedensburg Road, Oley, PA. 717/987-3459.

La Petite Auberge is known for its classical French dishes. Quaint setting. Moderate. Route 562 between Reading and Boyertown, PA. 717/689-5510.

The Lemon Tree Inn is a beautifully-decorated century-old restaurant in downtown Lancaster. The menu emphasizes traditional American dishes and some continental dishes. Moderate. 1766 Columbia Avenue, Lancaster, PA. 717/394-0441.

Mercersburg Inn The dining room is formal and the menu is a surprise—Swiss with a touch of French. Moderate. 405 South Main Street, Mercersburg, PA. 717/328-5231.

Virginia

Charlottesville

Not far from Charlottesville is an inn said by many to be the finest in the nation. **The Inn at Little Washington** is one of ten inns in America to win honors from *Relais et Chateaux*, the prestigious guide to small hotels, inns, and restaurants around the world. The inn added another honor in 1989 when it was awarded a five-star rating from the Mobil Travel Guide. The inn, in the small (population 200) village of Washington, VA, about an hour north of Charlottesville, offers stunning cuisine and elegant accommodations. Chef-owner Patrick O'Connell prepares a menu featuring regional meats and produce, and has won almost unanimous acclaim as owner of the best restaurant in the Washington (big and little) region. The eight rooms and two suites are furnished elegantly with many antique pieces. Both dinner (a fixed-price meal) and the rooms rate as expensive, but worth it for a very special occasion. Washington, VA 22747. 703/675-3800.

In the Charlottesville area

Auburn Hill Originally part of Monticello, this estate is made for horse-lovers. The guest house, a two-room cottage, is the former slave quarters. The real attraction is that Auburn Hill is an equestrian center, and rides and lessons can be arranged. Moderate. Write c/o Guesthouses, P.O. Box 5737, Charlottesville, VA 22905. 804/979-7264.

Boar's Head Inn This 175-room inn and sports club is larger than most of the inns listed in this book, but is included because it is an elegant, Williamsburg-style hotel set amid beautifully landscaped grounds made for evening strolls. The rooms are furnished with antique reproductions and carefully chosen fabrics and accessories. Moderate to expensive. The inn is on U.S. 250 two miles west of U.S. 29. Box 5185, Charlottesville, VA 22905. 804/296-2181.

Mayhurst Inn This exquisite Italianate Victorian mansion has an oval staircase that ascends four floors to a rooftop gazebo. The seven rooms and the rest of the house are furnished with antiques. Moderate, P.O. Box 707, Orange, VA 22960. 703/672-5597.

Nicola This two-centuries-old, one-room log cabin sits in a grove on a 180-acre farm. The rooms are furnished with antiques, the views are beautiful, and a tennis court is steps away. Moderate. Write c/o Guesthouses, Box 5737, Charlottesville, VA 22905. 804/979-7264.

Prospect Hill This plantation house's original section dates back to 1732. Today there are seven guest rooms furnished with antiques and country crafts. Moderate. R.D. 1, Box 55, Trevilians, VA 23170. 703/967-0844.

Silver Thatch Inn This white frame building began as a log barracks built for Hessian mercenaries during the Revolutionary War. Today the inn has seven antique-filled guest rooms and a fine dining room. Moderate. 3001 Hollymead Road (about six miles north of Charlottesville on U.S. 29), Charlottesville, VA 22901. 804/978-4686.

200 South Street The twenty guest rooms in this beautiful urban inn are furnished with canopy beds, antiques, and fireplaces. The inn is located a block off the Mall in the center of Charlottesville. Expensive. 200 South Street, Charlottesville, VA 22901. 804/979-0200

For dining:

Bull Alley serves American nouveau cuisine in a restored smokehouse. Great atmosphere. Moderate. 333 West Main Street, Charlottesville, VA. 804/979-0128.

The C&O Restaurant doesn't look like much, but it does blend into the neighborhood. The only indication that there is a restaurant here is the faded Pepsi sign giving the name. Hiding inside this misleading facade is food fine enough to win national acclaim. Downstairs in the tavern, varied fare is served at moderate prices. Upstairs, in two settings at expensive fixed-price rates, fine French and American nouvelle cuisine is served. Reservations required. 515 E. Water Street, Charlottesville, VA. 804/971-7044.

La Galerie, on U.S. 250 west of Charlottesville at the Crozet turnoff, serves fine French country cuisine and is popular with the area's gentry. It is very particular about guests reconfirming reservations. Expensive. 804/823-5883.

Historic **Michie Tavern** plays hosts to the Wine Museum on land once owned by Patrick Henry's father. The superbly restored 200-year-old tavern serves Southern favorites, but only at a luncheon buffet. It is closed for dinner. Inexpensive. Route 53, Monticello Mountain, VA. 804/977-1234.

The Ivy Inn looks like the historic old home that it is. Fine Virginia dishes and other American standards served at moderate prices. 2244 Old Ivy Road Charlottesville, VA. 804/977-1222.

The Old Mill is the main dining room in the Boar's Head Inn, and serves succulent Old Virginia dishes and more creative contemporary fare. Expensive. Reservations are suggested. The inn is on U.S. 250 two miles west of U.S. 29, Charlottesville, VA. 804/296-2181.

Silver Thatch Inn is known for its regional meat dishes and incredible desserts. Moderate. 3001 Hollymead Road (about six miles north of Charlottesville on U.S. 29), Charlottesville, VA. 804/978-4686.

Le Snail serves fine country-French meals in an old house in downtown Charlottesville. Moderate. 320 W. Main Street. 804/295-4456.

Middleburg/Leesburg

The Ashby Inn A popular restaurant, this is also a six-room inn. The guest rooms are furnished with early American pieces. Moderate. Routes 701 and 759, Paris, VA. 703/592-3900.

The Gibson Hall Inn This 157-year-old mansion was the stately home of the first mayor of the small town of Upperville. Oriental rugs, designer decor and a magnificent center hall greet visitors to the five rooms. If this is a very special weekend, book the third-floor lovers' retreat and soak away all cares in the Jacuzzi. Room rates are moderate. P.O. Box 225, Route 50, Upperville, VA 22176. 703/592-3514.

L'Auberge Provencale There are six elegant guest rooms furnished with Victorian and French antiques in this acclaimed restaurant. Moderate. White Post, VA. 22663. 703/837-1375.

The Laurel Brigade Inn This old inn in the center of historic Leesburg once booked rooms for less than $20 a night. Today, the five beautifully furnished rooms in the old stone building are still a bargain, making the inn one of the few to get into the inexpensive category. But the restaurant is the real draw here, serving regional fare at inexpensive/moderate prices. 20 W. Market Street (Route 7), Leesburg, VA 22075. 703/777-1010.

Red Fox Inn The Red Fox claims it is the oldest inn in the nation, and it just may be. The old stone foundation walls and timbers show the majesty of age without the deleterious effects. There are six rooms in the main inn and thirteen rooms (some with fireplaces) in the two annexes, the Stray Fox Inn and McConnell House. The main inn, in the center of the antique-filled village of Middleburg, dates from 1728 when the main inn was built by Joseph Chinn, George Washington's cousin. In the 1970s it was showing its age, but recent renovation has restored the elegance of the rooms and raised the quality of the cuisine in the popular dining room, which serves classic Virginian, Italian, and French dishes. Dinner prices are moderate; the rooms are expensive. 2 E. Washington Street, Middleburg, VA 22117. 703/687-6301.

The Windsor Inn Better known as a fine restaurant offering British pub fare in the center of Middleburg, the Windsor Inn is also home to four gaily decorated guest rooms. The dinner fare is moderate, the rooms are moderate/expensive. 2 W. Washington Street, Middleburg, VA 22117. 703/687-6800.

For fine dining:

The Ashby Inn features seafood, with sauteed scallops and shrimp winning acclaim. There are four dining rooms ranging from a rustic pub to a formal room. Willard Scott, our favorite star on NBC's "Today" show, raves about this restaurant. Expensive. Routes 701 and 759, Paris, VA. 703/592-3900.

L'Auberge Provencale is praised for its superb cuisine from Provence. Moderate. White Post, VA. 703/837-1375.

The Red Fox Tavern serves interesting regional dishes in an attractive room. Moderate/expensive. 2 E. Washington Street, Middleburg, VA. 703/687-6301.

Mosby's Tavern, another Red Fox operation, serves lighter fare in a former stable just a block from the Red Fox Tavern Inn. Inexpensive/moderate. 2 W. Marshall Street, Middleburg, VA. 703/687-5282.

1763 Inn is a cozy inn with three beautiful dining rooms, one with a fireplace and another overlooking a pond. The surprise is that the fare is German. Stick to that. The Bavarian Farmer's Platter, a feast of bratwurst, pork chop, and *kassler ripchen* (smoked pork loin), is wonderful, as is the goulash. Avoid the seafood. Rooms and dinners expensive. U.S. 50 between Upperville and Paris, VA. 703/478-1383.

The Windsor House, across the street from the Red Fox Inn, serves lamb chops, liver, and fish and chips. Moderate. 2 W. Washington Street Middleburg, VA. 703/687-6800.

Fredericksburg

Kenmore Inn This elegant white mansion in the heart of town has thirteen charming rooms. Moderate. 120 Princess Anne Street, Fredericksburg, VA 22401. 703/371-7622.

McGrath House There are three comfortable rooms in this carefully restored nineteenth-century home. Moderate. 225 Princess Anne Street, Fredericksburg, VA 22401. 703/371-4363.

Richard Johnston Inn This home has been elegantly restored and furnished with antiques. The nine rooms are moderate. 711 Caroline Street, Fredericksburg, VA 22401. 704/899-7606.

For fine dining:

Chimney's Tavern serves an American menu in an elegant colonial setting. Try the outdoor garden and pub. Moderate. 623 Caroline Street, Fredericksburg, VA. 703/371-9229.

Kenmore Inn serves traditional and trendy meals. Moderate. 120 Princess Anne Street, Fredericksburg, VA. 703/371-7622.

La Petite Auberge is known for its crabmeat dishes and other seafood. Moderate. 311 William Street, Fredericksburg, VA. 703/371-2727.

Old Mudd Tavern is a bit out of town, but this charming old house serves some interesting dishes. Stick to the basics. Moderate. Just off U.S. 1 in Thornburg, VA. 703/582-5250.

The Smythe's Cottage is a dining spot serving colonial fare in rooms decorated with country crafts. Moderate. 303 Faquier Street, Fredericksburg, VA. 703/373-1645.

North Carolina

Esmeralda Inn Legend has it that this rustic hillside lodge was once the hideout for Clark Gable, Mary Pickford, and other stars seeking a moment of privacy. The thirteen rooms are simply furnished, as are the six chalets on the grounds. Moderate. P.O. Box 57, Chimney Rock, NC 28720. 704/625-9105.

Flint Street Inns Two turn-of-the-century homes in Asheville's oldest district offer eight suites. Inexpensive. 100 and 116 Flint Street, Asheville, NC 28801. 704/253-6723.

Grove Park Inn This elegant mountain resort offers every activity and superb facilities. Moderate/expensive. 290 Macon Avenue, Asheville, NC 28804. 800/222-9793 in North Carolina, 800/438-5800 outside.

Hound Ears Club Meticulous facilities and service at this elegant, small resort that caters to an older crowd. Expensive. P.O. Box 188, Blowing Rock, NC 28605. 704/963-4321.

Old Reynolds Mansion This seventeen-room mansion was built partly before the Civil War and partly around the turn of the century. There are ten guest rooms, all decorated with antiques. Moderate. 100 Reynolds Heights, Asheville, NC 28804. 704/254-0496.

Ragged Garden Inn This turn-of-the-century home is surrounded by terraced gardens of roses, dogwoods, azaleas, and other flowering plants. The five guest rooms are furnished adequately, but the garden is the star here. Moderate. Sunset Drive, Blowing Rock, NC 28605. 704/295-9703.

Red Rocker Inn This Victorian hotel furnished with antiques has eighteen guest rooms. Moderate. 136 North Dougherty Street, Black Mountain, NC 28711. 704/669-5991.

For fine dining in the Asheville area, your best bets are to stay at the **Grove Park Inn** or the **Hound Ears Club**. Both serve exceptional food. Your other choices:

Green Park Inn specializes in beef and seafood served in a Victorian dining room. Moderate. Two miles south of Blowing Rock, NC., on U.S. 321. 704/295-3141.

New River Inn specializes in steaks and trout. Moderate. North Valley Road a mile north of the Blue Ridge Parkway in Blowing Rock, NC. 704/295-3056.

Ragged Garden Inn has European country decor and a menu to match. Good, but not great. Moderate. Sunset Drive, Blowing Rock, NC. 704/295-9703.

Chapter Two

The Magnificent Bay

This romantic getaway is the stuff of picture postcards: technicolor sunsets, harbors filled with white sails and luxurious yachts, colorful towns with intriguing shops and majestic old homes.

For four centuries, the Chesapeake Bay has lured travelers. The first Europeans to explore the 200-mile-long estuary were attracted not by its natural beauty, but by dreams of wealth. And wealth there was. The bay is filled with fish, waterfowl, and shellfish, and lined with safe harbors, fertile farmland, and navigable rivers. The tales these explorers spread back home captivated others, who braved the unknown to found small outposts in the New World. In time, these outposts grew into busy ports carrying the wealth of the New World back to the Old.

Despite the passage of the centuries, the bay still works its magic on travelers. Beauty, adventure, and excitement still await, but only if travelers choose carefully. The five towns we describe in this chapter are filled with wonders of man and nature.

A tour of the bay should start at the jewel on its western shore, the city founded in 1649 by Pilgrims and named Providence. Today it is known as Annapolis.

❦ ANNAPOLIS

Here are some of our memories of visits to this delightful city:

❦ One balmy summer night we sat at the open-air, dockside bar at the Annapolis Hilton, listening to the band while watching the passing boaters in the harbor cul-de-sac called "The Alley" do the nautical equivalent of cruising a drive-in. Out in the dark harbor, anchored sailboats bobbed gently, their lights throwing patterns of color on the water. Small water taxis, busy as the bugs that glide the surface of a lake, carried boaters to and from the vessels. And on land, a steady procession of celebrants wandered the City Dock area, inspecting the lively bars and restaurants. It was an evening of magic, one that made you feel that where you were was unlike anywhere else on earth.

❦ Rising before the sun is not one of our habits, but this time we had a reason. We had spent the night on the *Mystic Clipper*, a large schooner that sails the bay from City Dock four months a year. We had stumbled up on deck and were lining up for the early breakfast when we discovered an Annapolis we had never witnessed before. The harbor usually is a busy crossroad of sailboats, with boats arriving or departing at all times. This time it was eerily silent, swaddled in clouds of thick mist. Nothing moved save the fog, one or two ducks, and a jumping fish. The early wake-up time was forgotten in the beauty of the moment.

❦ And then there was the Saturday night in a recent December when, weary of tree-trimming, carolling, and holiday feasting, we decided to visit Annapolis for a change of pace. That was when we discovered the Annapolis Christmas parade. This parade, though, is on water, with more than seventy sailboats and motoryachts gaily decorated in surprisingly sophisticated displays of lights. The "floats" cruised through the harbor and surrounding waterways for several hours, sharing their lights and on-deck carollers with us and everyone on shore.

Talk with a sailor and sooner or later the conversation will turn to Annapolis, which brags that it is the sailing capital of the world. The hundreds of sailboats that crowd the bay every weekend are evidence that the claim is probably true. Annapolis is also the home of the U.S. Naval Academy, the tranquil and beautiful campus just a minute's walk from the City Dock. Almost overlooked in this nautical atmosphere is that Annapolis is also the capital of the state. All of these factors combine to make this town a colorful and exciting port to visit.

Walking is the best way to see the sights of Annapolis. All the attractions are within a few minutes of the **City Dock**, which is the center of activity in town.

At the City Dock you can watch the activity in the harbor or sign up for one of the cruises on a schooner or tour boat. On the other side of the harbor is Eastport, once an area of boatyards and blue-collar homes and now a district where expensive office buildings, condominiums, marinas, and fine restaurants are becoming the norm.

The dock is a busy world on weekends. Along the seawall are the low oystermen's skiffs, crabbing boats, old wooden schooners, and modern luxury yachts.

The sterns of the boats in the harbor attest to the international flavor of Annapolis. The name of the vessel and its home port is listed on the stern, and it is common to discover ships from ports all over the East Coast and from as far away as Europe and Australia in town for a visit.

Another attraction on the Alley is Fawcett's Boat Supplies, a ship's store that can equip sailors for a voyage around the world. It is fun to browse there, inspecting the sailing gear, hardware, and books. You can even buy charts for the South Pacific islands if you want to begin planning a voyage to Tahiti.

Just south of Fawcett's, on Spa Creek a few piers from the Hilton, is the posh **Annapolis Yacht Club**. The large flagpole there is the finishing line for the weekend sailboat races. Around five in the afternoon the sailboats come racing up through the harbor, heading for the finish line. The races are a colorful sight and worth catching from the seawalls and piers in Annapolis, Eastport, or from the walkway on the drawbridge over the creek.

From the dock, a fan-like maze of streets leads uphill to the circles —Church and State—that top the low hill overlooking the harbor. Main Street, the widest of the streets leading away from the dock, is lined with numerous restaurants and fine shops selling clothing, crafts, gifts, and art. **Market Place**, the low, white building across the Alley's dead end, sells everything from fresh crabs to imported delicacies.

If you walk north from Market Place, you come to the U.S. **Naval Academy**, where the remains of John Paul Jones are buried in the chapel. The deeds of Jones and other naval heroes are remembered in the **Naval Historical Museum**, where artifacts celebrating three centuries of naval history can be found. In May the campus is busy with parades, concerts, and a Blue Angels air show marking the commissioning of graduates as navy officers.

King George Street, Prince George Street, Maryland, and College avenues are lined with many historic homes, some of which are open for tours. The **Chase-Lloyd House**, built in 1769 by Samuel Chase, a signer of the Declaration of Independence, is at 22 Maryland Avenue. **Government House**, a Victorian mansion that is the home of the Maryland governor, is at College Avenue and Rowe Boulevard, just behind the State House on State Circle. The **Hammond-Harwood House** at 19 Maryland Avenue was built in 1764 and still is a stunning example of Georgian architecture. The **William Paca House** at 186 Prince George Street was owned by a former governor of Maryland who also signed the Declaration of Independence. Behind the house, at 1 Martin Street, is a beautiful formal garden of boxwoods, roses, a pond, and a Chinese Chippendale bridge.

No matter where you walk in the historic district, you always come back to a view of the water.

The harbor area also plays host to the annual boat shows that attract hundreds of boats worth millions of dollars—and thousands of sailors with Tahiti on their minds. The two four-day shows—one for sailboats and the other for power—take place in consecutive weeks in October.

The bay isn't overlooked in the festivities. Chesapeake Appreciation Days, held in October at Sandy Point State Park near the Bay Bridge, honors the state's oystermen with a weekend of food, fun, and entertainment.

The Bay Bridge, which connects Annapolis with the Eastern Shore of the bay, also has a day of its own in late May. One Sunday before the beach season begins, the bridge is opened to walkers. Shuttle buses carry the brave from the Navy Stadium in town to the bridge. Walkers are returned after they hike the six miles across the high span.

❦ CHESTERTOWN, MARYLAND

On the bay's Eastern Shore, about an hour from Annapolis, is Chestertown, founded in 1706 on the Chester River to advance trade in the Province of Maryland.

Chestertown today is a majestic river port whose main streets are lined with two-century-old homes, wonderful inns, and quality shops.

Water Street, the narrow lane that parallels the north bank of the river, hosts many of the old homes. The **Hynson-Ringgold House**, at Water and Cannon streets, was built in 1743 and expanded a generation later.

The **Customs House**, at Water and High streets, was built in 1746 and is known for its Flemish Bond brickwork. It was near this site on May 23, 1774, that citizens, outraged by taxes, boarded the port collector's ship and threw the imported tea into the river. That event is celebrated every year with parades, colonial craft exhibits, art shows, raft races, music, and food on the Saturday before Memorial Day.

Water Street between High Street and Maple Avenue is lined with numerous 200-year-old homes, but they are open only during the Candlelight Walking Tours in mid-September.

Open regularly for tours is the **Historical Society House** on Church Alley between Maple and High. This home, also called the Geddes Piper House, was owned by several Chestertown merchants, including William Geddes, the port collector whose brigantine was boarded by the tax rebels. The **Buck–Bacchus Store Museum** at High and Queen streets exhibits commercial and household articles from the nineteenth and early twentieth centuries.

For more old Federal and Georgian homes, fine shops, and shaded walks, roam the district bounded by Maple Avenue on the east, Kent Street on the north, and Cannon Street on the west. Take your time exploring. The **Chamber of Commerce** at 400 High Street has a brochure outlining a walking tour of the historic district. We enjoyed exploring these shops and admiring the old homes. The stroll ended at the White Swan Tavern on High Street, where we had tea and cookies.

In the flat farmland outside of Chestertown are other attractions. **Rock Hall**, on Route 20 beyond Chestertown, is a working seaport filled with commercial fishing vessels. Beyond Rock Hall, on Route 445, is the **Eastern Neck Wildlife Refuge**, a federal park that is home to hundreds of thousands of wintering geese, swans, and ducks. **Remington Farms**, on Route 20 north of Rock Hall, is a 3,000-acre wildlife research area with self-guided driving and hiking tours. It is closed during the hunting season.

Chestertown and the surrounding land make an attractive weekend tour in any season. By summer, the pleasures of the water are the lure. From fall to spring, the beauty of the land, the graceful flocks of waterfowl, and the slower pace draw visitors.

🐝 ST. MICHAELS, MARYLAND

This charming Eastern Shore town has a glorious history that dates back to the earliest days of the Colonies. In 1631 it was a trading outpost known as Shipping Creek, according to William Claiborne, who founded the first settlement in Maryland on Kent Island to the north in 1629.

Both Claiborne's settlement and Shipping Creek predate the founding of St. Mary's City, which is the official first colony in Maryland only because it was chartered.

Shipping Creek prospered, attracting Quaker settlers in the early years. In 1677, the name of the town was changed to St. Michaels after the town's new Episcopal parish, known as St. Michael the Archangel.

The town was an important center of shipping and shipbuilding. During the Revolution and the War of 1812, ships built in this town were responsible for the destruction or capture of hundreds of British vessels. The British didn't ignore this: on August 9, 1813, a British fleet gathered offshore to destroy St. Michaels shipyards and any boats in port. The citizens, though, outfoxed the Redcoats. By night, they blacked out all light in town, preventing the British cannon from finding a target. When morning came, the British gunners spotted lanterns through the thick fog, and the cannonade began. But the attack was fruitless; only one home was hit. The residents had raised lanterns to the tops of trees, giving the gunners false targets and throwing off their barrages.

After the war, the shipping and boatbuilding trade moved north on the bay to Baltimore, and St. Michaels began a long slumber.

Today St. Michaels is a reawakened port that attracts pleasure boaters as well as oystermen, crabbers, fishermen, and tour boats. It is a small town, and its main road—Route 33/Talbot Street—is lined with inns, shops, galleries, restaurants, and antique stores. The harbor, only a block from the center of town, is a lively area, with boats coming and going at all times.

The town is small enough to walk. We have particularly enjoyed picking up a loaf of bread or box of crackers and feeding the many geese, swans, and ducks that make the town harbor their home.

If you would rather ride, a surrey company offers a romantic horse-drawn carriage tour of town. And if the lure of the water is too much to resist, several cruise lines offer day sails and evening charters on the bay. A sunset cruise on the *Patriot* cruise boat is a pleasant way to end the day.

St. Michaels is also home to the **Chesapeake Bay Maritime Museum**, a waterside museum of eighteen buildings that have exhibits on boat-building, decoys, waterfowl, and bay history, and working examples of commercial fishing vessels used in oystering. Another town museum, the **St. Mary's Square Museum**, displays local memorabilia on the green around which the town was built.

Outside of St. Michaels are fields that in summer are full of farmers' labors and in winter are home to wintering geese. One winter weekend, while touring the countryside to photograph the flocks of Canada geese in the cornfields, we were delightfully surprised to find small groups of deer also feeding in the fields.

Another nearby attraction, at the end of U.S. 33 past St. Michaels, is **Tilghman**, a colorful, commercial fishing village definitely worth a visit. A drive there takes you through some beautiful farmland and past some antique shops worth a visit. East of St. Michaels, at the end of Bellevue Road, is the **Oxford-Bellevue Ferry**, the oldest in the nation, which will take you across the Tred Avon River to a lovely waterfront village called Oxford.

🐝 OXFORD, MARYLAND

The names of the town and river evoke pictures of a bucolic British countryside. The modern-day Oxford lives up to this picture. It is a small village dotted with some beautiful homes, anchored by a shipyard and famous inn, and lined with quiet streets and tall trees.

It wasn't always that way.

In the eighteenth century Oxford was a busy trading port, exporting tobacco and other products and importing goods and a cargo from hell: convicts, indentured servants, and slaves. The waterways around Oxford also were home to pirates. "Blackbeard" Edward Teach, Stede Bonnet, and other privateers hid out in these waters. Legends still exist that their buried treasures remain somewhere nearby, waiting to be found.

Oxford's contemporary treasures are more easily uncovered. Morris Street, which leads up from the ferry landing, is the location of several historic homes, including the **Barnaby House**, built in 1770, and the **Academy House**, which housed the officers of the Maryland Military Academy, whose director, Admiral Frank Buchanan, founded the U.S. Naval Academy. **The Grapevine House**, on Morris near Strand, is known for the still-producing vine that was brought from the Isle of Jersey in 1810. The **Customs House**, Morris and Strand streets, is a replica of the original built shortly after the Revolution. The **Oxford Museum**, at Morris and Market streets, displays nineteenth-century maritime history when it is open on weekends.

Oxford is smaller than St. Michaels, with fewer shops, restaurants, and attractions. Still, because of its beauty, it is worth a visit. We have fond memories of our hours there, strolling the town and feeding the ducks in the water off Strand Street.

Every August, the Tred Avon Yacht Club and the Chesapeake Bay Yacht Club of Easton sponsor a three-day regatta that livens up the town once again.

When you leave Oxford on Route 333, you will drive past the large estates owned by some of the industrial barons of the nation. Oxford, because of its proximity to the water and the abundance of waterfowl, has long drawn the gentry seeking sailing and hunting.

Route 333 leads you north to Easton, the county seat of Talbot County and the business center of the Eastern Shore.

❦ EASTON, MARYLAND

Easton is one of those wonderful towns that didn't destroy its past to build its present. In the town's center district, visitors can find eighteenth-century houses as well as Victorian masterpieces. And mixed in among both styles are fine shops, restaurants, and parks.

One of the prettier spots in Easton is on South Washington Street extension, where you will find the **Warner Wild Flower Sanctuary**, an eight-acre field that blossoms from spring to fall.

There are a number of fine old homes in Easton, most still private residences. They are not open for tours except on very special occasions.

One of the gems in Easton is the **Benjamin Stevens House** at South Lane and Harrison Street, built in 1794. A block away, at South and Talbot, is the **Talbot County Women's Club**, just three years younger. At Harrison and Dover streets is the **Bullitt House**, built in 1790, and nearby on Dover Street is the **Grymes Building**, built in 1794.

Other famous old homes include the **Thomas Perrin House** (1803) at 119 North Washington Street, **Foxley Hall** (1775) at Goldsborough and North Aurora streets, and the **Talbot County Court House** (1791) on North Washington at Federal Street. Opposite the courthouse is a row of shops whose buildings date from the late eighteenth century.

The **Third Haven Friends Meeting House** at 405 South Washington Street was built in 1682 and is believed to be the oldest frame house of worship in continuous use in America. Lord Baltimore attended services here.

The **Historical Society of Talbot County** has a museum with rotating exhibits depicting the early years in the county. The society also offers guided tours by reservation.

If Easton is the business center of the Eastern Shore, visitors must come away convinced that the currency is a duck.

Waterfowl are celebrated in almost every way possible here. Shops sell duck carvings, duck pictures, duck crafts, stuffed ducks, and more. Each November the **Waterfowl Festival** exhibits hundreds of decoys, paintings, and photographs of waterfowl.

Other annual events include the Easton Fly-Away in June, the largest air show in the state, and a jousting tournament held every August at St. Joseph's Church just northeast of town.

❦ TAKING THE TOUR

If you want to see the bay's sights at water level, the following sailing schools and cruise lines can help. The cost of two weekend days of classes is around $200 per student.

Sailing Schools

❦ Annapolis Sailing School offers weekend courses for beginners and novices. 601 Sixth Street, Annapolis, MD 21403. 800/638-9192.

❦ Chesapeake Sailing School offers weekend courses for all skill levels. 7074 Bembe Beach Road, Annapolis, MD 21403. 301/269-1594.

❦ Womanship offers classes mostly for women but does have some weekend courses for couples. Their motto: "We don't yell." 137 Conduit Street, Annapolis, MD 21403, 301/267-6661.

Cruise Lines

You can chart your own cruise through the yacht charter agencies, which can arrange for a boat of any length and a captain and crew to sail it for you. The cost depends on the size of the boat and the length of the cruise, but plan to spend at least $200 a day for boat and captain. We have had wonderful trips with the following: Adventures Float, whose offices are at 1415½ 21st Street NW, Apartment A, Washington D.C. 20036. 202/452-9563; and North-East Wind Yacht Charter, 326 First Street, Annapolis, MD 21403. 301/267-6333. Or try one of the following:

❦ The Mystic Clipper, a 125-foot-long schooner, makes one- and two-night cruises from the City Dock in Annapolis to St. Michaels or Tilghman Island. The cruises are only in May, June, September, and October. Reservations required for overnight trips. 800/243-0416.

❦ The Annapolitan II makes seven-hour round trips from the City Dock to St. Michaels and back, Memorial Day to Labor Day. 301/268-7600.

❦ Patriot Cruises, Inc. offers cruises at 11, 1 and 3 daily from May to October. Special evening charters available. 301/745-3100.

❦ Eastern Bay Charters offers day sails aboard a forty-foot schooner that sails at 9 and 2. 301/745-2329.

Annapolis Festivals

🦞 The Bay Bridge Walk takes place on a Sunday in late May.

🦞 The Maryland Renaissance Festival takes place from late July to Labor Day in nearby Crownsville. 301/267-6118.

🦞 The sailboat and powerboat shows are on consecutive weeks in October. 301/268-8828.

🦞 Chesapeake Bay Appreciation Days take place in mid-October at Sandy Point State Park on the bay near the west end of the bridge. Games, food, entertainment, and skipjack races.

🦞 The Christmas boat parade takes place on the last Saturday evening before Christmas.

🦞 Christmas in Annapolis is also celebrated with pub crawls, candle-light tours of the historic homes, special dinners, and other activities from Thanksgiving to the New Year. Call 301/268-8687.

Tours

Walking tours of Annapolis can be arranged by calling Historic An-napolis, Inc. (301/267-8149), Three Centuries Tours of Annapolis (301/263-5401), or the Town Crier pedicabs, which operate only during the summer (301/273-7330). Tours of the Naval Academy can be arranged by calling 301/263-6933.

The Historical Society of Talbot County offers guided tours of the city. The society is at 25 South Washington Street, Easton, MD 21601. 301/822-0773.

San Domingo Surreys has horse-drawn carriage tours of historic St. Michaels. You can also rent a carriage for private journeys. 301/745-3115.

Museums

The Chesapeake Bay Maritime Museum is on Mill Street on the waterfront in St. Michaels. It is open daily except January to March, when it is open weekends. 301/745-2916.

St. Mary's Square Museum is on The Green in St. Michaels. It is open weekends May to October. 301/745-9561.

The Naval Academy Museum is on the campus. The gate guard will direct you. It is open daily.

The Historical Society in Chestertown is open weekends May through October. It is on Church Alley near Queen Street. 301/778-3499.

The Oxford Museum is at Morris and Market streets. Hours vary. 301/226-5122.

The Historical Society of Talbot County Museum is at 25 S. Washington Street in Easton. It is open Tuesday through Sunday. 301/822-0773.

Useful Numbers

For more information, including more complete lists of attractions and festivals, write or call:

🦀 Tourism Council of Annapolis and Anne Arundel County, 6 Dock Street, Annapolis, MD 21403. 301/280-0445

🦀 Kent County (Chestertown) Chamber of Commerce, 118 North Cross Street, P.O. Box 146, Chestertown, MD 21620. 301/778-0416

🦀 Talbot County (Easton, St. Michaels, Tilghman, and Oxford) Chamber of Commerce, 7 Federal Street, P.O. Box 1366, Easton, MD 21601. 301/822-4606.

🦀 INNS AND RESTAURANTS

The bay towns have an abundance of wonderful inns and delightful restaurants. Here are our favorites, but first an explanation of how we break down our cost categories:

One night in an inn or hotel for two (often but not always including breakfast):

Inexpensive   Under $75
Moderate $75 to $125
Expensive   More than $125

Dinner for two (wine and drinks not included):

Inexpensive   Less than $25
Moderate $25 to $60
Expensive   More than $60

Annapolis

This colorful town offers a bounty of inns and restaurants. Here are our favorites:

The Historic Inns of Annapolis These five inns are all in the center of town, within a short walk of the City Dock and all in renovated eighteenth-century buildings. The **State House Inn** has nine rooms, some with Jacuzzis, in a brick house across from the Maryland State House. The **Robert Johnson House** has thirty rooms and two suites, and overlooks the governor's mansion. The **Reynolds Tavern** has four pretty rooms in the floors over the popular restaurant. The **Governor Calvert House**, a mix of Victorian and colonial architecture, has forty-nine rooms and two suites. The wedge-shaped **Maryland Inn** has forty-three rooms, four suites, and a pleasant surprise: a tavern with live jazz and other entertainment. The rooms are tastefully furnished with a mixture of antiques and reproductions. The room rates range from moderate to expensive, according to room size and building. For more information on any of the Historic Inns of Annapolis, write or call The Maryland Inn, Church Circle, Annapolis MD 21401. 301/263-2641.

The Ark & Dove This beautifully restored home offers several nice rooms furnished with period antiques and reproductions. Moderate. 149 Prince George Street, Annapolis, MD 21401. 301/268-6277.

The Charles Inn This inn is located on the picturesque Spa Creek, within walking distance of the Naval Academy and the inner harbor. All the guest rooms are furnished with antique pieces. You can drive in or sail in. Moderate. 74 Charles Street, Annapolis, MD 21401. 301/268-1451.

The Annapolis Hilton This 135-room hotel has a great location: on the dock right on the Alley and overlooking the harbor. Book a room on the back, where you can see all the action afloat. The waterfront bar is a great place on summer evenings. Expensive. 80 Compromise Street, Annapolis, MD 21401. 301/268-7555.

Note: If you are planning to visit during the boat shows in October or during Commissioning Week in late May, make your reservations very early—say six months to a year in advance. The town sells out very quickly at those times.

Our favorite restaurants include:

Café Normandie is a pleasant French bistro featuring seafood dishes with a Gallic accent. Try the desserts, particularly the crepes. Moderate. 195 Main Street. 301/263-3382.

Carrol's Creek Cafe serves fine regional American cuisine, particularly seafood and yummy desserts. Best of all, the outdoor deck is a fine place to spend an evening or afternoon, watching passing boat traffic while nibbling and sipping. Expensive. 410 Severn Avenue. 301/263-8102.

The Chart House is one of those chain restaurants that turns up on waterfronts. This one is no different, but the food (particularly the desserts) make it worth a visit. Moderate. 300 Second Street. 301/268-7166.

The Crate Cafe is a casual restaurant with a creative menu featuring egg dishes, seafood, and sandwiches. Leave room for dessert. Inexpensive/moderate. 49 West Street. 301/268-3600.

Griffins is a tavern cluttered with signs, paintings, and marvelous dark-wood decor. The tavern fare is among the best in town, but stick to the burgers and brunch-type dishes. Inexpensive. 18 Market Space. 301/269-1906.

Hampton House is a beautiful dining room. Lace and antiques set the stage, and the continental menu fulfills the expectations. Expensive. 200 Main Street. 301/268-7898.

Harry Browne's Restaurant serves some fine omelets and crepes in a room filled with art deco touches. Try dining in the garden out back. The upstairs room offers live music on weekends. Moderate. 66 State Circle. 301/263-4332.

Jason's is the new "in" place, where the boating crowd meets the BMW set. At least it is as we write this book, but trendy spots come and go with the tide. The food is worth a visit if you focus on beef and seafood. Live entertainment and dancing on weekends. Moderate. Sixth Street and Severn Avenue. 301/263-1770.

Marmaduke's Pub is where the real sailors drop anchor. It doesn't look like much and it seems to be more bar than restaurant, but the sailing crowd gathers here to watch videotapes of the day's sailboat races and munch on the food. Stick to the simple steak and seafood dishes. Moderate. Third Street and Severn Avenue. 301/269-5420.

McGarvey's Saloon is another fern bar, but the burgers and chili here are among the best in the region. Inexpensive. 8 Market Space. 301/263-5700.

Middletown Tavern serves fine American cuisine in the atmosphere of a colonial tavern. If the weather is good, dine outside on the porch. Moderate/expensive. 2 Market Space. 301/263-3323.

O'Leary's Seafood is a small, white-frame house on the waterfront between the shipyards. It is a cute place, with small tables covered with linen and decorated with flowers. The crab dishes and seafood are best here. Expensive. 310 Third Avenue. 301/263-0884.

Reynolds Tavern is a beautifully restored tavern in an eighteenth-century building. The menu is also restored, featuring such dishes as seafood and game pies. Moderate. 7 Church Circle. 301/263-6599.

The Treaty of Paris Restaurant in the Maryland Inn is perhaps the best in town. It serves continental cuisine in a very intimate and elegant setting. Expensive. Church Circle and Main Street. 301/263-2641.

Chestertown, Maryland

Brampton This meticulously restored, 130-year-old plantation house offers four bedrooms and a suite, all furnished with period antiques and fireplaces or Franklin stoves. The restoration of this inn is among the finest work we have seen. The place is beautiful! There are fifteen acres of grounds with century-old trees, boxwoods, and a grave headstone next to the drive. Ask about it. Moderate. RR2, Box 107, Chestertown, MD 21620. 301/778-1860.

Cole House This former general store and restored Victorian is in the town of Crumpton, about fourteen miles up river from Chestertown. It has three rooms, all furnished with antiques. Inexpensive. 7 Broad Street, Crumpton, MD 21628. 301/778-6155.

Great Oak Manor This elegant, twenty-five-room mansion is on the Chesapeake Bay, about eight miles from Chestertown. The mansion offers five guest rooms and four suites, all furnished tastefully with period pieces. For relaxation, guests can wander the twelve acres of lawn and gardens, swim from the beach, or use the nine-hole golf course, pool, and tennis courts at an adjacent marina. Moderate to expensive. P.O. Box 609, Chestertown, MD 21620. 301/778-INNS or 800/662-INNS.

Hill's Inn This century-old, beautifully restored Victorian in the center of Chestertown offers seven tastefully furnished rooms, shaded porches, and a wonderful, large parlor for relaxation. Inexpensive to moderate. P.O. Box 609, Chestertown, MD 21620. 301/778-INNS or 800/662-INNS.

The Imperial Hotel This small, three-story hotel was a rundown building until 1974, when George Dean, attorney for the Howard Hughes estate, bought it and refurbished it with antique reproductions and what seems to be half the world's supply of brass lamps. This quiet hotel is a perfect getaway spot, with sitting areas for drinks and conversation. The dining rooms are two Victorian parlors (one furnished in red, the other in green) where some stunning dinners are served. Behind the hotel is a carriage house housing a suite furnished in casual country decor. Moderate to expensive. 208 High Street, Chestertown, MD 21620. 301/778-5000.

Kent Manor Inn This beautifully restored, twenty-five-room inn is on Kent Island in the middle of 200 acres of soybeans and corn, about a half-hour from Chestertown. The rooms are luxurious, the outdoor gazebo bar a perfect setting for an evening chat, and the pool and grounds unusual finds at an inn. Expensive. Off Route 8 south of U.S. 50 on Kent Island. 301/643-5757.

The Lantern Inn This 85-year-old inn in the waterfront village of

Betterton, twelve miles north of Chestertown, is perfect for a quiet weekend. The four-room frame house has fourteen guest rooms, all furnished with antiques. Nearby is Betterton Beach, the only nettle-free beach on the bay. Inexpensive. 115 Ericsson Avenue, P.O. Box 29, Betterton, MD 21610. 301/348-5809.

Radcliffe Cross This elegant 260-year-old mansion was built by the Browns, a prosperous family of planters and merchants. There are two rooms in this mansion, both very spacious and filled with antiques. If you're looking for a romantic weekend, the century-old gardens may give you a hint: the boxwood-lined driveway that curves around to the entrance is shaped like a heart. Inexpensive. Quaker Neck Road, Chestertown, MD 21620. 301/778-5540.

Rolph's Wharf This cozy Victorian has five rooms, all elegantly furnished. The inn is on six acres of land on the bank of the Chester River, about five miles from Chestertown. Expensive. Rolph's Wharf Road, Chestertown MD 21620. 301/778-1988.

The White Swan Tavern This two-century-old inn offers five Federal-style rooms and a single Victorian suite. The common rooms are meant for socializing, games, or the soothing afternoon teas and delicious cakes and cookies. Take the time to examine the archaeological exhibit of artifacts found during restoration. Moderate. 231 High Street, Chestertown, MD 21620. 301/778-2300.

Fine dining (and a few stunning sunsets) in Kent County:

Fin, Fur, Feather Inn isn't a fancy restaurant, but the crab dishes and chowder are wonderful. Moderate. 425 Bayside, Rock Hall, MD. 301/639-7454.

Hemingway's has some fine seafood dishes, but the real attraction here is the sunset show on the bay. The restaurant is on Kent Island near the end of the Bay Bridge. Moderate. Pier One Marina, Stevensville, MD. 301/643-2722.

The Imperial Hotel serves creative cuisine in a Victorian atmosphere. The food is wonderful no matter what you order, and the ambience is very romantic. Service can be slow, but this just gives you more time to learn about your companion. Expensive. 208 High Street, Chestertown, MD. 301/778-5000.

Kent Manor serves creative and delicious seafood dishes in a restored eighteenth-century inn. Before dinner, have a drink in the outdoor gazebo bar or just sit under the huge shade trees in back. Entertainment some weekend nights. Moderate. The inn is on Route 8, just south of U.S. 50 on Kent Island. 301/643-5757.

Kitty Knight House is an inn on the Sassafras River north of Chestertown that dates back to the eighteenth century. The menu, though, is as current as a big-city dining room. The fare ranges from the bounty of the bay to more trendy dishes. Stick to the seafood. Moderate. Route 213, Georgetown. 301/648-5177.

The Narrows is alongside the Kent Narrows, just off U.S. 50 east of the Bay Bridge. If you can, get there at sunset and enjoy the moment on the back porch overlooking the drawbridge, channel, and marina. The ambience is pleasant but sporty. The tables are covered with linens and the walls are decorated with stuffed fish and waterfowl. The fare here emphasizes crab, but the steaks and veal dishes are wonderful. Moderate. Grasonville. 301/827-8113.

Old Wharf Inn serves seafood in a waterfront setting. Stick to the basics. Moderate. Cabin Street, Chestertown. 301/778-3566.

The River Inn features seafood in a waterfront location. Try dining out on the patio or deck. Moderate. Rolph's Wharf Road, Chestertown. 301/778-3227.

Rock Hall Inn is a basic steak and seafood house in a fishing community. Stick to the fish. Moderate. Main Street, Rock Hall. 301/639-7141.

St. Michaels, Maryland

Hambleton Inn This harbor-side inn has five rooms, all furnished with a mix of colonial and other pieces. Moderate. 202 Cherry Street, St. Michaels, MD 21663. 301/745-3350.

The Inn at Perry Cabin This elegant waterfront inn is a favorite with landlubbers and boaters. There are six rooms, all carefully decorated. Outside, huge trees shade the sprawling house, part of which dates back to the nineteenth century. A dock lures passing boaters, and the dining rooms and bar are famous in the region. Expensive. 308 Watkins Lane, St. Michaels, MD 21663. 301/745-5178.

Kemp House Inn This 180-year-old Georgian house offers seven rooms furnished with four-poster rope beds, fireplaces, fresh flowers, candles, and oil lamps. Moderate. 412 South Talbot Street (Box 638), St. Michaels, MD 21663. 301/745-2243.

Parsonage Inn This brick Victorian has seven rooms furnished with brass beds and Laura Ashley accessories. Moderate. 210 North Talbot Street, St. Michaels, MD 21663. 301/745-5519.

St. Michaels Inn This century-old brick colonial has eleven rooms, all furnished with antiques and reproductions. Moderate. 208 North Talbot Street, St. Michaels, MD 21663. 301/745-3303.

For fine dining:

The Inn at Perry Cabin is an attraction by itself. Enjoy the fine steaks, veal, and seafood dishes in the attractive waterfront dining room. Expensive. Route 33. 301/745-5178.

Longfellows is a small restaurant emphasizing fried oysters and crab. This is a popular stop for visiting boaters. Moderate. 125 Mulberry Street. 301/745-2624.

Martingham Harbourtowne Inn serves some interesting seafood dishes in a fancy setting. Expensive. Route 33. 301/745-9066.

St. Michaels Inn serves some fine dishes in a comfortable setting, but stick to the seafood. Moderate/expensive. 208 North Talbot Street. 301/745-3303.

The Tilghman Inn is a small place at Knapps Narrows in the village of Tilghman. The fare here is surprisingly sophisticated, featuring the bounty of the bay. Moderate. 301/886-2141.

Oxford, Maryland

1876 House This comfortable Victorian inn has three rooms, all furnished with tasteful period pieces. Expensive. 110 North Morris Street, Oxford, MD 21654. 301/226-5496.

Robert Morris Inn Part of the harborfront inn dates back to 1710; the rest to just after the Civil War. That means most of the thirty-three rooms are wonderful, with porches and water views. But some, including one we stayed in, are tiny. Book carefully. Moderate/expensive. 312 Morris Street, P.O. Box 70, Oxford, MD 21654. 301/226-5111.

There isn't much to choose from in this small town, but for fine dining try:

Pier Street is a marina restaurant, one where some dishes are wonderful surprises and other dishes are surprises of a different sort. Stick to the basic fish dishes. Moderate. Pier Street Marina. 301/226-5171.

The Robert Morris Inn is a fine country inn serving the standard dishes like crab imperial and stuffed flounder. The appetizers are wonderful, but the main dishes occasionally can miss. Keep it simple. Moderate. Strand and Morris streets. 301/226-5111.

Easton, Maryland

John S. McDaniel House This large Victorian offers five carefully-furnished rooms close to the waterfront and the shopping district. Inexpensive. 14 North Aurora Street, Easton, MD 21601. 301/822-3704.

The Tidewater Inn This large brick hotel holds some surprising sights: in hunting season, you are as likely to see a guest dressed in camouflage relaxing in the lobby with his hunting dog as a couple in formal evening wear. The 119 rooms and suites are furnished very tastefully. Facilities include a fine restaurant and a bar, a pool, and a location in the center of town. Expensive. Dover and Harrison streets, Easton, MD 21601. 301/822-1300.

For fine dining:

The Chambers serves the steak and seafood standards in three dining rooms decorated in eighteenth-century furnishings. Moderate/expensive. 22 West Dover Street. 301/822-5521.

Dover West serves regional fare in a comfortable setting that includes an outdoor cafe. Moderate. 14 West Dover Street. 301/822-2559.

Peachblossom attracts you before the meal comes. The smells of Italian cooking—fresh sauces, homemade breads—make it difficult to concentrate on the menu. Moderate. 6 North Washington Street. 301/822-5220.

The Tidewater Inn serves superb American and regional cuisine in the Hunter's Tavern or River Room. Moderate/expensive. Dover and Harrison streets. 301/822-1300.

The Washington Street Pub is a fine American saloon. Stick to basic pub fare and enjoy the casual atmosphere. Moderate. 20 North Washington Street. 301/822-9011.

Chapter Three

The Atlantic Shore

O nce upon a time, beach resorts were places for quiet contemplation. Religious orders, finding the sleepy towns perfect for introspection, built hotels and rustic camps and used them to reinvigorate the faithful.

Then the beaches were discovered by the sun-worshipping hordes from the city, and these quiet, religious retreats just plain went to hell.

Many of today's beach resorts are no longer peaceful getaways. All too often they are too big, too busy, and too jammed with both people and traffic.

There are four beach spots, however, that draw us back every year. The four are more than summer-month resorts. Long after the summer tans are only a memory, these resorts still offer their elegant inns, fine restaurants, stunning natural scenery, and enough off-beach activities to fill a rainy day.

We have walked their beaches and streets in all four seasons. The best time for these resorts, we found, is from September to May, when their attractions are not lost amid the summer rush.

❦ CAPE MAY, NEW JERSEY

Cape May has been a popular beach resort since the days of the Revolution. Presidents Lincoln, Grant, and other chief executives visited. Henry Ford and Louis Chevrolet are said to have raced their automobiles on the beach. And Wallis Simpson, the future Duchess of Windsor, made her debut here in the Colonial Hotel.

But none of these events did as much to ensure the popularity of the town as did the fire of 1878. The conflagration destroyed most of the town, very bad news at the time but a boon to wealthy Philadelphia residents who bought up the vacant lots and built magnificent Victorian mansions on them.

Over the years, many of the Victorian masterpieces disappeared or deteriorated. It wasn't until the early 1960s that some residents realized the extraordinary architectural wealth surrounding them. Civic groups pushed for the designation of 2.2 square miles in the center of the city as a National Landmark District. There are about 600 Victorian-era homes in that district today. Not all the homes were mansions, and not all have been restored, but enough of the Victorians have been refurbished to give visitors a taste of life in another era. Some of the renovated Victorians are now open as inns, a major factor in the rebirth of Cape May as a major ocean resort.

The inns' magnificent architecture is one of the reasons we enjoy strolling the streets of Cape May. The inns' decorative touches include stained- and leaded-glass windows and doors, gingerbread trim, towers, cupolas, broad porches, and other delights. The Victorians liked earth tones, and painted their homes to match. Brown, tans, greens, and yellows—usually in multiple combinations—are popular exterior colors. Some inn owners, though, have broken with tradition and painted their mansions in pinks, blues, and other pastels.

The beauty extends beyond the architectural majesty of the outside. Inside, the innkeepers usually have furnished the public rooms and guest bedrooms with Victorian period antiques, period art and crafts, and other beautiful items.

Though the inns are the jewels in Cape May's crown, the innkeepers don't welcome drop-in visitors. There are several ways to get a peek inside. At special times of the year, the inns are open for candlelight tours, Victorian Week activities, Christmas celebrations, and more. Trolley, gaslight, walking, and other tours of the inns and Cape May's historic district are offered year-round by the **Mid-Atlantic Center for the Arts**. If you are really determined to see the inside of a specific inn, call first and ask gently.

Self-guided tours of the historic district and outside inspection of the inns are possible any time. Stop by the **Welcome Center** at 405 Lafayette Street and pick up brochures that will guide you on a walking tour and tell you of the events in town. Most of the beautiful inns lie between the Welcome Center and the beach, a distance that can be covered in a 10-minute walk.

Some of our favorite inns are The Abbey, a towering Gothic-Revival house at Columbia Avenue and Gurney Street; Captain Mey's Inn at 202 Ocean Street; The Mainstay at 635 Columbia Avenue; and the Wilbraham Mansion at 133 Myrtle Avenue.

Another restored Victorian is the headquarters of the Mid-Atlantic Center for the Arts. The **Emlen Physick Estate** is a restored sixteen-room mansion that is a museum of Victorian life. It and the Center's art gallery in the former stables next to the mansion are worth a visit.

Cape May's festivals are well-known tourist attractions, not just diversions for beached-out visitors. These festivals include a Tulip Festival in May; a Promenade Art Exhibit in July; the Victorian Week festival of fashion shows, house tours, and entertainment in October; and the month-long Christmas celebration in December with tours, music, and more.

Shopping in Cape May was a bit disappointing, we thought. The three-block-long Washington Mall offers an assortment of shops, but few are exceptional. There are some antique shops and craft boutiques in town, but don't expect much.

Outside of town, **Cold Spring Village** is a restored farm village that demonstrates how life was in the 1850s. Buildings exhibit folk crafts, the art of blacksmithing, baking, food preparation, and more. **Wheaton Village** in Millville is a recreated Victorian village with demonstrations of glassblowing (the site once was a glass factory), pottery making, wood carving, and other arts. Take time to visit the **Museum of Glass** and admire the exhibits of art deco, art nouveau and other forms of glass art and glassware.

For nature lovers, Cape May has another side. Every fall, thousands of migratory birds stop here on their way to the Delaware and Chesapeake bays. Geese, songbirds, falcons, eagles, and more can be spotted in three popular birding areas nearby: **Cape May State Park**, the **Cape May Migratory Bird Refuge**, and **Higbee's Beach**.

If the sound of the visiting birds and fowl is too noisy, head north to the thirty acres of sculpted gardens and woods at **Leaming's Run Botanical Gardens**. There you will find twenty-five gardens, each with gazebos, benches, lily ponds and tall shade trees. One surprise at the gardens is a recreation of a small Colonial-era farm complete with garden, barn, and log cabin.

We almost forgot to mention that there is a beach in Cape May. It isn't as broad as it once was, nor as free. Beachgoers have to pay a small fee or obtain a beach pass from the inn or hotel in which they are staying. The beach is nice, but the rest of the town is a treasure even without the nearby surf. Try walking the beach-front promenade when the moon is out: On one side the surf, on the other the mansions of Beach Drive. It is a beautiful sight.

Finally, the **Cape May–Lewes ferry** runs several times every day, cutting short the distance between this New Jersey resort area and the next of our favorite beaches—Rehoboth Beach, Delaware.

❦ REHOBOTH BEACH, DELAWARE

The moment we fell in love with Rehoboth Beach remains crystal-clear in our memories. It was a clear August night and we were dining on the rooftop terrace of the now-defunct Café des Arts restaurant. In front of us was a dinner of surprising quality and interesting creativity. Below us was the boardwalk, the famed Dolle's Salt Water Taffy sign, and the beach. Then, as if for dessert, a huge orange moon began to rise over the ocean. What more could a couple ask of an evening?

Rehoboth Beach remains one of our favorite resorts, but not for its beach. This town has wonderful restaurants, an energetic arts center, some high-quality shops selling everything from avant garde art to fine clothing, and a small boardwalk that is just honky-tonk enough to enliven a Saturday night stroll.

And for beaches, you can choose the mob-scene in the center of town, where you will be within walking distance of Thrasher's French Fries, or drive a few minutes north or south of town to more secluded shores.

Rehoboth Beach came into existence a bit more than a century ago as a religious resort for the Methodist Episcopal Church. The early beginning probably contributed to the small-town atmosphere present today in Rehoboth Beach. This is a popular beach resort, but one with neighborhoods full of tall shade trees, landscaped yards, and fine old homes.

This feeling of community is seen in other ways. Culture in Rehoboth Beach is more than a Best Body on the Beach Contest or a noisy rock band in a beach-front bar. The **Rehoboth Art League**, with headquarters in a parklike neighborhood north of the center of town, sponsors art courses, exhibits, and concerts year-round. The beach crowd isn't ignored, either. Every Saturday afternoon during the season, concerts are held at the bandshell on Rehoboth Avenue and the boardwalk.

One of our favorite spots in town for walks is **Lake Gerar**, on First Street four blocks north of Rehoboth Avenue. The lake is home to many species of ducks and geese. We have picnicked on the banks of the lake, an event that always draws a crowd of admiring and hungry quackers.

Rehoboth Avenue and the paralleling streets of Baltimore and Philadelphia are the locus of activity in town. The finer shops like Carlton's (9 Rehoboth Avenue) and Muffie's (33 Baltimore Avenue) can be found on these streets, but don't overlook the small arcades that run between Rehoboth Avenue and Philadelphia and Baltimore avenues. They are home to boutiques selling gifts, jewelry, art, and other fine merchandise.

The downtown district is also where you will find restaurants that will enhance a romantic weekday. Blue Moon, Sydney's Side Street and Blues Place (also the best nightspot in town), The Back Porch Café, and others are all within a few minutes' walking distance.

For fun on the beach, volleyball, softball, and football games are played from seven to eleven every evening during the season on a lighted section of the sand between Rehoboth and Olive avenues.

Despite the blanket-to-blanket mob, we love this beach. Where else can you leave your towel and walk a few steps to Rehoboth Avenue and buy a bucket of Thrasher's fries? Surely more relationships have been sealed over Thrasher's fries than over a bottle of champagne. (If your beloved shares his or her fries, the relationship is certain to work out.)

For more seclusion, head six miles south of town to the **Delaware Seashore State Park**, a seven-mile strip of beach that will give you more privacy. Or you can head to **Cape Henlopen State Park**, on the north side of Rehoboth, where 2,684 acres of tall dunes and isolated beaches await.

🐚 CHINCOTEAGUE, VIRGINIA

If your idea of a romantic trip to the shore is to find a place where there are few crowds, then this small fishing village and the nearby beaches on **Assateague Island National Seashore** are for you.

Assateague Island stretches from just south of Ocean City, Maryland, to a bit beyond Chincoteague. Its thirty-seven miles of beach, dunes, scrub forest, and marshes are wild and undeveloped. Only a few miles of roads exist around the park centers, and most beach visitors never venture much more than a few hundred yards beyond the last parking lot.

This isolation and lack of access sets up several interesting possibilities. Nude bathing is common in some areas of the island, a practice that park authorities would rather not notice, for they would have to prosecute. And the isolation means that couples can enjoy the beach without the distractions of boom boxes, Frisbees, fishermen, and children.

The island is also home to a wide variety of wildlife. The best known are the herds of **wild ponies**, believed to be the stunted descendants of shipwrecked horses of Spanish conquistadores. The ponies share the island with thousands of migratory birds and tiny Sika deer.

Visitors can see the animals by taking one of the many **hiking trails** that start at the park offices at Assateague on the Maryland side or at the **Toms Cove Visitor's Center** near Chincoteague.

Back across the bridge to the island is Chincoteague, a rather plain village surrounded by a world of natural beauty. Chincoteague Bay and the surrounding marshland is home to countless migratory birds and waterfowl, and is the daily stage for some breathtaking sunsets.

The town became famous through Marguerite Henry's 1947 book *Misty of Chincoteague*, a classic children's tale about the wild ponies that roam Assateague Island. Every July, the Chincoteague Volunteer Firemen round up the ponies and force them to swim the inlet to Chincoteague. There, in a carnival atmosphere, some of the ponies are sold at auction to help raise funds for the fire department.

For a village with only 3,500 year-round residents, Chincoteague holds other surprises. There are a number of fine inns and even a few good restaurants.

But the main attraction in Chincoteague is not found in the inns, the Visitor's Center, the wild ponies, or the fishing fleet. The main attraction is the vast emptiness of the beaches. On one visit there we strolled past some surf fishermen cooking a breakfast just below the dunes. We watched them for a while and then continued our walk. Shortly, they disappeared from view. Then it dawned on us: we were all alone. No sunbathers. No fishermen. No boats offshore. No kites overhead. Completely, utterly alone.

Every couple should be so lucky once in their lives.

🐝 THE OUTER BANKS, NORTH CAROLINA

The Outer Banks are a long chain of narrow islands with a stark beauty and sense of isolation rarely found in the East. The attractions for travelers are subtle. On the surface, the Outer Banks offer little: There are few inns; the restaurants are only adequate. And nightlife? Well, what can you expect when the local papers list fishing piers under "Nightlife"?

No, the real attraction of the Outer Banks is in the barren beauty of the tall, wind-swept dunes at **Jockey's Ridge State Park** and the colorful hang-gliders flying over them. It is in the shipwrecks you discover on empty strands like Coquina Beach. It is in the marshland near the Hatteras Lighthouse that seems so empty until you stumble across the sunbleached timbers of a ship called the *Altoona* that made its last voyage off these shores in 1878. And it is in isolated villages like Ocracoke, whose way of life seems threatened by the needs of tourists.

The Outer Banks, islands stretching 175 miles from Cape Lookout, North Carolina, to Back Bay, Virginia, have been discovered. For many years, the few towns here were popular with fishermen but ignored by beach lovers. All that has changed. Despite the arrivals of resort communities, condominiums, and debates over development, the Banks remain a place apart from the rest of America. Privacy, empty beaches, a different way of life are the attractions here. For a tour of the Banks, the place to start is an island near the southern tip of the chain.

Ocracoke

Ocracoke has long attracted those seeking distance from civilization. The pirate "Blackbeard" Edward Teach used the island as his headquarters in the early 1700s. His raids against shipping led the Royal Navy to send an expedition to Ocracoke Inlet, where the sailors killed Blackbeard and routed his crew.

Ocracoke hasn't grown much in the centuries since. Even today there are only about 700 year-round residents on the island.

The conversion from an isolated fishing village to a tourist attraction has not always been easy. The recent construction of a new hotel in town caused much furor, with some residents denouncing it as a high-rise. The hotel is a modest three stories, which would hardly be noticeable in most resort areas, but it is a change that has shocked the citizenry on this isolated island.

A walk around the town gives evidence of how different Ocracoke is from your hometown. There are no movie houses, no McDonald's, no disco, no barber shop. The town seems frozen in time, somewhere around the end of World War II.

And beyond the small town's borders remain the other constants: the sea, the shore, and the dunes. Ever-changing, but ever the same.

At the other end of the ferry ride is another village, one where the twentieth century has made more inroads.

Hatteras

Hatteras is home to a vast fishing fleet that sweeps the warm Gulf Stream offshore. The presence of the fleet—both commercial and sport—always meant that Hatteras was more in touch with the present.

But not all the change went down smoothly. Oden's General Store, an old building that always smelled of fish, has moved, expanded, and started stocking such items as clothing and beach supplies. The humiliation surely was great, for the store changed its name to Nedo's. Behind Nedo's are the docks where many of the commercial vessels are berthed. You can watch the fish come off, heading for the packing house and the dinner tables inland. The rest of the village is quaint, its ties to the sea for its livelihood evident in the marinas and seafood houses.

North of Hatteras Village, in Buxton, is the **Cape Hatteras Lighthouse**, a 208-foot tower that is constantly threatened by the shifting sands. Near the lighthouse is the **Buxton Woods Nature Trail**, a three-quarter-mile path that takes you through wooded dunes, mazes of vines, and the marshes. It is a beautiful walk, but be careful to stay on the trail. The woods and marshes contain some dangerous reptiles.

You can also take the park road down to the shore. Don't try to drive to the beach unless you have a four-wheel-drive vehicle. Park near the fish-cleaning stands and walk to the pond, where colorful windsurfers are darting about, or over to the shore, where the powerful surf will entrance you.

From Hatteras north, you will pass through the **Cape Hatteras National Seashore**, made up of Ocracoke, Hatteras, and the southern half of Bodie Island. This seventy-mile stretch of mostly undeveloped seashore contains some of the most beautiful scenery on the Atlantic coast. Take time to pull off when you see parking areas. Do not pull off just anywhere; the soft sand on the shoulder will trap you.

On the beach, you might see anything from whales to porpoises, waterfowl to crabs. And most likely you will be all alone. At night, more surprises await on these secluded beaches. Overhead, more stars are visible than many urban dwellers imagine exist. And if there is a moon, the tireless surf turns to silver.

You won't be alone once you get north of Bodie Island, just past Whalebone Junction. **Nags Head**, a fine beach town in many ways, is now so busy it has two main roads. **Kitty Hawk** has the fabulous dunes and hang gliders, and **Duck**, on the far end, is the upscale part of the Banks.

From Nags Head, take Route 64 across the sound to **Roanoke Island**, the sight of the ill-fated first colony in America. At the north end of the island are the beautiful Elizabethan Gardens, a perfect place for a walk.

The main town on the island is **Manteo**, and the big change in town is The Waterfront, a development on Shallowbag Bay. It has some fine shops and is worth a visit. Our favorite spot, one we return to every visit, is the Christmas Shop and Island Art Gallery, a maze of rooms selling Christmas ornaments, fine art, and gifts.

The change in Manteo is part of the change in the Outer Banks. Development and all that means has come, and more is coming. Enjoy the emptiness of the Banks below Nags Head before it, too, becomes a faded memory.

Useful Numbers

For more information, including more complete lists of inns, write:

❦ Cape May Chamber of Commerce, Box 109, Cape May, NJ 08204. 609/884-8411.

❦ Rehoboth Beach Chamber of Commerce, 73 Rehoboth Avenue, P.O. Box 216, Rehoboth Beach, DE 19971. 302/227-2233.

❦ Chincoteague Chamber of Commerce, Beach Road, P.O. Box 258, Chincoteague, VA 23336. 804/336-6161.

❦ Outer Banks Chamber of Commerce, P.O. Box 90, Kitty Hawk, NC 27949. 919/261-3801.

❦ The Cape Hatteras Lighthouse is closed to the public, but the former keeper's house and a visitor's center have exhibits. Buxton, NC 919/473-2111.

❦ Ocracoke Island is reachable by a free ferry from Hatteras. Reservations are not required. 919/928-3841.

Festivals

In Cape May, New Jersey

The Tulip Festival is in May.

The Victorian Week of fashion shows, concerts, and other entertainment is in mid-October.

The Promenade Art Exhibit is in July.

The Fish Festival celebrates Cape May's role as a major fishing port. Activities include exhibits, seafood tastings, and more. It is in September.

Christmas in Cape May is a month-long festival with concerts, special tours, and other events.

For more information and schedules, call 609/465-7181.

In Rehoboth Beach, Delaware

Bandstand concerts are held Saturday afternoons from Memorial Day to Labor Day.

Cottage Tour of Art opens local homes to visitors in July. Indian Summer Festival offers a parade, a sidewalk art sale, antique show, and entertainment from late September to mid-October.

For more information, contact the Chamber of Commerce, 73 Rehoboth Avenue, Rehoboth Beach, DE 19971. 302/227-2233.

In Chincoteague, Virginia

Easter Decoy Festival is held Easter weekend.

The Pony Penning is held in late July.

The Oyster Festival is held over Columbus Day weekend in October.

The Waterfowl Open House is held during Thanksgiving week.

For more information, call 804/336-6161.

On the Outer Banks, North Carolina

The annual Rogallo Kite Festival is held every June at Kitty Hawk. 919/441-4124.

The Sand Sculpture Contest is held in July in Kill Devil Hills. 919/473-3493.

The New World Festival of the Arts is held in Manteo in mid-August. 919/261-3165.

Museums

In Cape May, New Jersey

Cape May Historic Society exhibits local memorabilia. The society is on the Shore Road, three-quarters of a mile north of Stone Harbor Road.

Cold Spring Village, 731 Seashore Road (two miles north of Cape May on U.S. 109) is open Memorial Day to mid-October. 609/884-1810.

The Emlen Physick Estate and the Mid-Atlantic Center for the Arts are at 1048 Washington Street. 609/884-5404.

Wheaton Village is at 10th and G streets in Millville, about thirty minutes from Cape May. 609/825-6800.

In Rehoboth Beach, Delaware

The Rehoboth Arts League is at 12 Dodds Lane in Henlopen Acres, on the north side of Rehoboth Beach. 302/227-8408.

In Chincoteague, Virginia

The Refuge Waterfowl Museum displays art of birds and waterfowl and an impressive collection of carved decoys. Maddox Road. 804/336-5800

Parks

Chincoteague National Wildlife Refuge is on Assateague Island. 804/336-6122.

Assateague Island National Seashore has its headquarters near Berlin, MD. 301/641-1441.

Cape Hatteras National Seashore has an information center at Whalebone Junction, where U.S. 158 and Route 12 meet in Nags Head. Route 1, Box 675, Manteo, NC 27954. 919/473-2111.

❦ INNS AND RESTAURANTS

The beach towns have a number of fine inns and restaurants. Here are our favorites, but first an explanation of how we break down our cost categories:

One night in an inn or hotel for two (often but not always including breakfast):

Inexpensive   Under $75
Moderate $75 to $125
Expensive   More than $125

Dinner for two (wine and drinks not included):

Inexpensive   Less than $25
Moderate $25 to $60
Expensive   More than $60

Cape May, New Jersey

The Abbey This Gothic-Revival inn dominates the center of the historic district of the New Jersey resort. The arched windows, Victorian furnishings and sixty-foot tower combine to turn a coal baron's mansion into one of the more striking inns in town. There are seven rooms in the main house, seven more in the cute McCreary Cottage behind the Abbey. All are furnished with a mixture of antiques, some Victorian, some not. If you can, book the Tower Room with its floor-to-ceiling windows. Moderate. Open April to November. Columbia Avenue and Gurney Street, Cape May, NJ 08204. 609/884-4506.

Captain Mey's Inn This inn ranks as one of our favorites. The nine rooms are decorated with Victorian furniture, fine touches like Persian rugs, and a wide mixture of eclectic art and collectibles. The breakfasts were memorable, the garden romantic, and the tea refreshing. We want to go back! 202 Ocean Street, Cape May, NJ 08204. 609/884-7793.

The Chalfonte This marvelous, 103-room hotel is the *grande dame* of town. For 123 years it has been a genteel retreat. The broad porches are made for resting and socializing, the King Edward Room Bar is acclaimed by some as the finest anywhere (we won't go that far), and its dining room is famed for its Southern cuisine. A stay here is like a stay in another time. The bed frames are iron, and there are few rooms with private baths. Rates include breakfast and dinner. Moderate. Open May to mid-October. 301 Howard Street, Cape May, NJ 609/884-8409.

The Duke of Windsor Inn This Victorian mixes molded ceilings, original brass beds, Tiffany windows, and eclectic furnishings in the nine guest rooms. Moderate. Closed in January. 817 Washington Street, Cape May, NJ 08204. 609/884-1355.

Mainstay Inn This Italianate villa is a stunning work of architecture: a wrap-around veranda, fourteen-foot ceilings with windows rising almost as high, brass gaslights, lace, giant mirrors, and more. The furnishings are exquisite and are a tribute to the meticulous restoration by the owners. There are eight rooms in the inn and five more in the adjacent cottage, a nice but modernized annex. Moderate. Open April to November. 635 Columbia Avenue, Cape May, NJ 08204. 609/884-8690.

Poor Richard's Inn The century-old home is magnificent, with deep bay windows and a hexagonal porch. Inside, the decor mixes Victorian with other periods, resulting in an eclectic and casual atmosphere. The nine rooms and two apartments are furnished with the same mix. Moderate. Open March to December. 17 Jackson Street, Cape May, NJ 08204. 609/884-3536.

The Queen Victoria This green Victorian is more relaxed than the

❦ Captain Mey's Inn is one of the marvelous Victorian inns in Cape May, New Jersey. *Photo by Barbara Radin-Fox.*

Abbey or Captain Mey's Inn. The twelve rooms are furnished with antiques, but the pieces are meant to be used, not just admired. (The inn is adding eleven new rooms with Jacuzzis.) Moderate. 102 Ocean Street, Cape May, NJ 08204. 609/884-8702.

Seventh Sister Guesthouse This inn looks like an artist's residence, and it is. Painter Jo-Anne Echevarria and her husband Bob Myers have furnished this Victorian home with abstract paintings, collages, and other modern art. There are six rooms, all tastefully furnished. Moderate. 10 Jackson Street, Cape May, NJ 08204. 609/884-2280.

The Victorian Rose Perfect for Valentine's Day, an anniversary or just a weekend of dreams, this two-story Victorian cottage celebrates roses. They are the stars of the garden and, in the off-season, decorate the Christmas tree. The ten rooms and two apartments are tastefully furnished with oak beds and dressers, caned chairs, and ceiling fans. Get the Green Room if you can. It has an Old Cape May bed, a clawfoot bathtub and a private porch. There is a cottage available for weekly rentals. Moderate. 715 Columbia Avenue, Cape May, NJ 08204. 609/884-2497.

The Wilbraham Mansion This twenty-four-room mansion has long been a tourist attraction in Cape May, and only recently became an inn. It is a wonderful mixture of the elegant—beautiful wood paneling, huge gilded mirrors, wonderful antiques, two Packer push-pedal organs— and the bizarre. Former owners added some unusual touches—exotic wallpaper; a huge, wrought-iron chandelier painted in day-glo colors— that current owners Pat and Rose Downes have decided to leave for the moment. The eight rooms are comfortable, furnished with wicker and some antique pieces. And the sole suite opens out to the indoor heated pool at the rear of the mansion. Moderate/expensive. 133 Myrtle Avenue, Cape May, NJ 08204. 609/884-2046.

Cape May is also blessed with many fine restaurants:

Alexander's is a beautiful restaurant whose decor—roses, lace, silver, crystal in four intimate rooms—is exceeded only by the quality of the fare. Rabbit, veal, and seafood are the treasures here. The only flaw is that you may have to bring your own wine. Call to see if they have a liquor license. Expensive. 603 Washington Street. 609/884-2555.

The Bayberry Inn is a one-room restaurant that looks like the large dining room of an old inn. The menu is unusual, featuring touches from the Caribbean as well as France. Bring your own wine. Moderate. Perry Street at Congress Place. 609/884-8406.

La Toque is a pretty French bistro with two personalities. By day it's a sandwich, salad, and omelet cafe, and by night an exciting and innovative cafe featuring beef and seafood. Moderate. 210 Ocean Street. 609/884-1511.

The Mad Batter is hard to label. At breakfast, lunch, and brunch the menu features egg dishes, crepes, and omelets. In the evening, though, the chefs turn creative, with dishes ranging from American nouveau to Oriental. It is all interesting and well-executed. If the weather cooperates, try dining on the outdoor terrace. Moderate/expensive. 19 Jackson Street. 609/884-5970.

Washington Inn is a longtime favorite of Cape May visitors. The menu is American standard, with no surprises but no failures. 801 Washington Street. 609/884-5697.

Rehoboth Beach, Delaware

The Corner Cupboard Inn This inn, on a lovely, pine-shaded lane about a block and a half from the beach, is like your grandmother's house—ten guest rooms filled with old furniture, but nothing too fancy. It is a warm, comfortable place, where you mingle with the other guests before the fireplace in the living room or outside on the veranda. Moderate/expensive. 50 Park Avenue, Rehoboth Beach, DE 19971. 302/227-8553.

The Gladstone Inn This three-story, white-frame house has that all-American look about it. There are six rooms and four apartments, all furnished simply but adequately. The inn is two houses from the beach and within walking distance of the business district. Moderate, and open only during the summer. 3 Olive Avenue, Rehoboth Beach, DE 19971. 302/227-2641.

The Pleasant Inn This beautiful inn with its broad front porch and gracefully landscaped lawn is a delightful find in this beach town. There are ten rooms and one carriage house, all close to the beach and business district and all pleasantly but not elegantly furnished. Moderate. 31 Olive Avenue, Rehoboth Beach, DE 19971. 302/227-7311.

Tembo Guest House This B&B located just a few minutes from the surf has six rooms furnished with a mix of antiques and contemporary pieces. Other inns have more elegant accommodations, but none has Amos the Turtle, the Official House Terrapin. Inexpensive. 100 Laurel Street, Rehoboth Beach, DE 19971. 302/227-3360.

Nearby Milford is a town worth visiting on a rainy day:

The Towers This Victorian mansion is elegant! All five rooms are decorated with French Victorian (is there such a thing?) antiques. Outside, a gazebo, pool, fountain, and lawn wait to soothe your travel-weary bodies. Moderate. 101 Northwest Front Street, Milford, DE 19963. 302/422-3814.

Rehoboth Beach has many fine restaurants:

Back Porch Cafe has been a favorite of ours since it opened in the 1970s. Try the omelets and seafood, but hope the weather will allow you to eat outdoors. Moderate. 21 Rehoboth Avenue. 302/227-3674.

Blue Moon is a beautiful restaurant with an inventive menu that is constantly surprising. The restaurant attracts a broad mix of diners, unlike the open-air bar, which draws a clientele that is mainly gay. Moderate/expensive. 35 Baltimore Avenue. 302/227-6515.

Camel's Hump is an oddity for beach resorts: it serves some excellent Middle Eastern dishes. Stick with the lamb. 21 Baltimore Avenue. Moderate. 302/227-0947.

Chez La Mer features the food of Provence in a pretty dining room. Moderate. Second and Wilmington Avenue. 302/227-6494.

Irish Eyes is a fine saloon that serves up pints as well as some fine sandwiches and steak and seafood specials. Moderate. 15 Wilmington Avenue. 302/227-2888.

Sydney's Side Street and Blues Place serves some creative, California-style dishes, heavy on the omelets and meat pies. Stick around after dinner for the best nightspot in town. Moderate. 22½ Wilmington Avenue. 302/227-1339.

Thrasher's French Fries is—okay, it's not a restaurant—it's the closest thing to fry heaven you will find. Buy 'em by the bucket. Cheap. 8 Rehoboth Avenue and other locations.

In nearby Bethany Beach:

Harbor Lights serves some fine seafood and steak dishes on the edge of the marsh. Get there in time for the sunset. Moderate. Route 1. 302/539-3061.

Nightlife

Rehoboth Beach and nearby Ocean City, Maryland, have several night spots worth mentioning.

Sydney's Side Street and Blues Place has some excellent live blues. The room is cramped but worth it. 22½ Wilmington Avenue, Rehoboth Beach. 301/227-1339.

The Lookout Lounge in the Ramada Inn in North Ocean City has been packing in visitors for years for the Admiral's cabaret show. The revue offers comedy, top-40 and show tunes, and dancing. 138th Street, Ocean City. 301/250-1867.

The Talbot Street Café has live rock, R&B, and reggae every weekend night. Funky atmosphere. 7 Talbot Street, in old Ocean City. 301/289-3806.

Chincoteague, Virginia

The Channel Bass Inn This inn is a big old house that fits right in with the casual surroundings of Chincoteague. But appearances are deceiving. The ten rooms and two suites are fine, all furnished comfortably with antique pieces, but what makes the Channel Bass Inn a surprise is the dining room, where superb (and expensive) dishes are served. Expensive. 100 Church Street, Chincoteague, VA 23336. 804/336-6148.

The Little Traveler Inn This 150-year-old house has a wonderful brick courtyard and rose garden, a back porch for bay-watching, and six rooms furnished with Victorian and other antique pieces. Moderate. 112 North Main Street, Chincoteague, VA 23336. 804/336-6686.

Miss Molly's This inn shares ownership with the Little Traveler just across the way, and is a large Victorian built by Miss Molly's father, a gentleman who made his fortune in clams. The seven rooms are furnished with antiques, and two are special: the Bay Room, with a view of that body of water; and the Blue Room, overlooking the main street in town. Moderate. 113 North Main Street, Chincoteague, VA 23336. 804/336-6686.

Year of the Horse Inn This spacious and sunny inn right on the bay has three rooms and a two-bedroom apartment. The decor, unlike the planned antiquities in many inns, is, well, mixed. There is everything from a wreath of peacock feathers to a Victorian fainting-couch draped with a fox fur. Check out the hat stand that sprouts gargoyles and the four-foot-tall rocking camel. Each of the guest rooms has a balcony facing the bay. Inexpensive. 600 South Main Street, Chincoteague, VA 23336 804/627-1983.

There are two inns in Snow Hill, Maryland, a lovely town with a surprising number of Federalist and Victorian homes about twenty-five miles north of Chincoteague on Route 12:

Chanceford Hall Bed & Breakfast Inn This large, 230-year-old house has five spacious guest rooms, all furnished with Williamsburg-style antique reproductions. All the beds are canopied. The inn has a heated lap pool, ten working fireplaces, and a sunroom for guests. Moderate. 209 West Federal Street, Snow Hill, MD 21863. 301/632-2231.

The Snow Hill Inn There are five rooms in this three-story frame house, which was built in stages between 1790 and 1850. Each room has a different decoration theme, but choose the Victorian Room, with its carved bed and private bath. Moderate. 104 East Market Street, Snow Hill, MD 21863. 301/632-3971.

In Berlin, Maryland, just off U.S. 50 five miles west of Ocean City, is perhaps the most elegant inn in the Eastern Shore and arguably its finest restaurant as well:

Atlantic Hotel There are sixteen elegantly furnished rooms in this Victorian masterpiece. Antique furniture, Oriental rugs, and fine works of glass decorate the rooms, halls, lounge, and dining room of this wonderful inn. Moderate. 2 North Main St., Berlin, MD 21811. 301/641-0189.

Dining in the Chincoteague area is limited, but there are two surprises:

Beachway is decorated to look like an old tavern. The menu, however, is more current. Stick to the seafood. Moderate. Maddox Boulevard, Chincoteague, VA. 804/336-5590.

The Channel Bass Inn is out of place in this small fishing village. The menu is continental, the prices are high, and the waiters wear tuxedos. The food lives up to the setting, though, if you stick to the seafood and crab. Expensive. 100 Church Street, Chincoteague, Va. 804/336-6148.

If you cannot get into the Channel Bass Inn, make the drive north to the **Atlantic Hotel**, where a surprisingly creative and wonderful menu awaits in the dining room. Seafood is the star of this romantic restaurant. Expensive. 2 North Main St., Berlin, MD. 301/641-0189.

The Outer Banks, North Carolina

The Berkley Center Country Inn This once was the Berkley Machine Works and Foundry, one of the few industrial sites on the isolated island of Ocracoke. Today, the factory has been converted into an inn, with eleven rooms furnished in simple but tasteful decor. There are four acres of grounds, and the inn is within a short walk of the ferry, a marina, and a usually empty beach. Moderate. P.O. Box 220, Ocracoke, NC 27960. 919/928-5911.

Outer Banks Bed and Breakfast This is one of the oldest buildings in the fishing village of Hatteras. The three rooms are cozy, but the atmosphere of the inn is welcoming, unlike some places on the Outer Banks. The best part of a stay here is the breakfast, where such surprises as apple soufflé pancakes with port and raspberry sauce; deep-fried french toast with apricot, sausage, and orange sour cream topping; scallop popovers in a white wine and cream sauce; and . . . well, there's a lot more. Inexpensive. P.O. Box 610, Hatteras, NC 27943. 919/986-2776.

Sanderling Inn This modern wood-and-glass inn is on the other side of the Outer Banks, where the old cedar-sided homes are being replaced by the latest in waterfront development. Duck, once a town visitors bypassed on the way to Nags Head, is now an "in" place among the BMW set. This inn, on a beautiful oceanfront spot, would be acclaimed in California or Florida, but on the Banks it seems out of place. Nevertheless, it is a lovely place to stay, even though it is—forgive the term—modern. There are sixty-one deluxe rooms, a restored U.S. Life Saving Station that serves as the bar, tennis courts, hot tubs, nature trails, and five miles of private beaches. Expensive. Route 319Y, five miles north of Duck. Mailing Address: Duck, NC 27949. 919/261-4111.

Scarborough Inn This two-story building is chock-full of antiques, including the bed the owner's mother was born in and some of the valuables her father, a member of the island's shipwreck commission, recovered from the ships lost in the treacherous Outer Banks waters. There are eleven rooms, all with two Victorian beds and a collection of antiques and craft pieces. The only drawback, if there is one, is that the inn is located on the main road in Manteo, about five minutes from busy Nags Head beach. Inexpensive. P.O. Box 1310, Manteo, NC 27954. 919/473-3979.

Fine restaurants are hard to come by down here. Banks visitors get up early and eat dinner early. Be warned.

The Back Porch in Ocracoke is in a rustic old building shaded by tall trees. Inside is a carefully decorated restaurant whose menu features fresh seafood—as long as it isn't fried. It's great! Moderate. 919/928-6401.

Café René is a new spot, just across the causeway from Nags Head. The menu is continental, featuring such dishes as roast duck and salmon *en croute*. Expensive. The restaurant is in The Waterfront development on Shallowbag Bay in Manteo. 919/473-1155.

The Froggy Dog is a cute spot, with aged cedar shingle siding and window boxes filled with flowers. It looks like a trendy spot for the tourists, but the locals love it for the biscuits, fried onion rings, and fried seafood. Moderate. On Route 12 in Avon. 919/995-4106.

Miller's Waterfront Restaurant serves excellent seafood and a great view of Roanoke Sound. Moderate. Milepost 16, the Bypass, Nags Head. 919/441-6151.

Sanderling Inn & Restaurant is famous for its Southern cuisine. The restaurant is a ninety-year-old former U.S. Lifesaving Station, an attraction in its own right. On Route 319Y, five miles north of Duck. 919-261-4111.

Weeping Radish Brewery and Restaurant makes our list if only for the name. This micro-brewery in Manteo makes its own suds to go along with the German fare: wieners, stews, and wurst. Moderate. On Route 64 in Manteo. 919/473-1157.

Chapter Four

Murder, Music, and More

Remember the old *Thin Man* movies? Myrna Loy and Dick Powell, she in her exotic gowns and he in his dashing tux, flitted from one glamorous nightspot to another, somehow managing to untangle a mystery and catch a murderer in between martinis.

Intrigue and mystery can add spice to a romance. Take those two spices, mix in an elegant old mansion, some strange characters, and one temporary corpse, and you have a recipe for an exciting weekend getaway, one where the two of you can play different roles—a vamp, say, or a rake—as you try to track down a killer.

The murder mystery is an exciting way to enliven a weekend. The program usually calls for a reception or cocktail party on the first evening so the guests can get acquainted and be assigned their "characters." At some mystery weekends, scattered in the crowd will be several ringers: actors chosen to pretend they are guests just like you but who will really be taking part in the "murder."

The guests are assigned their characters and are asked to play those roles at all times during the weekend. This "getting into a role" can go to some extremes: At The Towers in Milford, Delaware, guests are required to dress to fit the period theme of the weekend—Victorian or Roaring '20s, for example.

When everyone is in character, the murder takes place and the fun—the investigation—begins.

Murder Mystery Weekends are popular getaways in the Mid-Atlantic. Not as well known, but just as interesting, are other weekend activities that you can take part in: a Dickens weekend; a learn-all-about-being-an-innkeeper weekend; a weekend of listening to classical music, opera and ballet at a nineteenth-century Victorian spa; playing a role in a comedy or musical; sailing the Chesapeake Bay; taking a trip on a river raft or in a hot-air balloon; perfecting your cooking skills or trying your hand at making Victorian Christmas decorations.

These activities are usually offered in the off-season, between the end of fall and the beginning of the summer travel rush. They also often cost a fee in addition to that charged for lodging. Call or contact the hotel, inn, or spa for its latest schedule of events and fees.

❦ MURDER, ANYONE?

Chalfonte This stately Victorian mansion in Cape May plays host to murder every June. The homicide takes place in a Victorian setting where the clues all lead to a grand dinner dance and the unmasking of the villain.

The Chalfonte offers 103 rooms and is known widely for its Southern cuisine. Room rates for couples start at $74 and include breakfast and dinner. Write the hotel for more information about the summer programs and any fees.

Chalfonte—301 Howard Street, Cape May, NJ 08204. 609/884-8409.

Guesthouses and **Boxwood Tours** Every winter a grand country home in the rural counties outside of Philadelphia becomes the site of a murder. The subject varies, but the plot in the Manor House Murders always involves the uppercrust; a recent plot centered on a diplomatic summit on terrorism. The title: "Treaties, Traitors, and Treason."

Manor House Murders is a production of Guesthouses and Boxwood Tours, which changes the location of the murder mystery annually to one of the more than 100 homes, all private estates, in the Guesthouses registry. All of the Guesthouses are elegantly furnished and architecturally significant, and most are on Pennsylvania's or the National Register of Historic Places.

The Manor House Murders are held once each winter. The cost of the package is about $400 per person and includes two nights' lodging, dinner Friday, breakfast, lunch, and black-tie dinner Saturday, and breakfast and brunch Sunday. And a surprise or two.

Guesthouses and Boxwood Tours—RD 9, West Chester, PA 19380. 215/692-4575.

Harry Packer Mansion Murder is committed every weekend at this lavish mansion in Jim Thorpe, a small Victorian town in the Poconos. The proof, if you need it, is in the cemetery: the characters used in the Murder Mystery Weekends are—or rather, were—real, and some of the events in this murder are said to be taken from some true events.

This Murder Mystery Weekend is a two-night affair, beginning Friday evening with an orientation and assignment of characters and continuing through the unmasking of the villain at a formal dinner Saturday night.

In 1874, rail baron Asa Packer built the mansion as a wedding present for his son, Harry. The house is worth a tour, murder or not: Tiffany stained-glass windows decorate the dining room; hand-painted ceilings, carved mantles, and marble testify to the elegance of the building. There are seven guest rooms sharing three baths, and one suite with a private bath.

The murder mysteries are held every weekend from September to May; the cost is between $315 and $350 per couple, including breakfast Saturday and Sunday and dinner Saturday night.

Harry Packer Mansion—Packer Hill, Jim Thorpe, PA 18229. 717/325-8566.

Society Hill Hotels The murder mystery at these small Baltimore hotels takes participants throughout the city, with clues being found at such historic sites as the grave of Edgar Allen Poe or in dramatizations, such as a fight on the waterfront. The sleuths move around the city, riding a Baltimore trolley from one clue to another.

The Society Hill Hotels are three turn-of-the-century renovated townhouses located within several blocks of each other in downtown Baltimore. The three are known by their locations: West Biddle, famed for its restaurant and jazz bar; Government House, known for its two tower rooms; and Hopkins, near Johns Hopkins University and noted for its art deco suites.

There are sixty-nine nicely furnished rooms in the three hotels, all with private baths. The rooms in the West Biddle tend to be small.

The Murder Mystery Weekends are held once in the summer and again in late fall. The cost is $500 per couple and includes two nights' lodging and all meals.

Government House—eighteen rooms. 1125 North Calvert Street, Baltimore, MD 21205. 301/752-7722.

Hopkins—twenty-six rooms and ten suites. 3404 St. Paul Street, Baltimore, MD 21218. 301/235-8600.

West Biddle—fifteen rooms. 58 West Biddle Street, Baltimore, MD 21201. 301/837-3630.

200 South Street There are four Murder Mystery Weekends a year at this beautiful inn just a few minutes from the main shopping district of Charlottesville, Virginia. The mayhem takes place in February and March, perfect time for some quiet sleuthing indoors.

There are twenty rooms in this exquisite, 140-year-old inn. The interior touches are stunning: beautiful antiques, canopied beds, fireplaces, and Jacuzzis in some rooms. The price of the weekend varies according to the room. Room rates range from $70 to $100.

200 South Street—200 South Street, Charlottesville, VA 22901. 804/979-0200.

The Towers This ornate Victorian mansion is an elegant scene for murder, but twice a month from October to April a homicide is committed.

The fun extends beyond the murder mystery. The theme for the weekend varies. It could be a Victorian Murder, or a Roaring Twenties Murder, or a 1940s Murder. The guests, ready or not, *must* dress to suit the theme for the weekend.

The five rooms in this mansion are all lovingly decorated in French Victorian. The cost of the Murder Mystery Weekend is $350 per couple and includes lodging for two nights, two parties, two breakfasts, one dinner, and brunch.

The Towers—101 NW Front Street, Milford, DE 19963. 302/422-3814.

The American Zephyr This elegant art deco train turns murder into a federal offense: it happens on the rails between Washington and New York.

Once a month the three rail cars (an observation car, a coach, and a dining car) that make up the Mystery Train link up to a regular Amtrak train and go to New York or Washington.

The one-day train leaves Washington's Union Station at 7:20 A.M. (an hour that might explain the homicide) and returns at 9:50 P.M. In between, guests get assigned roles to play, the victim gets done in, and the sleuthing begins. The murderer is caught, but not before a brief interlude in Manhattan or Washington—long enough for a quick shopping trip, lunch, or a matinee.

The cost of the one-day trip is $195 per person and includes ticket, continental breakfast, and snacks. The Washington-to-New York trip is offered once a month, the New York-to-Washington trip five times a year.

The ultimate Zephyr Murder Train may be the three-day, two-night trip in April from Washington to The Homestead, the fabulous, five-star Hot Springs, Virginia, resort. Guests leave Friday, and the murder mystery begins. After arriving at The Homestead, guests take part in two days of the annual Wine and Food Festival at the resort, then board the train Sunday and begin investigating the murder once again. The Zephyr cars are attached to the Amtrak Cardinal, which takes you through some stunning mountain scenery. The cost of this trip is $699 per person, all meals, lodging, mystery, and train fees included.

American Zephyr, Inc.—Suite 602, 806 15th Street NW, Washington, DC 20005. 202/737-0818.

🍎 VICTORIANA

Atlantic Hotel In the small Maryland town of Berlin just a few minutes from the beach, this newly renovated High Victorian is a magnificent sixteen-room, antique-filled hotel built in 1895.

On the last weekend in November, the Atlantic hosts a Dickens Party. The staff dresses in period costumes, the guests in black tie. Horse and buggy rides are offered, a special dinner menu provides such temptations as roast goose and plum pudding, and a three-piece group plays dinner music while a live jazz trio holds out anachronistically in the lounge. The Dickens Party costs about $50 per couple. Room rates are $70 and up.

The Atlantic Hotel—North Main St., Berlin, MD 21811. 301/641-0189.

Chalfonte If the architecture of this Victorian-era hotel in the historic town of Cape May, New Jersey, intrigues you, attend the Victorian Architecture 101 weekend in June.

You can earn academic credit at this hands-on course on preservation. Also included are tours of the historic Victorian estates in the beach resort.

The best part of this program is the location: a 103-room hotel that is the essence of Victorian style and Southern hospitality. Write for more

❧ The Chalfonte Hotel in Cape May is the site of music weekends, Victorian celebrations, and other exciting diversions. *Photo by Barbara Radin-Fox.*

information about the program and any fees. Room rates for couples start at $74 and include breakfast and dinner.

Chalfonte—301 Howard Street, Cape May, NJ 08204. 609/884-8409.

Harry Packer Mansion Every August this magnificent Poconos mansion turns back the clock to the 1870s, when Harry Packer and Augusta Lockhart were married in a wonderful Victorian ceremony.

On the second weekend of that month the wedding of the first owners of the Packer Mansion is recreated so guests can enjoy the ceremony and festivities. There is no extra charge for the Wedding of Harry and Augusta Weekend beyond the regular room rates of $75 to $110 a night.

Harry Packer Mansion—Packer Hill, Jim Thorpe, PA 18229. 717/325-8566.

🐞 CHRISTMAS

Harry Packer Mansion Enjoy a Victorian Christmas Ball in an elegant 1874 mansion built as a wedding present for the son of a railroad magnate.

A string ensemble plays at the Christmas Ball. It is held in December, but the date varies. This elegant inn in the Poconos has seven guest rooms and one suite. There is no additional charge for the Christmas Ball beyond the regular room rates, which are $75 to $110 a night.

Harry Packer Mansion—Packer Hill, Jim Thorpe, PA 18229. 717/325-8566.

Queen Victoria Learn about the customs, folklore, and decorations of a Victorian Christmas in this Cape May inn of the same period.

The Decorating Workshop Weekend takes place from the first Thursday to the first Saturday in December. Museum curator Connie Hershey lectures on the customs of the season with an emphasis on the Victorian era. Other workshops focus on the folklore of the season and help you make your own decorations. The weekend concludes with a tree-decorating party (with three trees adorned in different aspects of Victoriana).

After the Decorating Workshop Weekend ends, a Dickens Extravaganza takes over from the first Sunday to the first Tuesday in December.

Lectures, dramatic readings from Charles Dickens' works, and Victorian entertainment lead up to a gala Dickens feast. These events are sponsored by the International Dickens Fellowship and the Victorian Society in America.

The Queen Victoria is a twelve-room inn; eleven of those rooms had Jacuzzis added in 1989. All are furnished with period pieces. The Decorating Workshop Weekend is $25 per couple plus the usual room charge of from $65 to $100 per night. It includes a reception, luncheon, and tree-decorating party. The cost of the Dickens Extravaganza varies.

Queen Victoria—Ocean Street, Cape May, NJ 09204. 609/884-8702.

❦ DRAMA

River House Have you ever wanted to play a role in a Broadway comedy or musical? Well, you can audition in this Virginia inn during one of its winter Theater Weekends.

Once a month, November to March, a Theater Weekend is held with a theme—Simon Sampler, Thurber Carnival, or Musical Medley, for example. The guests have an opportunity to rehearse and take part in staging part of one of the classics. The main performance is Saturday night with a Sunday matinee as an option.

The weekend costs $95 per person plus a lodging rate of $60 to $80 per night. That includes two wine and cheese parties, two dinners, two brunches, afternoon tea, and lodging.

River House—Boyce, VA 22620. 703/837-1476.

❦ HEALTH AND FITNESS

Chalfonte The grand Victorian lady of Cape May, New Jersey offers several summer programs emphasizing fitness.

A Performance Enhancement Workshop is designed to improve your confidence and achieve peak performance in sports and performing arts.

A Walking Wellness Weekend helps you both lose weight and improve cardiovascular function.

The times and fees for these summer programs vary. What doesn't is the majestic old hotel, whose 103 rooms offer comfortable accommodations and whose dining room is famed for its Southern fare. Room rates for couples start at $74 and include breakfast and dinner.

Chalfonte—301 Howard Street, Cape May, NJ 08204. 609/884-8409.

Coolfont This small West Virginia resort offers a Fitness Weekend to get your bodies into better shape, and a Massage Workshop Weekend that will help you enjoy each other a bit more.

The resort, a modern establishment surrounded by beautiful wooded hills, offers motel-like rooms and private chalets, and such recreational facilities as an indoor swimming pool, hiking trail, cross-country skiing trails, tennis, boating, and horseback riding.

The Fitness Weekend costs $190 per person in the winter and $230 in the summer. The Massage Workshop costs $450 per couple. Both prices include two nights' lodging, all meals, and activities.

Coolfont Recreation, Inc.—Berkeley Springs, WV 25411. 304/258-4500.

❦ GARDENS

Guesthouses and Boxwood Tours Enjoy a Spring Splendor Weekend with a tour of the marvelous Philadelphia Flower Show guided by an expert from the Philadelphia Horticultural Society, and lectures at Longwood Gardens and Winterthur, two of the celebrated Du Pont estates in the Brandywine Valley area.

In the summer, a Garden Party Weekend takes guests on a comparative tour of the gardens at Longwood and Winterthur and those at Hagley and Nemours, two other Du Pont estates.

Guests stay at one of the 100 country estates that are part of the Guesthouses association. All are private homes, usually historic and decorated with taste and style.

Guesthouses and Boxwood Tours weekends cost about $300 to $400 per person, including lodging for two nights, all meals, and some transportation.

Guesthouses and Boxwood Tours—RD 9, West Chester, PA 19380. 215/692-4575.

Rosehill Farm This bed and breakfast is also a working rose nursery, raising more than 70,000 miniature rose bushes in seventy varieties. There are six greenhouses to tour and rose experts waiting to offer advice on your garden.

There are five guest rooms in the farmhouse on the Sassafras River on the Eastern Shore of Maryland. The rooms are furnished simply but adequately. Room rates are $40 per night, breakfast included.

Rosehill Farm—Gregg Neck Road, Box 406, Galena, MD 21635. 301/648-5538.

Williamsburg Every April this Colonial masterpiece holds a four-day conference on gardening, with activities ranging from seminars on flower arranging, garden planning, and caretaking to tours of the famed gardens of Colonial Williamsburg and nearby estates.

The non-tour events take place in the Williamsburg Lodge Conference Center. Instead of staying there, get an elegant room in the five-star Williamsburg Inn or the Colonial Taverns. These rooms are expensive ($105 to $168 per night for a couple). The symposium fee is $170 per person and covers all activities except meals and optional tours.

Garden Symposium Registrar—Colonial Williamsburg Foundation, P.O. Box C, Williamsburg, VA 23187. 804/220-7255.

🍂 SPORTS

Biking Inn-to-Inn This association of bed-and-breakfast inns on the Eastern Shore of Delaware, Maryland, and Virginia offers custom-designed bicycle tours of the flat farming region, with stops planned in elegant waterfront inns and colonial plantation homes. The cost varies according to the inns selected. Write for tour maps and descriptions of the custom weekend trips.

Biking Inn-to-Inn on the Eastern Shore, Inc.—c/o Spring Garden Bed & Breakfast, Route 1, Box 283-A, Laurel, DE 19956. 302/875-7015.

Bright Morning This small bed and breakfast is located on the main street of the small town of Davis, the highest community in West Virginia.

The inn, through its Blackwater Outdoor Center, offers a number of activities in the surrounding Canaan Valley, a wilderness area that attracts hikers, campers, rafters, and skiers. Among the activities you can arrange while staying at the inn are:

🍂 Cross-country ski lessons and tours, with moonlight tours available when the moon cooperates.

🍂 Backpacking in all seasons, with day and overnight trips and tours to see spring and summer wildflowers and the fall foliage.

🍂 Cave explorations.

🍂 Whitewater canoe and raft tours, one-day and overnight trips.

🍂 Trout fishing trips in the spring and fall.

🍂 Rock climbing trips.

🍂 Hiking trips.

All of these activities are directed by qualified guides. There may be fitness and clothing requirements; check before booking a trip. The fees vary, but range from about $100 a couple for a day trip to double that for overnight trips.

The Bright Morning Inn has seven bedrooms and one suite, all furnished with country antiques. Room rates range from $65 to $95 per couple, breakfast included.

Bright Morning—William Avenue, Davis, WV 26260. 304/259-5119.

Guesthouses and **Boxwood Tours** Hot-air ballooning, fox hunting, polo, and steeplechase races are offered at the country estates of this country house association.

The Up, Up and Away Weekend of hot-air ballooning is hostage to the summer weather. Every attempt is made to schedule a weekend when winds are usually light, but the balloons go up only if weather conditions permit. In short, you may not go aloft.

The Foxes and Hounds Weekend kicks off the autumn hunt season. Guests go to the hunt and to the black-tie Hunt Ball. Steeplechase Weekend is a three-day event with either the Pennsylvania Gold Cup or the Radnor Race the main event.

In the Polo & Pimms weekend, a polo match and gourmet tailgate dinner top off a weekend of touring the historic and cultural sites in the region.

Guesthouses rates are $300 to $400 per person and include meals and lodging in the association's 100 historic, country mansions.

Guesthouses and Boxwood Tours—RD 9, West Chester, PA 19380. 215/692-4575.

Jordan Hollow Farm This two-century-old colonial Virginia horse farm offers horseback riding lessons, Western and English saddle, and beginner and advanced trail rides on the farm's forty-five acres and on the trails crossing the farm into the foothills of the Shenandoah National Park.

If riding the horse is not your style, try driving one of the buggies hitched up to a horse or pony. In the winter, the brave may want to attempt a local sport in which the horses pull skiers.

The farm has sixteen guest rooms. Room rates are $60 to $70.

Jordan Hollow Farm—Route 2, Box 375, Stanley, VA 22851. 703/778-2285.

The Sterling Inn Cross-country skiers and other winter sports enthusiasts will enjoy the Winter Getaway packages at the Sterling Inn in the Poconos Mountains.

Guests can use the cross-country trails on the property or enjoy ice skating and sledding. Downhill ski resorts are just a few minutes away. The Winter Getaway packages include use of the trails and a cross-country lesson, but not equipment. Bring your own or rent skis from Sterling's cross-country shop.

There are sixty-seven rooms in several buildings in this 149-year-old inn. All are decorated tastefully but not elegantly.

The Winter Getaway package is about $120 per person and includes two nights' lodging, two breakfasts, two dinners, and one cross-country ski lesson.

Sterling Inn—South Sterling, PA 18460. 717/676-3311.

❦ ON THE WATER

Guest Yachts This water-borne bed and breakfast operation is part of Guesthouses. It offers an opportunity to sample a romantic weekend on board a large sailboat and allows both of you to choose how much sailing you want. For example, you can spend the night on board a luxurious sailboat and then enjoy the facilities of the Great Oak Landing Resort (tennis, golf, swimming pool, private beach, windsurfing, and daysailing) on the Eastern Shore of Maryland. Or you can spend the night aboard and take a half- or all-day cruise or two-day sail with an overnight stop in another port on the bay.

All the boats are large—thirty-four to thirty-nine feet—Pearson sailing yachts. All have heads and showers, stereos, and other comforts. The rate depends on the cruise you choose, but ranges from $140 per couple for one night on board with no sailing to $700 for two nights (one at dock and the other at another anchorage) and two days of sailing.

Guest Yachts—RD 9, West Chester, PA 19380. 215/692-4575.

The Inn at Mitchell House This inn and the Echo Hill Outdoors School have a weekend package that offers two nights' accommodations at the inn and a day's sail on the historic skipjack *Elsworth*.

On the skipjack, one of the few remaining sailing oyster ships still working the Chesapeake Bay, guests can catch oysters and eat the delightful shellfish. Oyster season falls during the off-season months, so Skipjack Weekends take place from October to April. Dress warmly.

The inn, a manor house built in 1743, is on the Eastern Shore of Maryland about seven miles outside the charming town of Chestertown. There are five guest rooms in the inn, all furnished with antiques. Three of the rooms have fireplaces.

Rates for the weekend are the standard room rate ($75 to $90 per night) plus $70 per couple for the *Elsworth* cruise.

The Inn at Mitchell House—Box 329, RD2, Tolchester Estates, Chestertown, MD 21620. 301/778-6500.

The Mystic Clipper This modified version of the famed *Baltimore Clipper* sails the Chesapeake Bay for four months a year—May, June, September, and October. The 125-foot schooner, whose home port is Annapolis, sleeps up to forty-eight passengers in cabins that are cramped for landlubbers but spacious for old hands.

Most of the cabins have two single, staggered berths set into the side of the hull. The toilet and showers are shared. One cabin, though, has a queen-size bed.

The *Mystic Clipper* makes one- to five-night cruises. The ports visited—St. Michaels, Oxford, Baltimore, and other Chesapeake Bay cities—depend on the wind. The sail is not a rail-in-the-water thriller. The ship does heel in a wind, but not enough to unsettle newcomers.

The *Mystic Clipper*'s fares range from about $90 to $130 for a one-night cruise up to more than $250 per person for a two-night weekend voyage. The five-night cruise costs more than $500 per person. The rates include all meals.

Mystic Clipper—800/243-0616.

❦ FOOD AND WINE

Chalfonte Enjoy a summer weekend of wine-tasting that focuses on a varietal wine produced both domestically and abroad.

This majestic Victorian hotel offers 103 rooms and notable Southern cuisine. Room rates for couples start at $74 and include breakfast and dinner. Write the hotel for more information about the summer programs and any fees.

Chalfonte—301 Howard Street, Cape May, NJ 08204. 609/884-8409.

Channel Bass Inn This elegant inn in the quaint fishing village of Chincoteague, Virginia, offers four-day cooking classes where chef/owner James S. Hanretta teaches guests how to make sauces, prepare vegetables, make a shellfish and saffron rice dish, a crab soufflé, and an almond amaretto dessert.

The Sunday-to-Wednesday program is offered weekly from January to May. Tuition is $750 per person and includes three nights' lodging and most meals. $350 deposit required.

Channel Bass Inn—100 Church Street, Chincoteague, VA 23336. 804/ 336-6148.

The Towers Chocoholics, take note! This Milford, Delaware, Victorian mansion has a Chocolatiers Weekend in which everything served—from coffee to breads to main course—is flavored with chocolate.

The weekends are offered twice a month from October to April. The Towers is a majestic Victorian with five guest rooms, all decorated in period finery. The Chocolatier Weekend rate is $200 per couple.

The Towers—101 NW Front Street, Milford, DE 19963. 302/422-3814.

🐦 MUSIC

Bedford Springs Hotel The Bedford Springs Festival offers about three summer weeks of symphony concerts, ballet, jazz, pop, and chamber music at this splendid old hotel.

The 242-room Bedford Springs Hotel is a Victorian survivor of the grand old days when majestic hotels were built around springs thought to have healing powers. The hotel's magnesia springs have been drawing guests since 1804.

The music festival in the south-central Pennsylvania resort is staged at an amphitheater tent in a meadow near the hotel, and at other times in the hotel itself.

The Bedford Springs Hotel rates range from $125 to $160 per couple and include breakfast and dinner. Admission to the events at the festival is separate in most instances.

Bedford Springs Hotel—Bedford Road, Bedford, PA 15522. 814/623-6121. The music festival number is 412/391-5460.

Chalfonte This venerable Cape May Victorian has a number of special music weekends during the summer. They include:

🐦 Concerts by Candlelight
🐦 A Weekend with Gilbert & Sullivan
🐦 Bluegrass and Folk Music
🐦 Victorian Marionette Opera
🐦 Victorian Dances

The times, length, and fees for these summer programs vary. What doesn't is the stately old hotel, whose 103 rooms offer comfortable accommodations. Room rates for couples start at $74 and include breakfast and dinner.

Chalfonte—301 Howard Street, Cape May, NJ 08204. 609/884-8409.

Orkney Springs Before the Civil War, these Shenandoah Valley springs were owned by a local figure by the name of Lee—Robert E. Lee. In the 1850s, the first frame buildings were erected at the site. They are gone, but the five-story main hotel and its fabulous 50-by-100-foot Grand Ballroom, which was erected in 1873, are still in existence.

The spa operated until the 1950s, when the Episcopal Diocese of Virginia bought the hotel, outbuildings, and surrounding 950 acres for use as a retreat. Once a year, though, the place is open to the public for the Shenandoah Valley Music Festival, held over several weekends from mid-July to Labor Day.

Events at the festival include symphony orchestra concerts, arts and craft shows, and a black-tie ball in the hotel.

The rooms in the hotel and other buildings are simple, but the grounds are beautiful, the springs are still bubbling and can be sampled, and the festival recalls a simpler time.

Room rates are about $50 per person per night, all meals included.

Orkney Springs Hotel—Orkney Springs, VA 22845. 703/856-2198. Shenandoah Valley Music Festival, 703/856-2198.

Williamsburg The performing arts in the eighteenth century are the subject of Learning Weekends in Colonial Williamsburg every March.

The four-day lectures and workshops include numerous recitals, a candlelight concert, tours, an opera, and more.

The non-tour events take place in the Williamsburg Lodge Conference Center. Instead of staying there, get a room in the five-star Williamsburg Inn or the Colonial Taverns. These beautiful rooms are expensive ($105 to $168 per night for a couple). The symposium fee is $200 per person and covers all activities but not meals and optional tours.

Colonial Williamsburg Foundation—P.O. Box C, Williamsburg, VA 23187. 804/220-7255.

❦ ARTS, CRAFTS, AND ANTIQUES

Chalfonte This National Historic Landmark offers a variety of summer art workshops in a Victorian setting that has changed little since the hotel was built in 1876.

During the summer, the Chalfonte has these weekends:

❦ A Watercolor Workshop

❦ A Photography Seminar

❦ Oil Painting with artist Charles Movalli

❦ Rug Hooking and Quilting

The times, length, and fees for these summer programs vary. What doesn't is the stately old hotel, whose 103 rooms offer comfortable accommodations. Room rates for couples start at $74 and include breakfast and dinner.

Chalfonte—301 Howard Street, Cape May, NJ 08204. 609/884-8409.

Guesthouses and **Boxwood Tours** Enjoy an interpretive tour of the Brandywine Valley as seen by three generations of Wyeth artists.

The weekend package includes two nights' lodging, two breakfasts and two dinners, admissions to local attractions, and some surprises.

Guesthouses and Boxwood Tours weekends cost about $300 to $400 per person, including lodging for two nights, all meals, and some transportation.

Guesthouses and Boxwood Tours—RD 9, West Chester, PA 19380. 215/692-4575.

Williamsburg Four Colonial Weekends explore the eighteenth century American's style, from clothing to manners. The three-day forums are held in January, February, and March.

The non-tour events take place in the Williamsburg Lodge Conference Center. Instead of staying there, get a room in the five-star Williamsburg Inn or the Colonial Taverns. These rooms are expensive ($105 to $168 per night for a couple). Call or write for the symposium fee.

Colonial Weekends Reservations—P.O. Box B, Williamsburg, VA 23187. 804/220-7255.

❦ HISTORY

Williamsburg The History Forum explores the important influences on the early years of this nation. The four-day symposium in November includes speeches, panel discussions, tours, and dramatizations.

The non-tour events take place in the Williamsburg Lodge Conference Center. Instead of staying there, get a room in the five-star Williamsburg Inn or the Colonial Taverns. These beautiful rooms are expensive

($105 to $168 per night for a couple). Call or write for the symposium fee.

Colonial Williamsburg Forums Registrar—P.O. Box C, Williamsburg, VA 23187. 804/220-7255.

❦ INN-KEEPING

Lord Proprietors' Inn This North Carolina guesthouse runs inn-keeping programs every winter. The three-day seminar covers all aspects of running an inn. The fee is $400 per couple and includes lodging, meals, and tuition.

The inn has twenty rooms, all furnished with antiques, some of which are for sale.

Lord Proprietors' Inn—300 N. Broad Street, Edenton, NC 27932. 919/482-3641.

Wedgwood Inn This Bucks County, Pennsylvania, inn offers three-day Inn School Programs that will teach you all you want to know (and maybe a bit you don't) about running a guest house.

The seminars last from Friday evening to Sunday and the course program is designed to give you the information you need about the business aspect and daily routine of running an inn. Class sizes are limited. The fee is $395 for a couple and does *not* include lodging. Friday dinner is included.

The Wedgwood Inn is two buildings, one a Classic Revival and the other a gabled Victorian. The inn has ten rooms, two suites, and a carriage house. Rates are inexpensive to moderate (up to $125), depending on the room.

Wedgwood Inn—11 West Bridge Street, New Hope, PA 18938. 215/862-2570.

❦ MISCELLANEOUS

Chalfonte The stately Victorian hotel in Cape May has a number of summer programs that resist easy categorization. They include Beach Picnic Weekends, Journal Writing, and more. For details, write the hotel.

The Chalfonte offers 103 comfortable rooms and fine Southern cuisine. Room rates for couples start at $74 and include breakfast and dinner.

Chalfonte—301 Howard Street, Cape May, NJ 08204. 609/884-8409.

❦ THE RESORTS

The grand resorts of the Mid-Atlantic—The Homestead, Greenbrier, Wintergreen, The Hershey Hotel, The Tides Inn, and the Williamsburg Inn—have numerous theme weekends. For a more detailed look at those resorts and their special weekends, see Chapter 5, "The Grand Resorts."

Chapter Five

The Grand Resorts

For more than two centuries, the grand resorts of the Mid-Atlantic have lured visitors seeking an elegant retreat from the worries of the world.

The first resorts of the region were modest inns built around thermal and mineral springs whose waters were thought to have healing powers. As "taking the waters" grew in popularity, the resorts built larger, more lavish hotels and added finer services and a wide variety of entertainment.

Over the generations, these resorts attracted the wealthiest and most powerful families in the nation. The guest registries ring with names from another age: Pierce, Buchanan, Lee, Du Pont, Vanderbilt, Roosevelt, Rockefeller. In time, the resorts' very elegance became the main attraction, and the springs that gave them birth served as only a minor lure. Many of these grand spas are gone now, victims of changing travel patterns. A few from the golden age still exist, joined by a new generation of resorts designed to accommodate the changing needs of the twentieth-century traveler.

There are nine resorts in the Mid-Atlantic that we love to visit. Two of them—the Homestead and the Greenbrier—trace their heritage back to the first years of this nation. Those two and a third—the Williamsburg Inn—offer the finest in lodging, food, sports facilities, and entertainment. They are ranked by the *Mobil Travel Guide* among the top dozen resorts in the country.

The other six resorts range from a lavish 1930s Spanish-style hotel whose name is synonymous with chocolate to a mountaintop resort whose 11,000 acres contain some of the most beautiful scenery in the Mid-Atlantic.

❦ THE TOP THREE

The Homestead, the Greenbrier, and the Williamsburg Inn share a level of quality in service and lodging—simply, *the best*. But they differ in size, facilities, and other, subtler, ways. The rates vary widely, depending on the season. Holiday periods are the busiest and thus the most expensive. All three resorts have some weekend and weeklong packages with incredible savings. Ask about them.

The Greenbrier

This West Virginia resort has roots that reach back to the early years of the nineteenth century, when Stephen Henderson, a wealthy New Orleans sugar planter, and other southern gentlemen built simple frame cottages on the hillside overlooking a sulphur spring in the rough mountains of what were then the western counties of Virginia.

Henderson's cottage was a simple two-story house that overlooked the "folly," a stone cupola sheltering the non-thermal sulphur springs. The cottage survived the years, and today serves as a modest museum that gets its name—the **Presidents' Cottage Museum**—from its famous guests: presidents Buchanan, Pierce, Tyler, and Fillmore.

The presidential connection is important to the Greenbrier, but there is one room in the Presidents' Cottage Museum that says more about this resort and how it sees itself than any of the presidential memorabilia.

In the cottage is the Lee Room, a shrine to Robert E. Lee, who was a frequent visitor to the resort in the years after the Civil War. The Lee Room contains a massive mural depicting major battles in the war, with Lee and his horse, Traveller, as the main figures. In the entrance lobby two other prints—one of Lee and the other of his esteemed comrade in arms, Stonewall Jackson—complete the connection with the South.

The Greenbrier once played a major role in southern society. Before the tragic war between the states, a grand white frame hotel on the grounds known as **The Old White** served as the social center of the

South. Families came to spend the summer season, allowing belles and beaux to meet and marry.

During the Civil War, the hotel was a prize taken and lost by both sides, usually being used as a hospital by the forces holding it. After the war, in a meeting that assured the resort's ascendancy in the southern heavens, Lee and his top generals had a reunion at the Greenbrier in 1869, a moment captured for all time in a famous photo that hangs in the cottage.

The plantation gentry of the South were not the only notables to visit. The Fords, Armours, and Vanderbilts also visited, often traveling to the resort in their private railway cars.

Time and modern fire codes did to The Old White what a civil war could not: In 1922 the famous old hotel was declared unsafe and was razed. It was replaced by a grand white hotel, the one that exists today. This hotel's journey through the Depression and decades since hasn't always been smooth. During World War II, the army bought the resort and used it as a hospital. After the war, the grand hotel, battered and run down by its military service, was reacquired by its longtime former owner, the C&O Railroad (now CSX), and refurbished to its previous elegance.

The passage of time has not erased the memories of Old White. A plaque on the grounds reads: "Here gathered from the North and South great generals, famous statesmen and philanthropists, lovely ladies and reigning belles who left upon the silken shore of memory images and precious thoughts that shall not die and cannot be destroyed."

Today's Greenbrier is a worthy successor to The Old White that inspired those thoughts, even though the ties to the South are a bit distant today. The Presidents' Cottage Museum and the plaque keep the memories kindled, but the atmosphere of the Greenbrier is that of the finest major metropolitan hotel. The facilities and amenities are among the best in the land, but the ambiance is perhaps *too* correct, *too* formal.

The Greenbrier today is not *the* grand hotel of the South, but it is a *grand hotel*. Elegance—from the lobby to the 700 rooms, from the spa to the dining rooms—shines from every corner at the Greenbrier. The resort is a popular destination for honeymooners, families, and leaders of government and industry, who hold annual conventions in White Sulphur Springs.

There are 6,500 acres of grounds at the Greenbrier, gently rolling fields and hills landscaped with more than 80,000 flowering bulbs, bushes, and trees. The activities seem to outnumber the blossoms. You can shoot a round of golf or skeet, go trout fishing and horseback riding, play tennis indoors or out, jog, hike, bike, swim, and bowl. The Greenbrier has a top-flight diagnostic clinic that attracts many captains of industry for their annual checkups, and a newly refurbished health spa where baths, massages, and saunas can make you feel whole again.

The Greenbrier also offers numerous theme weekends, from programs of music, antiques, the spa, food and wine to seminars on investing and classes in dancing.

ɧ **The Greenbrier** The surprise is that even with all the Greenbrier offers, the cost is reasonable. There are many weekend packages offering great savings at this resort, but the basic rate is about $130 to $180 per person per night. That includes breakfast and dinner, the seminars and usually the weekend activities, dancing at dinner, films, the afternoon tea in the lobby, and swimming. Use of the spa, golf course, and many of the sports facilities is extra. Amtrak's Cardinal runs from Washington to the train station across the street from the Greenbrier's grounds. White Sulphur Springs, WV 24986. 304/536-1110.

The Homestead

Virginia's Valley of the Warm Springs, near the West Virginia state line, has been a resort area since the 1600s, when the Indians are said to have used the thermal waters there. The springs attracted Thomas Jefferson, who in 1787 in his *Notes on the State of Virginia* wrote that the springs "relieve rheumatism. Other complaints . . . have been removed or lessened."

The two kinds of thermal springs—hot and warm—brought visitors seeking relief and cures in the healing spas. The first inn was built at the springs in 1766, and legend says it was called the Homestead. The present hotel, a majestic 600-room red-brick Georgian, was built in 1902, replacing one that was destroyed by fire.

The Homestead's ties to the southern aristocracy are not as deep as those of the Greenbrier, but the Homestead retains a southern ambience that is missing at its West Virginia counterpart. Soft accents and down-home courtesy are found here. This atmosphere can be traced to the ownership of the Homestead. Unlike the Greenbrier, which is owned by the CSX Corporation, the Homestead has been owned and operated by one family—the Ingalls—from the late 1800s through the present day. This single-family ownership means that tradition is revered over change at the Homestead.

These traditions can be found in many areas. For example, the spa

❦ The Homestead, a five-star resort featuring the finest accommodations, services and food. *Photo by John M. Gazzola Jr.*

here is not as elegant as the new gold, mirrored, and green-and-white tiled spas at the Greenbrier. You get the same services, but the atmosphere remains much like that which your mother would have experienced had she visited the Homestead a generation ago.

The gentility of the past is not forgotten in the theater, where movies from the 1930s and 1940s are favored (although a 1950s Hitchcock sneaks in every once in a while). Ask why modern films are not shown and you are told, "Well, the language and scenes of nudity are upsetting to our guests, who come here for a civilized visit."

Other traditions include an afternoon tea and concert in the long, stately lobby and a staff that quickly learns your name and never seems to forget it. On our second visit, we were greeted by name at the entrance to the dining room by Jerry, the captain, whom we had met only once during a visit a year before.

In the huge dining room filled with chandeliers, columns, a dance floor, and bandstand, you will see another heart-warming sight rarely witnessed at modern resorts. Families—sometimes three generations—will be seated at large tables, reenacting some family ritual of retreat and reunion at this gracious resort.

Over the years the Homestead has attracted the rich and famous, including numerous presidents and such society figures as Marjorie Merriweather Post and Mrs. Cornelius Vanderbilt. During World War II, the resort served briefly as an internment center for Japanese diplomats rounded up after the attack on Pearl Harbor.

The elegance found at all Mobil five-star resorts is evident throughout the Homestead, from the public rooms to the spacious and elegantly furnished guest rooms.

Woven in with the elegance is a world of activity. The Homestead has three golf courses; tennis courts; a quaint, seventy-eight-year-old indoor and outdoor pool; bowling alley; a charming movie theater that puts the Greenbrier's auditorium to shame; a lively night club; organized activities; and 15,000 acres of grounds for riding, fishing, hiking, jogging and, in the winter, skiing and ice skating.

The Homestead prides itself on its golf courses, where tournaments are often played. Sam Snead, the seemingly ageless pro, makes his home in Hot Springs, and served as the Homestead's professional for a number of years. The Sam Snead Tavern in town is a post-round meeting place for golfers and others attracted by the congenial atmosphere and fine food.

Other activities are not neglected at this resort. There are many theme weekends from fall to spring offering special programs on wine, Virginia food, music, and antiques.

In the small village of Warm Springs just a few miles from the resort hotel are two historic **bath houses** now owned and operated by the Homestead. These two simple frame houses are shaped like small, round circus tents with holes in the tops where the spring's steam escapes. They have attracted bathers for more than two centuries; legend has it that Thomas Jefferson designed the men's bathhouse. Among the first guests were Alexander Hamilton and George Washington.

The men and women bathe separately in these warm springs. They can soak nude if they wish, and women have the option of wearing cotton rompers that look like the original bathing suits the spa's guests used to wear.

The waters are wonderful, relaxing, and much as they were two centuries ago when other generations soothed away their cares here.

That's the way it was—and that's the way it still is—in the Valley of Warm Springs, where the elegant Homestead resort still remembers what is important in life: living well.

🐝 **The Homestead** There are many golf, tennis, and ski packages available that offer great savings. The basic rate is about $140 to $190 per person per night. That includes breakfast and dinner, dancing, movies, the pools, nightclub, games, and other activities. Use of the spa, golf course, and other sports facilities is extra. Amtrak's Cardinal from Washington stops in Covington, and the Homestead buses guests the twenty miles to the resort. Hot Springs, VA 24445. 703/839-5500.

The Williamsburg Inn

This fifty-two-year-old hotel in southeastern Virginia is fit for a king. Actually, several kings. Its guests have included Queen Elizabeth II and Prince Philip; the emperor and empress of Japan; kings from Saudi Arabia, Sweden, Morocco, and Thailand, five U.S. presidents, and numerous other world leaders.

This 235-room inn is magnificent, a resort where luxury is common in a setting of uncommon beauty. The attention to detail, inside and out, makes this inn worthy of its top rating. The inn was the creation of John D. Rockefeller and his wife, Abby, the two major patrons of the restoration of Colonial Williamsburg.

The Rockefellers wanted a hotel next to the historic district, but not just an ordinary inn. They wanted a hotel that guests would feel was a home away from home. The attention to detail—landscaping, brick arches, interior appointments, inlaid and painted decorations—was tremendous. The result was superb.

The hotel is majestic, a three-story white-washed post-colonial Regency-style building that doesn't dominate its surroundings as the Homestead does. Inside, guests are welcomed into a lobby filled with warmth, from the greetings of the gracious staff to the fires crackling in the fireplaces flanking the room. The furnishings are reproductions of Regency-style antiques, elegant but not intimidating. These chairs and sofa were made for sitting.

At the back of the lobby, doors and windows open to the shaded terrace, lawn bowling green, and one of the two golf courses. A nature center of ponds and ducks and a charming swimming pool, looking more like those found at exclusive private clubs than those at hotels, are just a short walk to the right.

Other sports facilities await: another pool and golf course (both the eighteen-hole and nine-hole courses were designed by famed golf architect Robert Trent Jones), badminton, miniature golf, tennis courts, croquet, shuffleboard, and cycling and jogging paths.

Inside, the rooms live up to the expectations raised in the lobby. Regency reproductions and tasteful appointments make one feel like a guest in a mansion rather than in a hotel.

The Regency Dining Room at the inn is noted for its fine cuisine, featuring fresh seafood and regional specialties. During dinner, a small combo plays for those who like to dance between courses. On Sundays, the room hosts a sumptuous brunch with music provided by the Williamsburg Chamber Players.

Our favorite memory of the inn came during a visit one cold and snowy Christmas season. Frozen by the elements, we walked to the front door, where a uniformed doorman greeted us and opened the doors to the gracious lobby. There, just a few steps away, was a golden vision of light, warmth, beauty, gaily decorated Christmas trees and wreaths, and smiling guests.

We felt we had arrived at a manor, where we and others were honored guests for a weekend of yule celebrations.

Most of all, despite the elegant setting, we felt at home.

❦ **The Williamsburg Inn** There are a number of packages available that include some meals and tickets to Colonial Williamsburg. Inquire about them, for they will save you money. Usual rates are $145 to $180 per couple per night, meals not included. Reservations are a must. For the popular Christmas season, make them far in advance. P.O. Box B, Williamsburg, Va. 23187, Call 800/HISTORY.

A visit to any of these three inns is always a special moment. If we had our wishes, we would visit the Greenbrier in June when the rhododendrons are in bloom, the Williamsburg Inn around Christmas, and the Homestead, our favorite of the three, for skiing and its fabulous party on New Year's Eve.

❦ A HALF-DOZEN DELIGHTS

These six resorts would rank high in anyone's book. They offer a wide variety of surroundings and facilities, with one common denominator: all will make your romantic weekend very special.

The Boar's Head Inn

This beautiful colonial-style inn is a wonderful surprise in the gentle hills just east of Charlottesville, Virginia. The inn and adjacent sports club are located on some wonderful grounds made for weddings (we have witnessed several there), afternoon daydreaming, and moonlight strolls around the lake.

There are 175 rooms in the Boar's Head, all furnished with antique reproductions and carefully chosen accessories. The sports club offers tennis, squash, racquetball, platform tennis, and some exercise facilities. Hot-air ballooning, horseback rides, and golf can be arranged at the front desk.

Outside, a terrace restaurant overlooks the lake and the ducks and geese that call it home. A row of shops offers some fine gifts and accessories. The landscaping is particularly beautiful, with fountains, rock gardens, tree groves, and a labeled garden waiting to tempt you to linger for a moment.

The dining room and pub are first class. The Old Mill Dining Room, named after the ruins of an 1834 grist mill on the grounds, serves some excellent regional dishes and Virginia wines. The pub on the lower level serves up live entertainment and dancing almost every evening.

The owners of the inn are John and Felicia Rogan. Felicia Rogan is the owner of Oakencroft Vineyards just a few miles away, and each October a Bacchanalian Wine Festival is held at the inn, with dancing, a feast, and sampling of the state's wines.

❦ **The Boar's Head Inn** Rooms are $100 and up, with some weekend packages available. Box 5185, Charlottesville, VA 22905 804/296-2181.

Grove Park Inn

The resort on Sunset Mountain in the Blue Ridge Mountain chain near Asheville, North Carolina, has been luring travelers since 1913 with its awesome views of nature and its excellent sports facilities.

There are 510 guest rooms in the stone-and-red-tile hotel set between the golf course and the wooded slope of Sunset Mountain.

Grove Park's tone is set in the Great Hall, a massive lobby flanked by two huge stone fireplaces that suggest a majestic mountain lodge. The atmosphere is genuine: all the facilities at Grove Park, from the public areas to the guest rooms, are grand.

The guest rooms are spacious, all tastefully appointed and furnished, often with wonderful Mission Oak antique pieces. Outside, the views are stunning, from the mountain behind to the golf course and valleys below.

Five restaurants wait to serve you, and an open-air terrace is a perfect spot for a meal or a drink while watching the setting sun seemingly set the mountains on fire.

Recreational activities are the strong suit at this resort. There is an eighteen-hole golf course, tennis courts, indoor and outdoor swimming pools, and a sports complex with indoor tennis, racquetball, squash, and a complete exercise and aerobics room with weight stations.

Romance is another hallmark of Grove Park, for every February the inn hosts a Valentine's Weekend and Sweetheart Ball. Couples might also enjoy a special horse-drawn-carriage ride through the dark, pine-scented forests and past some of the old stone buildings on the grounds.

Other theme weekends include an arts, crafts, and antiques festival; a jazz festival; a festival of flowers; a Mother's Day weekend celebration; a Christmas celebration that fills the entire month of December; and a New Year's Eve celebration. The latter two events are new at Grove park, for the inn only began staying open year-round in 1984.

Grove Park has hosted industrialists and diplomats, actors and entertainers, presidents and vice presidents (George Bush visited in 1986, Dan Quayle in 1988).

🎦 **The Grove Park Inn** There are package plans for tennis and golf, but the one you want is called Romance for Two, which offers two nights' lodging, champagne, flowers, chocolates, use of the Nautilus center and pool, and a tour of the nearby Biltmore Estate for $269 per couple. Normal rates are $100 to $155 per person. 290 Macon Avenue, Asheville, NC. 28804 800/438-5800. In North Carolina call 800/222-9793.

Hotel Hershey

An unknowing passerby would be puzzled by this grand, Spanish-style mansion on a modest hill in the middle of the lush farming region of central Pennsylvania. But this magnificent hotel is a monument to the man who gave it its name: Milton S. Hershey, founder of the chocolate empire based in the town of the same name.

It was during the Depression that Hershey ordered the construction of the 250-room hotel. For him, the move was practical: it enabled him to keep his labor force employed at a time of economic hardship.

Hershey handed his architect a picture postcard of a small Mediterranean hotel that he and his family had visited, and ordered him to use the design. And, he told architect D. Paul Witmer, make sure the hotel has a fountain, a patio, tiled floors, and a dining room without corners. "In some places, if you don't tip well, they put you into a corner," Hershey said. "I don't want any corners."

Out of this came a masterpiece, an elegant hotel that mixes the ornate beauty of a Spanish mansion with the natural beauty of the location. The cornerless Circular Dining Room has stained glass and picture windows that look out on two pools and a wide veranda overlooking the formal gardens. The Fountain Lobby looks like the courtyard of a mansion in Madrid, decorated with colorful tiles; a fountain; an oak-railed balcony; and huge urns of plants, trees, and flowers.

After dinner, we have enjoyed relaxing in the Fountain Lobby or walking on the veranda, watching the sun set and families of bunnies hopping out of their hiding places.

The Hotel Hershey's rooms are spacious and furnished with antique reproductions. Recreation facilities include whirlpool and sauna, indoor and outdoor pools, an exercise room, five golf courses, lawn bowling, tennis, shuffleboard, horseback riding, hayrides, sledding, and cross-country skiing.

Nearby are other attractions linked to the Hershey name. The twenty-three-acre **Hershey Gardens** on the hillside near the hotel have more than 40,000 tulips, 40,000 roses, a number of rare trees and bushes, and six theme gardens. In the town are **Hersheypark**, an old-fashioned amusement park; **ZooAmerica**, a wildlife center; and **Chocolate World**, a tour of how the sweet stuff is made that ends in a wonderland of chocolate bars, ice cream, and other diet-busting delights.

Romance is not neglected in this very romantic hotel. Theme weekends range from "A Romantic Weekend" around Valentine's Day to weekends centered on big bands, murder mysteries, jazz festivals, the fabulous fifties and sixties, and more. Best of all is the weekend in February called The Great American Chocolate Festival: three days of dining, wining, dancing, and tasting.

And even when there isn't anything special going on, the Iberian Lounge has live music and dancing almost every night.

❦ **The Hotel Hershey** The golf, Hersheypark, and the theme-weekend packages offer great deals that include meals and activities. The basic rate is $93 to $105 per person breakfast and dinner included, or $101 to $113 per person all meals included. P.O. Box BB, Hershey, PA 17033. 800/437-7439.

Hidden Valley

This four-seasons resort in the Laurel Highlands of south-central Pennsylvania has matured into a wonderful resort offering fine golfing, tennis, and cross-country and downhill skiing in a ruggedly beautiful setting.

Our visits to Hidden Valley have taken place in the winter, a time when many Mid-Atlantic ski resorts are bursting at the seams with traffic, bus groups, and long lift lines. Not so here.

Hidden Valley attracts couples and families. It is not a singles-oriented resort, the kind that has a surplus of bars and a shortage of civility.

Hidden Valley's attractions are excellent accommodations, natural beauty, nightly entertainment, some organized activities for those who need help getting started, short lift lines during ski season, and some surprisingly fine restaurants.

Add to those features 25,000 acres of state park land and you have a resort that blends the best of a planned community with the rugged beauty of a mountain forest. Hidden Valley's carefully-thought-out plan allows the resort to merge with, rather than dominate, its surroundings.

Other amenities include a mountaintop golf course; tennis courts; a base lodge with a restaurant, grill, shops and theater; a health club with a pool; racquet ball court; sauna and tanning salon; and enough hiking trails to wear out even the hardiest trekker.

For cross-country ski buffs there are sixty kilometers of patrolled and groomed trails in and around the resort and the Laurel Highlands parks. The cross-country center just outside the entrance to Hidden Valley can arrange rentals and lessons.

What we enjoyed most, though, was the lodging: a spacious Four Seasons Suite with a fireplace in the living room, a large bedroom, a tiny kitchen area, and a balcony overlooking the striking, snow-filled woods.

Hidden Valley is a jewel, one where privacy and quiet pleasures can be cherished. For a couple, that is a very important asset.

🍷 **Hidden Valley** There are a number of golf and ski packages available. Inquire about them. Basic rates for the Four Seasons Suites, including breakfast and dinner, ski pass, use of the health club, and a Saturday night reception, start at $240 per person for two nights. Other lodging is available in rooms, townhomes, and houses. 1 Craighead Drive, Somerset, PA 15501. 800/458-0175.

The Tides Inn

This is a golf and water sports resort with a thick Virginia accent. Our memories of this small resort on a creek just a few minutes' cruise from the Chesapeake Bay are not of the golf, though there are three eighteen-hole courses and one nine-hole course. And not of the tennis, although there are more than a half-dozen courts. And not even of the resort's fleet of boats, from canoes and Sunfish all the way up to a large motor yacht used for dinner cruises.

No, our memories center on the food.

If you are on a diet, the Tides food can be dangerous to your health. Guests have their own "bread girl" and "butter girl," and a choice of numerous rich dishes ("Order any or all of them. Whatever you want"). It's almost too much.

And don't count on the staff to help. The southern hospitality is thicker than the gravy here. You'll feel guilty if you don't try just a bit of everything.

Enough is enough. The Tides Inn is wonderful for a weekend, particularly if you like water sports and golf.

Activities include a freshwater pool, a small beach that is unusable after the nettles come up the bay in early summer, daily cruises, and nightly games and dancing to a live band.

The rooms at the Tides, either in the main hotel or the two-story buildings flanking it, are spacious. Most have a view of the water and some have large, sunken bathtubs.

Mix it all together—sports, scenery, a cruise, and all too much fine food—and you have a great weekend. If you can still move after a day of meals at the Tides.

🐝 **The Tides Inn** The golf package plans can lower the rates, but normal charges are $190 to $240 per couple per night, all meals included. Irvington, VA 22480. 800/438-5000.

Wintergreen

This glorious resort in the Blue Ridge Mountains just east of Charlottesville, Virginia, offers a feast for lovers of nature.

There are 11,000 acres to Wintergreen, most of them undeveloped wilderness. Nature is Wintergreen's centerpiece, with a full-time naturalist and staff not only guiding the resort development but offering weekly programs and field trips on such subjects as wild flowers, the animals of the forest, the geology of the mountains, and the stars in the clear skies overhead.

We rarely rise at dawn, but the exception is when we visit this resort. There, at about 3,800 feet elevation, the sun comes over the mountain chains and spreads pinks and golds over the meadows and hills, turning snow-covered ski runs into pastels that bleach into a gleaming white.

On one ridge lookout, called Raven's Roost, you can stand on a wooden platform and gaze *down* at the migrating hawks and waterfowl. Or you can look west and see the mountains of West Virginia more than fifty miles away.

This mountain resort is large enough to have two golf courses, one on the mountaintop and the other on the upland valley floor—separated by almost half a mile of elevation. In the summer there is about fourteen degrees' difference in temperature between Devil's Knob, the highest golf course in Virginia, and Stoney Creek, the new course at Wintergreen that is 1,400 feet lower in elevation. Both are championship courses. In the winter, guests can ski and golf on the same day, paying for a greens fee or a lift ticket, but not both.

The golf courses attract not only the duffers, but herds of deer, a common sight on the fairways and in nearby woods. Sightings of bear and other animals are not unusual.

Other recreational facilities include ten ski slopes, some of them the steepest in the Mid-Atlantic; twenty-two tennis courts; one lavish indoor pool and five outdoor pools; a sixteen-acre lake for swimming, boating, and fishing; stables and riding trails; hiking paths; and the Wintergarden spa and exercise facility.

Nature activities include a highly acclaimed wildflower symposium every May for which Wintergreen won the National Environmental Award from the American Hotel and Motel Association, and jeep safaris that take guests through the undeveloped 6,700 acres of the resort, to areas that are rarely visited.

The lodging here is in condominium apartments, townhouses, homes, a twelve-room country inn called Trillium House and a larger inn at the shopping and restaurant complex. The condos we have stayed in are simply stunning, offering breathtaking views of the mountain ranges and luxurious accommodations.

The big surprise at Wintergreen is the quality of the food. **The Trillium House**, the **Garden Terrace**, and the **Copper Mine Restaurant** serve some surprisingly high-quality dinners.

The hidden star, if your diet can take it, is down in the valley at the **Rodes Farm Inn**, a small restaurant set in a red brick former girls' school at the base of a mountain. There, Marguerite Wade serves country-style food like Grandmother used to make. You'll love it.

✾ **Wintergreen** There are a number of packages that include tennis fees, golf green fees, ski lift tickets, and more. The basic rates range from $129 per person for a studio to $156 for a one-bedroom apartment. Wintergreen, VA 22958. 800/325-2200.

How We Rate Them

- ❦ *Best Overall Resort* The Homestead
- ❦ *Most Romantic* The Williamsburg Inn for elegance; Wintergreen for nature-lovers
- ❦ *Best Skiing* Wintergreen
- ❦ *Best Value* Hotel Hershey, Boar's Head Inn, and Hidden Valley
- ❦ *Most Luxurious Accommodations* Greenbrier
- ❦ *Best Food* Tough call, but the Homestead beats out the Tides Inn. That's not counting the Rodes Farm Inn, which, if it were a resort, would be in a class by itself.
- ❦ *Best Location* Wintergreen and the Grove Park Inn: The mountains are stunning.
- ❦ *Best Theme Weekends* Hotel Hershey

Chapter Six

Wine Country

There is nothing more romantic than a fine wine, nor more intoxicating than a relationship in full bloom. To savor both, we suggest a weekend tour of the wine-growing areas in the Mid-Atlantic.

These wineries have long been overshadowed by their cousins in California's Napa Valley and France's legendary viticultural regions. But the Old World's grand wine grapes—the *vitis vinifera*—are grown today in the vineyards of the Mid-Atlantic. Once there were many wineries in the region, but blight, neglect, and, most of all, Prohibition, destroyed them. The vineyards that exist today are less than a half-century old, young by European standards, and the vines are just beginning to produce the quality of grapes needed to make fine wines. In recent years, some of the regional wines have won acclaim from nationally known critics.

There are five regions in the Mid-Atlantic where visitors can tour the wineries, sample the vintages, and explore some beautiful attractions nearby. These wine regions are in the Virginia countryside around Charlottesville and Middleburg, in the rolling hills of central Maryland, in the Amish and Wyeth country of southern Pennsylvania, and in Bucks County, Pennsylvania, north of Philadelphia.

The vineyards in these areas welcome visitors for tastings and tours of the wineries. Some of the wineries are also settings for more lavish events ranging from concerts and dinners to murder-mystery parties and renaissance fairs.

The time for these tours is in the fair-weather months of April to October, for there is an annual rhythm to the vineyards. Winter is the slow season, the time when the winemaster is busy testing his vintages, moving the wines from huge holding tanks to oaken casks, and pruning the dark, twisted vines on the hillside rows of trellises. During these months, most of the wineries are closed to visitors.

Between April and October, the wineries are open every weekend, and festivals seem to happen at the pop of a cork. The season-ending harvest festivals take place between late August and October, depending on the location of the vineyard.

The wineries described in this chapter were chosen for the quality of their wines, the beauty of their location, the fun offered at their festivals, and other nearby attractions. Enjoy the wines, but sample selectively; overindulgence detracts from romance. The five areas in which these wineries are located are filled with other diversions—beautiful scenery, antique and craft galleries, quaint inns, and fabulous restaurants. We hope you will take the time to enjoy those, too, for each region is filled with enough activities to round out your weekend.

A tour of Mid-Atlantic wine country should start in the beautiful, rolling hills of central Virginia. This is where it all began more than two centuries ago, when Thomas Jefferson and George Washington tried to grow European wine grapes on their estates, Monticello and Mount Vernon. Their efforts failed—disease destroyed Jefferson's vineyard and Washington's wines turned to vinegar—mainly because the two statesmen were preoccupied with the Revolution. Though their vines withered, their dreams did not. Today, their vision inspires a new generation of Virginians, and the forty wineries in the state produce enough bottles to rank Virginia fourth nationally in wine production.

❦ VIRGINIA

The heart of the Virginia wine industry can be found in the gentle hills surrounding Charlottesville, where winemakers have found the climate and soil hospitable to the grand European grapes.

Just northwest of Charlottesville, on Barracks Road, is **Oakencroft Vineyards.** This winery is set in a small valley between two hills on the estate of Felicia and John Rogan.

Oakencroft is an unusual vineyard for several reasons. First, it is owned by a woman, Felicia Rogan, who is president of the Jeffersonian

Wine Grape Growers Society and whose husband is a developer and owner of the four-star Boar's Head Inn in Charlottesville. Second, its winemaker is a woman, Deborah Welsh. Lastly, the winery itself is a stunning redwood and stone building with a wine-tasting room filled with antiques and art.

The winery's surroundings are like a park. We particularly enjoyed strolling down to the lake that is home to ducks and geese. Another pleasant walk is up the hill behind the winery, where the vineyard is. There, in the rows of vines at the summit, we found a beautiful vista of the Rogan farm and surrounding estates. The vineyard, stretching down the hillside to allow drainage and air flow, is a perfect place to take a picture of the rows of grapes, the winery, and the gentle valley.

Oakencroft annually produces about 45,000 bottles of Cabernet Sauvignon, Seyval Blanc and a Chardonnay that has won critical acclaim. Oakencroft is different from other wineries on the tour. It is a winery —a wine factory, in short—but the handmade tiles, the antiques, the art, and the refinement of the decor in its main room are unique. Take time to explore Oakencroft before heading south of Charlottesville to **Montdomaine Cellars**, a 100,000-bottle-a-year operation in a huge warehouse.

The wines produced by Montdomaine—Chardonnay, Riesling, Cabernet Sauvignon, Merlot, and others—come from the vineyards of the cellar's shareholders. The winemaker, Shep Rouse, can often be found in the winery and, time willing, will explain how wine is made from grapes.

North of Charlottesville is a more picturesque winery: **Barboursville Plantation**, a 100,000-bottle-a-year operation that traces its roots back to one of the first leaders of Virginia and one of the oldest wine families of Italy. This was once the estate of James Barbour, governor of Virginia from 1812 to 1814. In 1976, Gianni Zonin of the Zonin wine family and company of Italy planted the first *vinifera* vines on the estate. Today, Adriano Rossi is the winemaker. He produces Cabernet Sauvignon, Merlot, Riesling, Chardonnay, and other varietals from the grapes on Barboursville's fifty acres of vineyards. If it seems unusual to find an Italian making wine on a Virginia estate, it shouldn't: Jefferson's winemaker was Filippi Mazzei from Tuscany.

The Barboursville winery is farmlike and functional, its tasting room lacking the artistic touches of Oakencroft. Barboursville makes up for the lack of antiques with a hearty welcome for visitors, an excellent selection of wines often accompanied by cheese and crackers, a tree-shaded table for a picnic, and some local history.

In a grove of trees down near the vineyards is another setting perfect for a picture. There you will find the haunting brownstone ruins of the Barbour mansion, the Jefferson-designed greathouse destroyed by a Christmas-Day fire in 1884. The memories of that day don't hang heavy over the present-day estate, for every year it holds a Christmas open house in early December.

A bit farther north, on U.S. 29 ten miles south of Culpeper, is **Prince Michel Vineyards** in Leon, the largest winery in the state with an annual production of close to 300,000 bottles. This winery is in a modern, ranch-style brick building that is deceptive; at the back is a large winery, hidden from view because it is on a slope. Visitors to Prince Michel can sample the wines, tour a museum and gift shop, see the winery in operation, or watch a video show on wine making.

The museum is filled with wine-making artifacts, old photographs, and antique wine goblets and bottles. The slide show helps explain how the winemaster turns grape juice into a memorable vintage. The gift shop sells wine, of course, but also linens, silver and pewter pieces, and wine-serving items.

Like Barboursville's Zonin family, Prince Michel's winemaker has a long viticultural heritage. Joachim Hollerith, the winemaker and general manager, came to Virginia from the Rheinpfalz region of Germany, where his family has been making wine for 300 years.

Farther north on U.S. 29, on the bypass near Culpeper, is **Dominion Wine Cellars**, where visitors can tour the winery and taste the Chardonnay, White Riesling, Johannisberg Riesling, and Cabernet Sauvignon.

The other Virginia wine region we like to visit is in the horse country, about an hour west of the Washington metropolitan area. Two of the wineries are near Middleburg and the third is outside Leesburg, two quaint eighteenth-century towns filled with old inns, antique shops, boutiques, and craft outlets where horses and foxes appear to be the dominant theme.

Just a few country lanes outside of Middleburg is **Meredyth Vineyards**, where Archie Smith, Jr., his son Archie Smith III and the rest of the family produce more than a dozen varietals and blends, with an annual bottling of almost 200,000.

The Smiths are not like the Zonins and Holleriths; their winemaking experience is fairly new. Archie Jr., was an advertising executive and writer, and his son was a lecturer at Oxford. Both changed careers to found the winery to save the family farm.

Meredyth is a popular winery, known for more than its fine wines. Its Tasting Trellis Pavilion, located downhill from the winery next to the vineyards, is used for weddings and large parties. And the winery itself, a small warehouse-like bottling factory with a gift shop that sells wines and Virginia food specialties, is used for candlelight dinners, murder mystery parties, theme tastings, and festivals.

Another Middleburg winery is **Piedmont Vineyards and Winery**, whose main house was built before the Revolution. Piedmont produces Chardonnay, Semillon, and other blends, and opens its facilities for candlelight dinners, tastings, and festivals. Each August, the Middleburg Wine Festival is held here, attracting many of the state's wineries for a competition and offering music, food, and entertainment.

The Leesburg-area winery, **Willowcroft Farm Vineyards**, is located between Middleburg and Leesburg in a rustic barn overlooking the Blue Ridge Mountains. Visitors are welcome to tour the winery and taste the vintages, but the owners suggest calling 703/777-8161 and making an appointment.

The major reason there are so many wineries in Virginia is strong state support. Virginia aggressively markets and promotes the wineries, as illustrated by the grape-cluster road signs that guide visitors to the vineyards. Look for these signs during your tour; they were a big help in guiding us to the wineries, which are often found down unmarked country lanes.

That strong state support is lacking in Pennsylvania and Maryland and, not surprisingly, there are fewer wineries in these two states. But the ones there make up for their lack of numbers in the robustness of their festivals and the beauty of the surrounding countryside.

❦ MARYLAND

In the Maryland farmland north of Washington, near the village (actually more a crossroad anchored by a bait shop/gas station) of Sunshine is a vineyard and winery whose Cabernet Sauvignon was said by one wine critic to rank with the best of California and France. **Catoctin Vineyards**, a small operation located in a stone and timber barn, offers tastings, sales, and interesting conversation with the resident winemaster, Robert Lyon.

If wine festivals are what you seek, continue north to the Blue Ridge foothills of Maryland. Near the town of Mt. Airy is **Berrywine Plantations**, which produces twenty-five semisweet fruit and grape wines but is also known for its festivals. Berrywine hosts a strawberry/Scottish festival in June, a Razz/Jazz Fest in July, a medieval encampment in the autumn and more, with the theme keyed to the harvest.

Quieter but more traditional in the vintages they produce are the nearby **Elk Run Vineyards** and **Loew Vineyards**. These two wineries produce Chardonnay, Riesling, and Cabernet Sauvignon.

🦌 PENNSYLVANIA

From Mt. Airy it is but a few hours' drive to the Wyeth and Amish country of southern Pennsylvania. In this verdant farm country are three wineries that we found offer fine vintages and more activities than a traveling taster could expect. At **Chaddsford Winery** in Chadds Ford, winemakers Lee and Eric Miller turned a beautiful, century-old stone and frame barn (ask them to show you the unused part of the barn) into a winery and tasting and sales rooms. The Millers buy their grapes from other vineyards and produce Cabernet Sauvignon, Chardonnay, Chambourcin, and Riesling.

Chaddsford also offers tasting evenings; dinner parties; concerts of jazz, country, and classical music; and weekend festivals centered around a seasonal or harvest theme.

Allegro Vineyards in the small town of Brogue near York is known by wine critics as a small operation that produces some fine Cabernet, Chardonnay, and Seyval.

Of all the vineyards mentioned in this chapter, none offers more for the eye, the ear, or the tastebuds than the **Mt. Hope Winery and Estate** in Lancaster County. Visitors can tour a beautiful thirty-two-room sandstone mansion built in 1800 and furnished with Victorian furniture and accessories. The adjacent vineyard and winery operation produces 300,000 bottles of twenty-five varietals—including champagne.

If that isn't enough, Mt. Hope is also the scene of a spring Scottish festival; a rock and roll fifties weekend (with Chuck "The Truck" Romito, the winery president, as master of ceremonies); and a summer-long Renaissance Festival complete with a queen and her court, a jousting tournament, jesters, games, Shakespearean drama, and music. Fall and winter are not neglected either, with candlelight dinners, tastings, and other events. It's a fun weekend, no matter the season.

The last wine region well worth visiting is Bucks County, a well-known tourist stop in the countryside north of Philadelphia. Bucks County is celebrated for its beautiful eighteenth-century homes and farms; parks; covered bridges; and villages filled with antique shops, tasteful boutiques, and galleries. It is also known for its wineries.

Bucks County Vineyards, located on a farm that dates back to a 1717 William Penn grant, produces more than 200,000 bottles a year. The vineyards offers tours and tastings and one oddity: a wine and fashion museum featuring the original costumes of Broadway and Hollywood stars. The link between wine and the stage may seem a bit obscure, but the winery's president, Arthur Gerold, once owned a major theatrical company. Among the costumes in the museum are a dress worn by Julie Andrews in "My Fair Lady," clothes worn by Marlon Brando in "The Godfather," and more. In addition, the winery has a cheese and bread shop, a perfect excuse to stop for a small snack and a glass of wine at the patio tables outside.

Other area wineries include **Buckingham Valley Vineyards**, which also has picnic tables for a lunch stop, and the **Peace Valley Winery**, boasting one of the more elegant buildings in the region. Both allow self-guided tours of the vineyards and regular tastings.

There are more wineries in the five regions described here, and you can pick up brochures at most of the wineries listing others in the area. Take time to explore anything interesting along the way, and save the wine you buy for drinking when the driving is done.

🍒 TAKING THE TOUR

Winemaking in Virginia is celebrated in the Virginia Wine Museum at historic Michie Tavern, on Route 53 near Jefferson's Monticello south of Charlottesville. The museum is open every day except holidays. Call 804/977-1234. The Virginia Wine Festival is held every June at the Northern Virginia 4-H Center in Front Royal. Call 800/658-8830 for the exact dates.

Maryland holds a wine festival in September at the Carroll County Farm Museum in Westminster. Call 301/848-7775.

Pennsylvania has numerous local festivals. For information about them or any of the numerous wine festivals in the Mid-Atlantic, write or call the following groups:

🍒 The Wine Marketing Program, Virginia Department of Agriculture and Consumer Services, Division of Markets, P.O. Box 1163, Richmond, VA 23209 or call 804/786-0481.

🍒 The Maryland Department of Agriculture, Marketing Services, 50 Harry S Truman Parkway, Annapolis, MD 21401 or call 301/841-5770.

🍒 The Pennsylvania Travel Bureau of Development, Department of Commerce, 416 Forum Building, Harrisburg, PA 17120 or call 800/ VISIT-PA.

The wineries listed here are usually open for visitors on weekends from spring through fall. Here are directions to them:

Virginia

Barboursville Plantation In Barboursville. From the intersection of routes 20 and 33, take Route 20 south 200 yards, turn left on Route 678, drive a half-mile to Route 777, turn right and drive 500 yards to the first driveway. Turn right and go to the vineyards. 703/832-3824.

Dominion Wine Cellars In Culpeper. The wine cellars are on the U.S. 29 bypass. 703/825-8772.

Meredyth Vineyards In Middleburg. At Middleburg's blinking light on U.S. 50, turn south and drive two and a half miles to Route 628, then turn right and drive two and a half miles to the winery. 703/687-6277.

Montdomaine Cellars In Charlottesville. Take Route 20 twelve miles south of I-64, turn right on Route 720 and drive a half-mile to the vineyard. 804/971-8947.

Oakencroft Vineyards In Charlottesville. Take U.S. 29 north to Barracks Road, then go west three and a half miles to the winery on the left. 804/296-4188.

Piedmont Vineyards and Winery In Middleburg. The winery is three miles south of Middleburg on Route 626. 703/687-5528.

Prince Michel Vineyards In Leon. The winery is on U.S. 29 ten miles south of Culpeper. 703/547-3709.

Willowcroft Farm Vineyards In Leesburg. Take U.S. 15 south from Leesburg, turn right on Route 704 and make an immediate right on Route 797, a dirt road. Drive three and one-tenth miles to the winery. Call for an appointment. 703/777-8161.

Maryland

Berrywine Plantations In Mt. Airy. From I-70, take Exit 60 and drive north four and a half miles on Route 675. Turn right on Glisans Mill Road and drive three and seven-tenths miles to the vineyards. 301/662-8687.

Catoctin Vineyards In Brookville. Take New Hampshire Avenue north from I-495, the Washington Beltway, and drive fourteen miles to Greenbridge Road. Turn right; the vineyard is at number 805. 301/774-2310.

Elk Run Vineyards In Mt. Airy. The vineyard is midway between Baltimore and Frederick on Route 26 (Liberty Road). 301/774-2513.

Loew Vineyards In Mt. Airy. The winery is on Route 26, three and a half miles east of Route 75 at number 14001. 301/460-5728.

Pennsylvania

Allegro Vineyards In Brogue. From I-83 near York take Exit 6E to Route 74 south. Follow Route 74 for fifteen miles through Red Lion to Brogue. Turn right at the Allegro sign and drive two miles to a second Allegro sign, then turn left and drive three-quarters of a mile to the vineyards. 717/927-9148.

Buckingham Valley Vineyards In Buckingham. The winery is on Route 413, two miles south of Route 202. 215/794-7188.

Bucks County Vineyards In New Hope. The winery is on Route 202, one mile north of Lahaska. 215/794-7449.

Chaddsford Winery In Chadds Ford. The winery is on U.S. 1 five miles north of Route 52, about fifteen miles northwest of Wilmington. 215/388-6221.

Mount Hope Winery and Estate In Mannheim. The estate and winery are sixteen miles north of Lancaster on Route 72. 717/665-7021.

Peace Valley Winery In Chalfont. 300 Limekiln Road, two miles from Route 313. 215/249-9058.

❦ INNS AND RESTAURANTS

The vineyard regions are blessed with numerous inns and restaurants that will enhance a wine-country romantic weekend. Here are our favorites, but first an explanation of how we break down our cost categories:

One night in an inn for two (often but not always including breakfast):

Inexpensive   Under $75
Moderate $75 to $125
Expensive   More than $125

For dinner for two (wine and drinks not included):

Inexpensive   Less than $25
Moderate $25 to $60
Expensive   More than $60

Virginia

Between Middleburg and Charlottesville is an inn considered by many to be the finest in the nation. The **Inn at Little Washington** is one of ten inns in America to win honors from *Relais et Chateaux*, the prestigious guide to small hotels, inns, and restaurants around the world. The inn added another honor in 1989 when it was awarded a five-star rating from the *Mobil Travel Guide*. The inn, in the small (population 200) village of Washington, about an hour north of Charlottesville, offers stunning cuisine and elegant accommodations. Chef-owner Patrick O'Connell prepares a menu featuring regional meats and produce, and has won almost unanimous acclaim as the owner of the best restaurant in the Washington (big and little) region. The eight rooms and two suites are furnished elegantly with many antique pieces. Both dinner (a fixed-price meal) and the rooms rate as expensive, but worth it for a very special occasion. 703/675-3800.

In the Charlottesville area:

Boar's Head Inn This 175-room modern inn and sports club is owned by the Rogans of Oakencroft Vineyards. It is larger than most of the inns listed in this book, but is included because it is an elegant, Williamsburg-style hotel set amid beautifully landscaped grounds made for evening strolls. The rooms are furnished with antique reproductions and carefully chosen fabrics and accessories. The inn has shops selling fine crafts and gifts; a health club; tennis, squash, and racquetball courts; ballooning; a lake with geese and ducks; an outdoor patio cafe—staffed by a St. Bernard named Bruno—overlooking the lake; a fine restaurant; and live music and dancing every evening. Each October, a Bacchanalian Wine Festival is held at the inn, with dancing, a feast, and sampling of the state's wines. Moderate/expensive. The inn is on U.S. 250 two miles west of U.S. 29. Write Box 5185, Charlottesville, VA 22905. 804/296-2181.

High Meadows This seventeen-room inn mixes the Federalist style of its first builder and the Victorian style of a later owner who added to the house. The inn is on twenty acres with its own vineyard and gardens. The rooms are furnished nicely with antiques and country furniture. Every evening, the Great Hall that joins the two halves of the house is used for a tasting of local wines. Following that, a six-course dinner of regional fare is served by candlelight in the dining room. The inn is on Route 20 south of Charlottesville. Moderate for both rooms and dinner. Route 4, Box 6, Route 20 South, Scottsville, VA 24590. 804/286-2218.

Silver Thatch Inn This white frame building began as a log barracks built for Hessian mercenaries during the Revolutionary War. Today the inn has seven antique-filled guest rooms and a fine dining room. Moderate. 3001 Hollymead Road (about six miles north of Charlottesville on U.S. 29), Charlottesville, VA 22901. 804/978-4686.

200 South Street The twenty guest rooms in this urban inn are furnished with canopy beds, antiques, and fireplaces. The inn is located a block from the center of Charlottesville. That's the only drawback for an inn that would be a stunner in a country setting. Expensive. 200 South Street, Charlottesville, VA 22901. 804/979-0200.

In the Middleburg/Leesburg area:

The Gibson Hall Inn This 157-year-old mansion near Middleburg was the stately home of the first mayor of the small town of Upperville. Oriental rugs, designer decor, and a magnificent center hall greet visitors to the five rooms. If this is a very special weekend, book the third-floor lovers' retreat and soak away all cares in the Jacuzzi. Moderate. Write P.O. Box 225, Route 50, Upperville, VA 22176. 703/592-3514.

The Laurel Brigade Inn This old inn in the center of historic Leesburg once booked rooms for less than $20 a night. Today the five beautifully furnished rooms in the old stone building are still a bargain, making this inn one of the few to get into the inexpensive category. The restaurant is the real draw here, serving regional fare at inexpensive/moderate prices. 20 West Market Street (Route 7) Leesburg, VA 22075. 703/777-1010.

Red Fox Inn The Red Fox claims it is the oldest inn in the nation, and it just may be. The old stone foundation walls and timbers show the majesty of age without the deleterious effects. There are six rooms in the main inn and thirteen rooms (some with fireplace) in the two annexes, the Stray Fox Inn and McConnell House. The main inn, in the center of the antique-filled village of Middleburg, dates from 1728, when the inn was built by Joseph Chinn, George Washington's cousin. In the 1970s it was showing its age, but recent renovation has restored the elegance of the rooms and raised the quality of the cuisine in the popular dining room, which serves classic Virginian, Italian, and French dishes. Dinner prices are moderate; the rooms are expensive. 2 East Washington Street, Middleburg, VA 22117. 703/687-6301.

The Windsor Inn Better known as a fine restaurant offering British pub fare in the center of Middleburg, the Windsor Inn is also home to four gaily decorated guest rooms. The dinner fare is moderate; the rooms are moderate/expensive. 2 West Washington Street, Middleburg, VA 22117. 703/687-6800.

For fine dining in Virginia's Wine Country:

The C&O Restaurant just opposite the old train station in Charlottesville is one of those places where appearances are misleading. The old red brick townhouse doesn't look like much, but it does blend into the neighborhood. The only indication that there is a restaurant here is the faded Pepsi sign displaying the name. Hiding inside this misleading facade is food fine enough to win national acclaim. Downstairs in the tavern, varied fare is served at moderate prices. Upstairs, in two seatings at expensive fixed-price rates, fine French and American nouvelle cuisine is served. Reservations required. 515 East Water Street, Charlottesville, VA. 804/971-7044.

La Galerie, on U.S. 250 west of Charlottesville at the Crozet turnoff, serves fine French country cuisine and is popular with the area's gentry. It is very particular about guests reconfirming reservations. Expensive. 804/823-5883.

Historic **Michie Tavern** plays hosts to the Wine Museum on land once owned by Patrick Henry's father. The superbly restored 200-year-old tavern serves southern favorites, but only at a luncheon buffet. It is closed for dinner. Inexpensive. Route 53, Charlottesville, VA. 804/977-1234.

The Ivy Inn looks like the historic old home that it is. Fine Virginia dishes and other American standards served at moderate prices. 2244 Old Ivy Road, Ivy, VA. 804/977-1222.

The Old Mill is the main dining room in the **Boar's Head Inn**, and serves succulent Old Virginia dishes and some more creative fare. Expensive. Reservations are suggested. The inn is on U.S. 250 two miles west of U.S. 29 in Charlottesville, VA. 804/296-2181.

Silver Thatch Inn is known for its regional meat dishes and incredible desserts. Moderate. 3001 Hollymead Road (about six miles north of Charlottesville on U.S. 29), Charlottesville, VA. 804/978-4686.

Le Snail serves fine country French meals in an old house in downtown Charlottesville. Moderate. 320 West Main Street. 804/295-4456.

The Red Fox Tavern serves interesting regional dishes in an attractive room. Moderate/expensive. 2 East Washington Street, Middleburg, VA. 703/687-6301.

Mosby's Tavern, another Red Fox operation, serves lighter fare in a former stable just a block away from the Red Fox Inn. Inexpensive/moderate. 2 West Marshall Street, Middleburg, VA. 703/687-5282.

The Windsor House, across the street from the Red Fox Inn, serves lamb chops, liver, and fish and chips. Moderate. 2 West Washington Street, Middleburg, VA. 703/687-6800.

Maryland

Bed and Board at Tran Crossing In the heart of Frederick's restored area of Federal and colonial homes is this very small B&B in a three-story Victorian townhouse. The public rooms are furnished with antiques while the two guest rooms, which share a bath, have more modern furniture. This inn is close to the historic homes and antique shops of

Frederick as well as to the wine country to the east. Moderate. 121 East Patrick Street, Frederick, MD 21701. 301/663-8449.

The Inn at Buckeystown This inn is in a century-old Victorian mansion with an adjacent cottage in a former church. The nine guest rooms and one cottage are furnished with Victorian antiques. Lovers swear by the suggestive decor of the Love Room and the made-for-snuggling Fireplace Room. At the cottage, beautiful stained-glass windows, a private hot tub, and a cozy loft bed await. Expensive, but rates include breakfast and a five-course dinner. 3521 Buckeystown Pike (Route 85), Buckeystown, MD 21717. 301/874-5755.

The Strawberry Inn This small inn began life as a farmhouse in the mid-nineteenth century. Today the two-story white frame house anchors the small downtown of New Market, a city filled with antique and craft shops. The five rooms, all with private baths, are furnished with Victorian pieces. Inexpensive. 17 Main Street, New Market, MD 21774. 301/865-3318.

The Summer House This two-room cabin sets on a sixty-acre farm near the two-century-old main house outside Westminster, in the center of Maryland's wine country. Downstairs in the cabin is an antique-filled living room and a fireplace; upstairs is a four-poster bedroom and a full bathroom. The adjacent pond and weeping willows serve as peaceful neighbors. Moderate. Write The Traveler in Maryland, P.O. Box 2277, Annapolis, MD 21404. 301/269-6232.

The Turning Point Inn This large Edwardian home is both a popular restaurant and a five-room inn furnished with country antiques and crafts. All the rooms have private baths. Visitors should sample the dining room's offerings. Moderate. 3406 Urbana Pike (Route 355, in the center of the village of Urbana), Frederick, MD 21701. 301/874-2421.

Fine dining in Maryland requires a bit more searching:

The Inn at Buckeystown serves five-course dinners featuring game and fish served in a creative manner. Adding to the meal are the Victorian china and silver. Inn guests get preference here, but call anyway. Expensive. 3521 Buckeystown Pike (Route 85), Buckeystown. 301/874-5755.

The Turning Point Inn features some outstanding seafood dishes in an airy dining room and deck overlooking the Frederick County farmland and Sugar Loaf Mountain. 3406 Urbana Pike (Route 355 in the center of Urbana), Frederick. 301/874-2421.

Bushwaller's in downtown Frederick serves American cuisine in the dark-wood atmosphere of the new American saloon. Inexpensive/moderate. 209 North Market Street. 301/694-5697.

Di Francesco's serves classic Italian dishes. 26 North Market Street, Frederick. 301/695-5499.

For other options, we suggest strolling the low-numbered blocks of North Market Street in downtown Frederick, where you will find a large selection of restaurants, none of which are outstanding but most of which are fine.

Pennsylvania

The Amish country and Brandywine Valley of Pennsylvania are loaded with good restaurants and superb inns. Here is a list of some of the best near the wineries:

Cameron Estate Inn Only a few minutes from the Mt. Hope Winery, this spacious eighteen-room inn is surrounded by farmland laced with trout streams and hiking trails. All but two of the rooms have private baths; all are filled with antiques and reproductions. The dining room's menu of American and continental cuisine has won acclaim. Inexpensive/moderate. Write RD #1, Box 305, Mount Joy, PA 17552. 717/653-1773.

Donegal Mills Plantation There are seventeen rooms in this eighteenth-century mansion, all furnished with period antiques. Adjacent to the inn is a restaurant in an old mill and a semirestored village that is a tourist attraction. Moderate. Trout Run Road, P.O. Box 204, Mount Joy, PA 17552. 717/653-2168.

The Fairville Inn Located about ten miles from Chadds Ford between Longwood Gardens and Winterthur, this inn offers fifteen rooms in the main house and the new country-rustic annexes. The rooms are comfortable, all with private baths and five with fireplaces. Moderate. The inn is in Fairville, on Route 52 near the village of Mendenhall. Write P.O. Box 219, Mendenhall, PA 19357. 215/388-5900.

General Sutter Inn This twelve-room inn is on the square in Lititz, a picture-perfect community with a chocolate factory, pretzelmaker, and a surprising number of eighteenth-century houses. The inn is a quaint place, something you might find as the setting for a Victorian novel; the lobby is filled with exotic birds in cages and the main decorating theme in the rooms is wicker. Still, it is a fine place, with a nice dining room and garden plaza. Inexpensive. 14 East Main Street, Lititz, PA 17543. 717/626-2115.

Hamorton House You drive three-quarters of a mile down the entrance road before you come to this 140-year-old fieldstone mansion, thirty-four rooms of which are filled with seventeenth- and eighteenth-century antiques. The mansion in Glen Mills is elegant, the perfect setting for a romantic weekend. There are six guest rooms, four with private baths, and one suite. Take time to walk the grounds, for the paths lead you to sculptures, a gazebo, and a wishing well. Moderate. Write Guesthouses, RD 9, West Chester, PA 19380. 215/692-4575.

The Log House at Battle Hill The twenty acres of meadows surrounding this restored eighteenth-century, two-room log cabin makes this a special spot in Chadds Ford. There are two lakes, a pool surrounded by hedges for your private enjoyment, and evening walks through the lantern-illuminated lawn. Expensive. Write Guesthouses Bed & Breakfast, R.D. 9, West Chester, PA 19380. 215/692-4575.

The Mill House This 1766 stone house, furnished with early American antiques, is set on a mill stream with a humpbacked bridge. There are three rooms, all tastefully furnished with period pieces. Outside, you may bump into some of the peacocks strolling the grounds. Inexpensive. 313 Osceola Mill Road, Gordonville, PA 17529. 717/768-3758.

Sweetwater Farms This fifty-five-acre sheep and horse farm has nine rooms in the old stone farmhouse. Six rooms have private baths, but all are exquisitely furnished with country antiques and decorations. Moderate. Box 86, Sweetwater Road, Glen Mills, PA 19342. 215/459-4711.

For fine dining in Amish country:

The Cameron Estate Inn is operated by Betty Groff, whose Amish fare at Groff's Farm is famous in the region. At the estate the menu is continental and still noteworthy. The Sunday brunch is exceptional. Moderate. Donegal Springs Road, R.D. 1, Box 305, Mount Joy, PA. 717/653-1773.

General Sutter Inn serves surprisingly good American fare, but take time, if weather permits, to have a cocktail on the garden patio that overlooks the town square. Moderate. 14 East Main Street, Lititz, PA. 717/626-2115.

Groff's Farm is a restaurant in an old stone farmhouse that serves authentic Pennsylvania Dutch fare. That includes some of Betty Groff's own creations, such as Chicken Stoltzfus (chunks of chicken in a cream sauce on a bed of light pastry) and black raspberry tarts. Reservations required for dinner. Moderate. Pinkerton Road, Mount Joy, PA. 717/653-2048.

The Lemon Tree Inn is a beautifully decorated century-old restaurant in downtown Lancaster. The menu emphasizes traditional American dishes and some continental dishes. Moderate. 1766 Columbia Avenue, Lancaster, PA. 717/394-0441.

For fine dining in the Brandywine Valley:

The Chadds Ford Inn has been serving food and drink since the early 1700s. The menu is very creative, but the kitchen lives up to its promises. Favorites include braised quail, veal chops with shiitake mushrooms, and salmon en croute. Moderate. The inn is at the intersection of routes 1 and 100, Chadds Ford, PA. 215/388-7361.

Buckley's Tavern is two restaurants. In the front room, a pub serves light sandwiches and pasta dishes. In the elegant back dining room, an eclectic menu offers surprises from Thai dishes to French standards. Stick to the back room. Expensive. Route 52 in Centreville, DE, just over the Pennsylvania state line. 302/656-9776.

The Dilworthtown Inn serves classic continental cuisine (chateaubriand, filet mignon bearnaise, shrimp provençal) in a carefully restored 230-year-old inn. While there, visit the Dilworthtown Country Store next door. Briton's Bridge at Old Wilmington Pike, West Chester, PA. 215/399-1390.

The Bucks County area is filled with enough inns and restaurants for an entire book. Here are some of our favorites:

The Inn at Fordhook Farm This 220-year-old stone mansion was once the summer home of the Burpees, the family whose seeds are famous. The Burpees still own the farm and use it as an inn and small conference center. There are five bedrooms in the main house and two bedrooms in a carriage house, all tastefully furnished with antiques and oriental rugs. Around the buildings are sixty acres of gardens and croplands. Moderate. 105 New Britain Road, Doylestown, PA 18901. 215/345-1766.

The Inn at Phillips Mill This is a small inn, only five rooms in a stone building that is more than two centuries old. All five rooms are cozy, but are tastefully furnished with country furniture and accessories. Moderate. North River Road (Route 32), New Hope, PA 18938. 215/862-2984.

Pineapple Hill This inn is located in a farmhouse built around 1800. The five rooms and two suites are furnished with country furniture and antiques, while the common rooms serve as showplaces for many country arts and crafts. Inexpensive/moderate. 1324 River Road, New Hope, PA 18938. 215/862-9608.

1740 House This picture-perfect inn overlooks the Delaware River. The twenty-four rooms in the stunning frame main house are carefully decorated, and all have private baths. Canoeing, ice-skating, a pool, and walks along the Delaware Canal are available for the guests' enjoyment. Moderate. River Road, Lumberville, PA 18933. 215/297-5661.

Wedgwood Inn This inn is made up of two buildings—a classic revival stone house built around 1830 and a gabled Victorian built just after the Civil War. There are ten rooms, two suites and a carriage house, all furnished with an interesting mix of old furniture and some Victorian pieces. Inexpensive/moderate. 111 West Bridge Street, New Hope, PA 18938. 215/862-2570.

For fine dining in Bucks County:

The Black Bass Hotel serves some very fine French and American dishes in a country-inn atmosphere. Expensive. River Road, Lumberville, PA. 215/297-5770.

Centre Bridge Inn is a resurrected inn. The original 1706 building burned down and was rebuilt in the 1950s. But this inn on the canal serves a wide variety of meats and seafood, all well-prepared. Expensive. Routes 32 and 263, New Hope, PA. 215/862-9139, 215/862-2048.

The Golden Pheasant serves a continental menu, specializing in game dishes. Expensive. River Road, Erwinna, PA. 215/294-9595.

The Inn at Phillips Mill serves excellent French cuisine, with special dishes available for vegetarians. Outdoor dining in the summer. Moderate. North River Road, New Hope, PA. 215/862-9919.

The Sign of the Sorrel Horse serves some stunning continental dishes, from magnificently creative appetizers through dessert. Our dinner wrecked our diets. The dining room is in a building built in 1749. In the summer you can dine on the veranda overlooking the forest, a flower garden, and a pool with a fountain. Expensive. R.D. 3, Old Bethlehem Road, Quakertown, PA. (We urge you to call for directions, for we found it only after some difficulty.) 215/536-4651.

For more inns, restaurants and nearby attractions in the wine country, turn to Chapter 1, "The Beauty of the Mid-Atlantic."

Chapter Seven

A Tale of Four Cities

The Mid-Atlantic's four major cities—Baltimore, Philadelphia, Richmond, and Washington—are many things: exciting, amusing, entertaining and, at times, exasperating. Romance is not a term that often comes to mind when discussing them, but romantic they can be, for they are filled with wonderful sights, glorious museums, superb restaurants, and quaint hotels and inns. Better yet, after years on the critical list, these cities are experiencing a renaissance.

A generation ago, Baltimore, Richmond, Washington, and Philadelphia were sad examples of urban blight: business and industrial centers were dying from a combination of population shifts, foreign competition, and the flight to the suburbs.

Today, the downtowns of these cities are alive again, filled with enough vibrant attractions to satisfy a long-time resident or weekend visitor.

The secret to making your visit to any of these cities romantic is to set limitations. You cannot do it all or see it all. Choose a theme—museums, theaters, nightlife, or shopping—and then plan your trip around it.

This chapter is a sampler of these four cities, with our favorite sites, inns, and restaurants. Not every museum, boutique, historical park, and garden walk is mentioned. Just those we think are romantic and fun.

❦ BALTIMORE

Baltimore's past, present, and future are found on the seawalls around its harbor. The magnificent deep anchorage on the Patapsco River just upstream from the Chesapeake Bay lured Lord Baltimore in the early 1600s. Over the centuries since, the harbor turned the small settlement into a major seaport that ships out coal, steel, and other products to ports around the world.

Like many other industrial giants, Baltimore fell on hard times. The steel mills closed, the auto plants dwindled, the harbor traffic slacked off, and rot set in.

Thanks to inspired local leadership, the harbor proved the source of the renaissance in Baltimore. Factories, warehouses, and pier terminals on the Inner Harbor were razed and replaced with shops, restaurants, and hotels. This development spread, bringing "gentrification" to Federal Hill, a historic neighborhood just west of Fort McHenry, and to Fell's Point, where the tugboats still dock next to the road.

Baltimore's wonders go beyond new developments. Its two fine art museums are often overlooked by art lovers heading to Washington, Philadelphia, or New York. The **Baltimore Museum of Art** (33rd and North Charles streets) has the largest Matisse collection in the nation, along with numerous Picasso, Renoir, Cezanne, and Gauguin paintings and works by other post-impressionists. The collections at the **Walters Art Gallery** (600 North Charles St.) span some 6,000 years, from early Egyptian art to art deco and art nouveau, and include one of the finest private collections of oriental art in the nation.

The **National Aquarium**'s white Beluga whales and their finny friends entertain visitors at their modern building next to **Harborplace**, the Rouse Company development that led to the rebirth of the Inner Harbor. Today this waterfront is a busy world of shops, hotels, restaurants, food markets, ice-skating rinks, a science museum, an amphitheater for concerts, sailing ships, and passing yachts.

South of the Inner Harbor is **Federal Hill**, the historic area of "twilight's last gleaming" fame. This neighborhood just west of Fort McHenry is changing, with the old brick townhouses and shops being renovated into upscale residences, galleries, and restaurants. East of the Inner Harbor you come to **Little Italy**, a neighborhood of narrow streets, narrow rowhouses, and wonderful bistros and restaurants, and then **Fell's Point**, our favorite neighborhood in Baltimore.

Fell's Point traces its roots back to the early 1700s, when the Fell brothers from England set up their trading business here. Things haven't changed much since then. The streets are still narrow and bear names

—Bond, Thames, Shakespeare, Lancaster—that testify to the origins of the point's first residents.

Most of the buildings in the area where the tugboats tie up are more than a century old, and many predate the War of 1812. Up until a generation ago, Fell's Point was a slum of waterfront bars, ship's stores, and shabby housing. The drunken sailors have gone and many of the waterfront bars now have ferns in their windows, but the tugboats remain, tied up just cobblestone steps away from newer attractions. While most of the houses are private and cannot be visited, one—the 234-year-old Robert Long House at 812 South Ann Street—has been restored and is open on Thursdays from 10 A.M. to 4 P.M.

Other attractions in Fell's Point include antique shops, junk bazaars, the exotic China Sea Marine Trading Company at 1724 Thames Street; the remarkable Admiral Fell Inn at 888 South Broadway across from the tugs; some surprisingly good restaurants; and one of Baltimore's regional delights, the Broadway Market, a feast for the eyes and nose.

Farther east, an old industrial area known as Canton Harbor is being reborn into a major complex with a marina, galleries, shops and housing.

While the waterfront holds Baltimore's heritage, there are other areas that are worth visiting. **Mount Vernon Place**, between St. Paul and Cathedral streets a few steps north of the Walters Art Gallery, is one of the more beautiful city squares in the Mid-Atlantic. Renovated Victorian townhomes, parks, and art galleries line the neighborhood around the square.

North Howard Street (the 700 to 800 blocks) and West Read Street (the 200 block) are the oldest antique market areas in the state, with more than three dozen shops selling everything from books and jewelry to furniture and silver.

If shopping is on your list, the shops at Harborplace are inviting, but don't miss those at the Brokerage, a mall of nineteen restored Victorian buildings at Market Place and Water Street just four blocks from Harborplace.

Baltimore's cultural life has not been neglected. Not far from where the infamous block of strip joints and seedy bars once existed are the **Lyric Opera House** (527 N. Charles St.), home to the Baltimore Opera Company; the **Joseph Meyerhoff Symphony Hall** (1212 Cathedral St.), where the Baltimore Symphony Orchestra plays; the **Morris Mechanic Theater** (Baltimore and Charles streets), where top plays are staged; and the **Peabody Conservatory of Music** (1 E. Mount Vernon Pl.), where operas, orchestral concerts, and recitals are presented.

The **Convention Center and Festival Hall** just west of the Inner Harbor play host to the Baltimore Wintermarket, a huge craft show that draws more than 500 artisans from around the nation every February, and to international festivals almost every weekend in the summer.

Nightlife, like the rest of the city, is undergoing a change for the better. Blues Alley Jazz (1225 Cathedral St.) serves up fine creole seafood as well at the live performances of such stars as Phyllis Hyman, Sara Vaughan, Ramsey Lewis, and Wynton Marsalis. Danny's (Charles and Biddle streets) and the Cafe Park Plaza (810 N. Charles St.) also serve up light jazz.

For more variety, try the Fishmarket on the Inner Harbor a few steps east of the National Aquarium. This renovated waterfront building is home to six nightclubs offering music from rock to blues, from disco to country. One small cover charge allows you to visit all of the clubs. Ltl Ditty's in the Brokerage offers sing-along. For more sedate entertainment, try the 13th Floor at the stately Hotel Belvedere (Charles and Chase streets), where the view is matched by the quality of the live entertainment.

Getting around Baltimore to see all these sights is fairly easy. The Inner Harbor Trolley travels around the sights from Fell's Point to Harborplace and north to Mount Vernon Place. At twenty-five cents, the price can't be beat. If you have the time, take a cruise around the harbor on one of the water taxis that shuttle between the sights.

🍃 PHILADELPHIA

Often overlooked by travelers heading to Washington and New York, Philadelphia has triumphed over rejection to become a vibrant and exciting metropolis, the fifth largest in the nation.

The history of rejection goes back centuries. In 1682, William Penn founded the city on the bluffs above the Schuylkill and Delaware rivers. Penn envisioned a utopia, a "greene countrie towne" where personal freedoms would be assured. This atmosphere of freedom attracted intellectuals, writers, and philosophers whose works and words stirred resentment against the heavy hand of the English king.

This politically charged cauldron bubbled over on July 4, 1776, when the Declaration of Independence was signed at the State House (now Independence Hall). Eleven years later the U.S. Constitution was drafted there. Philadelphia served as the capital of the new United States until 1800, when the political capital of the nation was moved to Washington. That rejection was compounded by the ascendancy of New York City as the economic capital of the new nation.

Philadelphia, its history, and its heritage survived those affronts, and today offer more attractions than any visitor can see in a weekend.

The City of Brotherly Love has several outstanding museums, a busy cultural life, many neighborhoods and parks worth strolling, fine shopping, excellent restaurants, and a park that holds this nation's heritage.

Independence National Historic Park is a square mile of history, a large urban green perfect for walking, relaxing, and sight-seeing. At the Visitors Center at 3rd and Chestnut streets you can sign up for guided tours and get more information on the park. Within the park you can tour **Independence Hall**, where there is always a line; **The Liberty Bell Pavilion; Liberty Hall**, the oldest subscription library in the nation; the eighteenth-century **Todd House** and **Bishop White House; Carpenters' Hall**, where the Continental Congress met; **Old City Hall**, first home of the U.S. Supreme Court; **Congress Hall**, where the first five congresses met, and other historic buildings.

Ben Franklin, the city's favorite son, is not forgotten. **Franklin Court** was once owned by him and today is a tribute to his life. Franklin is buried a few steps north, in the **Christ Church Burial Ground**, 5th and Arch streets.

Washington Square, the park at 6th and Walnut streets, was one of five originally planned by William Penn. Today it is also the site of the **Tomb of the Unknown Soldier of the American Revolution**.

Another historic area, **Society Hill**, is directly south of Independence Park. The neighborhood, bounded by Front, 6th, Walnut, and Lombard streets, got its name because it was the headquarters of a group of merchants known in Penn's day as the Society of Free Traders. Back then, the neighborhood was a hill. Over the years, erosion leveled the hill and the area of historic rowhouses became a cherished residential neighborhood that today is a lovely, romantic area in which to walk.

Philadelphia's historical sites do not overshadow its numerous museums. Those we put on our don't-miss list are the **Philadelphia Museum of Art** (26th St. and Benjamin Franklin Parkway), the third largest in the nation with thousands of paintings, sculptures, drawings, and prints; the **Rodin Museum** (22nd St. and the Franklin Parkway), which has one of the largest collections of Rodin's sculptures and drawings outside of France; and the **Philadelphia Art Alliance**, on lovely Rittenhouse Square, which has three floors of galleries displaying everything from avant-garde to traditional works of art.

The Norman Rockwell Museum (601 Walnut St.) displays hundreds of the works of one of America's best-known artists; the **Mummers Museum** (2nd St. and Washington Ave.) displays costumes from the traditional New Year's Day parade; and the **University Museum of Archeology and Anthropology** (33rd and Spruce streets) has archeological exhibits from cultures around the world.

The Philadelphia Flower Show every spring is among the finer such shows in the nation. If you miss it, try visiting the **Morris Arboretum** (Hillcrest Avenue near Germantown Avenue), one of the nation's top Victorian landscape gardens, or the **Pennsylvania Horticultural Society** (325 Walnut St.), the producer of the flower show, where you can view an eighteenth-century garden.

If you have come to the city for a little shopping, you don't have to go far from the sights to break your budget. The **Bourse**, at 21 South 5th Street just east of the Liberty Bell Pavilion, was built as a grand mercantile exchange in the early years of this century. Now restored, the Bourse is home to numerous shops and more than a score of restaurants and eateries. **Rittenhouse Square**, at 18th and Walnut streets, is beautiful, particularly during the spring, and is a center of shops, boutiques, salons, and galleries. Chestnut Street, between 6th and 18th streets, is also a shopper's paradise, with many fine clothing stores. The king of all the shopping areas may be the **Reading Terminal Market** (12th and Filbert streets), a maze of more than 700 shopping stalls.

Antique enthusiasts will enjoy a walk down Pine Street between 9th and 18th streets, and Chestnut Street between 7th and 18th, where antiques from early American art and furniture to more contemporary collectibles can be found. Don't miss our favorite shops: Alfred Bullard (1604 Pine St.) for eighteenth- and nineteenth-century furnishing; Schaffer's (1032 Pine St.) for stained glass; and Frank S. Schwarz & Son (1806 Chestnut St.), which has some wonderful early American paintings and antiques.

Antiques are also the subject of the annual **Philadelphia Antiques Show**, held each April in the 103rd Engineers Armory, 33rd Street north of Market.

Our favorite shopping area is **South Street** between 6th and Front streets. This narrow road is a carnival, bustling with people and lined with avant-garde shops selling everything from fine art and antiques to T-shirts and the latest uniform in punk rock. Between the tempting stores are ethnic restaurants that are some of the undiscovered wonders in town.

Almost as active as South Street is Philadelphia's cultural and nightlife scene. The **Academy of Music** (Locust and Broad streets) is the home of the Philadelphia Orchestra, the Philadelphia Pops, the Opera Company of Philadelphia, and the Pennsylvania Ballet. The **Annenberg Center** (3680 Walnut St.) presents high-quality theater, concerts, and dance. The **Forrest Theater** (1114 Walnut St.) and the **Walnut Street Theater** (9th and Walnut) present top-flight drama and musicals.

For band and dance music, your best bet is to head to one of the hotels. The Hershey Philadelphia Hotel (Broad and Locust streets), the Sheraton Society Hill (One Dock St.), The Warwick (17th and Locust streets), and the Top of Centre Square (1500 Market St.) have live entertainment most nights. For more contemporary sounds, try the Beverly Hills Bar and Grill in the Bourse (21 S. 5th St.) for live rock music, or the Lautrec Restaurant/Borgia Cafe (408 S. 2nd St.) for live jazz. And if you just want some quiet music in an intimate atmosphere, try the Society Hill Hotel's piano bar (301 Chestnut St.).

Getting to all these places is fairly easy. The historic area, Society Hill, and South Street are on the east side of town, all within walking distance of one another. Most of the large museums are clustered around the Benjamin Franklin Parkway near Fairmont Park and Logan Circle. The best plan is to stay near the museums or the historic area and walk to all nearby attractions. Then take a taxi to another area. Don't drive around in Philadelphia; parking is difficult to find and expensive.

❦ RICHMOND

Rebellion and Richmond seem to have gone hand-in-hand. In 1775, Patrick Henry, addressing Washington, Jefferson, Randolph and other prominent Virginians, asserted: "Give me liberty or give me death!"

Those rebels went on to make history, but another Richmond rebellion almost a century later led to the destruction by fire of most of the capital of the Confederacy during the final days of the Civil War. The most recent rebellion was a generation ago, after some had written Richmond off as out of touch with the times and declining because of backward-thinking leadership.

Richmond not only survived those desperate times, but today it pulsates with new energy. Exciting new buildings crown its hilly center city. Elegant shops, stylish boutiques, and fine restaurants fill the renovated riverfront warehouse district known as Shockoe Slip. The historic west end of town remains proud as always, but the fringe areas, where decay always starts, have been reborn as new businesses, and residents have brought their vitality back to the city.

Richmond's museums offer many cultural diversions. The **Virginia Museum of Fine Arts** (Boulevard and Grove avenues) houses a large collection of art deco, art nouveau, and imperial Russian Easter eggs and jewels created by Fabergé. The **Valentine Museum** (1015 E. Clay St.), whose name makes it a must stop on a romantic weekend, has a collection of costumes, decorative arts, and textiles. The **Museum and White House of the Confederacy** (1201 E. Clay St.) has the world's largest collection of Confederate artifacts and documents.

Grand old mansions are major sights in Richmond. **Agecroft Hall** (4305 Sulgrave Rd.), a wonderful Tudor manor house built in England in the late fifteenth century, was dismantled and rebuilt here in the 1920s. Many of the furnishings are from the Tudor period. The adjacent **Virginia House** (4301 Sulgrave Rd.) is a Tudor house built of materials from Warwick Priory, which was built in England about the year 1125. Both houses and their lovely gardens are open for visits, but you will need reservations for Virginia House. **Wilton** (S. Wilton Rd. off Cary St.) is a Georgian mansion built by William Randolph, a colonial leader of the eighteenth century. The furnishings are authentic to the period. The Governor's Mansion is open for tours only during Historic Garden Week at the end of April.

Other stately homes can be found on **Monument Avenue**, a lovely boulevard and interesting walk along a street dotted with monuments to Confederate heroes.

Finally, no romantic trip to Richmond would be complete without seeing the graceful swan bed at **Maymont**, a splendid Victorian mansion and 100-acre park (Hampton St. and Pennsylvania Ave.). This mansion is filled with colorful decorations, lace, and superb Victorian art and furniture. Take time to stroll the grounds, which overlook the falls of the James River, and don't miss the Swan Lake, where you can feed gaggles of geese. If the weather cooperates, take a carriage ride around the grounds.

The **falls on the James River** are the reason the city is where it is. Boats couldn't travel farther up the river, so a frontier outpost was created at the falls. Visitors can walk on the pathway along the Kanawha Canal Locks on the north shore starting at 12th and Byrd streets. Or you can get a closer look at the falls. Richmond is unique among major cities: you can shoot the white water within sight of the downtown skyscrapers. The Richmond Raft Company (804/222-RAFT), Alpine Outfitters (804/794-4172), and the James River Experience (804/323-0062) can arrange for raft, kayak, or canoe trips through the rapids.

Shoppers will be delighted by the choices in Richmond. **Shockoe Slip** (12th and Cary streets) and **Main Street Station** (14th and Franklin streets) are two renovated areas now filled with boutiques, galleries, and restaurants. On the other side of town, the **Fan District** (Main and Cary streets between the Boulevard and Belvidere) is dotted with galleries, craft and antique shops, and restaurants.

🐝 The lovely garden sculpture at Maymont, the magnificent Victorian estate in Richmond. *Photo by Barbara Radin-Fox.*

Some stores and galleries we enjoyed were Elements (100 Shockoe Slip) for fine wood, metal, fiber, and glass crafts; Z Rosa (225 W. Main St. and 12th and Main streets) for whimsical, colorful, amusing folk art from Central America and the Caribbean; and Martha's Mixture (3445 W. Cary St.) for antiques.

Nightlife in Richmond centers on the restaurants. Great jazz and blues can be found at Benjamin's (2093 W. Broad St.), top-40 music and dancing in the downstairs room at the Tobacco Company (1201 E. Cary St.) with live music upstairs, and a wide range of live entertainment at Sam Miller's Warehouse (1210 E. Cary St.).

You may want to consider side trips. Not far east of Richmond, along both banks of the James River, are stately colonial-era plantations. These greathouses and grounds, open for tours, offer romantic strolls and marvelous river views. (For more details see Chapter 8, "A Change of Pace.")

Getting around Richmond is far easier than in any other city in this chapter. Traffic is manageable and parking is plentiful.

🥂 WASHINGTON, DC

Long scorned by American cities as a company town where red tape was the main industry, and ridiculed by other nations as a capital without taste or culture, Washington has finally attained the style and pizzazz expected of a world capital.

The renaissance was a long time coming, but its arrival has changed the face of this city. New museums, theaters, restaurants, shops, and galleries seem the norm now. Consider this:

🥂 Dining a generation ago usually meant fried food (fish or chicken). Now Washington has restaurants serving superb French cuisine as well as Cuban, Ethiopian, Italian, Korean, Chinese, Japanese, Afghan, Vietnamese, Persian, and Cambodian.

🥂 Theater once seemed to be a dirty word in Washington. That began to change with the arrival of the Kennedy Center for the Performing Arts in the 1960s, but has reached the point today that the Kennedy Center finds itself competing with the fine productions at Arena Stage, National Theater, Ford's Theater, and a score of other stages. In addition, Embassy Row is the center of plays, concerts, films, opera, and other activities you do not have to be a senator or cabinet secretary to attend.

🥂 Washington has always had many museums. But in one generation the National Gallery of Art has added an East Building; the new National Air and Space Museum, and the Hirshhorn Museum line the opposite side of the Mall, the park between the Capitol and the Lincoln Memorial; and the National Museum of African Art, the Arthur M. Sackler Gallery of Oriental Art, the National Museum of Women in the Arts, and other new galleries have opened.

With so much to see, where does a couple start?

Making a visit to Washington romantic is simple but time-consuming. Visit some of the museums filled with beautiful art, mix in walks in the parks and through some eclectic neighborhoods, and finish with a romantic dinner in an elegant restaurant.

The time to visit, if you can choose, is early April, when the city is tinged with pink and white cherry, dogwood, and tulip blossoms. The blossoms' lifespan is brief—only a week or so if it rains—so don't be disappointed if you miss them. The city has enough wonders to delight a couple.

Let's start with the museums. In Washington, unlike most other cities, almost all the museums are free. The Mall in downtown Washington is lined with museums of history, technology, air and space, and historic documents. For a little romance however, you may want to focus your visit on the **National Gallery of Art**, both the East and West buildings (Constitution between 3rd and 7th). There you will find the latest touring exhibits from other nations as well as 800 paintings and sculptures by European old masters and impressionists. On Sundays at 7 P.M. (except during the summer) free concerts are held in the East Garden Court of the West Building.

Other major museums on the Mall are the **Freer Gallery of Art** (12th and Jefferson Dr. SW), where you will delight to oriental art and James McNeill Whistler's Peacock Room, a fantasy world of gilded panels, painted leather walls, and other surprises; the **Hirshhorn Museum and Sculpture Garden** (8th and Independence SW), a collection of late nineteenth- and twentieth-century art and sculpture; and two new museums, the **National Museum of African Art** (950 Independence Ave. NW), where more than 6,000 textiles, sculptures, pieces of folk art, and jewelry illustrate the culture of that continent; and the **Arthur M. Sackler Gallery** (1050 Independence Ave. SW), an underground gallery featuring Chinese and Persian art over many centuries.

Away from the Mall are other excellent museums. The **Folger Shakespeare Library** (201 East Capitol St.) is known not only for its rare manuscripts but also for its concerts, readings, and an elegant Tudor gallery of carved wood walls and doors. The **National Museum of American Art** takes you from the colonial era to the present, and the nearby **National Portrait Gallery** displays works from all periods of American history. Both museums are in the Old Patent Office Building (7th and G streets NW).

The relatively new **National Museum of Women in the Arts** (1250 New York Ave. NW) is a beautiful building that showcases the works of women artists from the United States and other nations, while the **Corcoran Gallery of Art** (17th and New York Ave. NW) features American art, particularly landscapes, as well as impressionists and photographs. The nearby **Renwick Gallery** (17th and Pennsylvania Ave. NW) features crafts and decorative arts.

Other works of art can be found at **Hillwood** (4155 Linnean Ave. NW), the former home of the late Marjorie Merriweather Post. Hillwood is a forty-room museum filled with Post's collection of Fabergé jeweled objects, textiles, porcelains, and furnishings of eighteenth-century France and imperial Russia. The ninety Fabergé pieces include two imperial Russian Easter eggs. A rustic lodge on the twenty-five-acre estate displays 188 American Indian artifacts. Hillwood is open daily except Sunday and Thursday.

Dumbarton Oaks (1703 32nd St. NW) is a Georgetown mansion displaying some fine Byzantine and pre-Columbian art. Don't miss the elegant gardens at 3101 R St. NW.

The most romantic museum, though, is tucked away in a mansion just off tree-lined Embassy Row. The **Phillips Collection** (1600 21st St. NW) is acclaimed for its collection of French impressionists, American modernists, and post-impressionists. On Sunday afternoons in the wood-panelled main salon, visitors are entertained by a concert. The building, the art, and the Sunday concerts make this museum by far the most romantic in town.

The White House, the Capitol, and the Supreme Court are interesting buildings to visit, but not very romantic. The Washington, Lincoln, and Jefferson memorials are decidedly more romantic at night, when a tour by car can make a visit very special. (As a general rule, do not walk around the open fields and wooded areas on the Mall at night. Unlike the restaurant and shopping districts, it can be unsafe.)

You can get a marvelous view of downtown Washington from the Bell Tower at The Pavilion at the **Old Post Office** (12th and Pennsylvania Ave. NW), a renovated historic structure now home to offices, shops, restaurants, and an atrium stage for entertainment. Another recently renovated historic structure is **Union Station** (1st and Massachusetts Ave, NW), a marble marvel now filled with shops, boutiques, movie theaters, and restaurants.

Not all the attractions are encased in marble. Several neighborhoods are vibrant centers of shops, grand homes, unusual galleries, and interesting restaurants. **Capitol Hill**, the neighborhood east of the Capitol, is lined with renovated Victorian townhouses and dotted with galleries and restaurants. **Georgetown**, once a slum and now one of the posh addresses, is a busy circus that is best visited during the day. The shops along M Street from 28th west to 34th Street are worth your time, but the scene at night approaches gridlock for people as well as cars. Go only if you are going for dinner or entertainment.

The most exciting and eclectic of the neighborhoods is **Adams-Morgan**, whose anchor is 18th Street and Columbia Road NW. This area is a United Nations of art galleries, book stores, restaurants, and nightclubs. It is always crowded, but where else can you eat Ethiopian, Jamaican, or Cuban cuisine; see avant-garde art; browse through shops dealing in

1950s collectibles; watch a tap dancer on the bar in a French bistro; and listen to Irish, folk or Latin music, all within a few blocks?

For romantic walks during the day, try the park on the Potomac River near the Kennedy Center; Rock Creek Park, which bisects the city; or the C&O Canal from Georgetown into Maryland. And try to drive across the Potomac to the George Washington Parkway, which offers some stunning views at river level directly across from the Mall and other interesting views from overlooks as the parkway climbs on its way to McLean, Virginia.

Antique shops and art galleries abound in Georgetown, Adams-Morgan, and around Dupont Circle. For more antiques, head out Connecticut Avenue to Howard Avenue in Kensington, Maryland, where more than seventy shops selling everything from country furnishings to fine European antiques can be found on Antique Row.

There are two side trips that are fun: to Bethesda, Maryland, and Alexandria, Virginia, both about thirty minutes from the Mall by car or Metro, the Washington area's modern subway. In **Alexandria**, the Torpedo Factory on King Street at the waterfront houses studios and shops of numerous artists, while King Street and its cobblestoned cross-streets are lined with restaurants, nightclubs, antique shops, boutiques of every stripe, and historic old homes. A bit farther south on the George Washington Parkway is **Mount Vernon**, the plantation home of George Washington.

Bethesda is a thriving suburban crossroads that is now filled with some fine restaurants. For a varied selection of restaurants, drive or walk on Wisconsin Avenue, where Italian, Romanian, Tex-Mex, Japanese, and Chinese restaurants are located, or dare to go into the Bethesda Triangle, a maze of streets bounded by Wisconsin and Old Georgetown Road where even more choices wait.

Nightlife in the Washington area is eclectic. You can choose a play, opera, or concert at the **Kennedy Center**, or view other plays and musicals at the **National Theater** (13th and Pennsylvania Ave. NW), **Ford's Theater** (511 10th St. NW), and **Arena Stage** (6th and Maine SW). And that doesn't even mention the productions at the **American Playwrights' Theater** (1742 Church St. NW), **The Folger Theater** (201 E. Capitol St. SE), **Source Theater** (1835 14th St. NW), or the **Studio Theater** (1501 14th St. NW). Or the concerts at the **Lisner Auditorium** (730 21st St. NW); **Wolf Trap Farm Park** (1551 Trap Rd. in Vienna, VA); the **Capital Centre**, a big indoor arena just off the Beltway in Landover, Maryland; and countless other halls, auditoriums, and clubs.

Throughout the 1980s, the most popular show in Washington has been Stephen Wade's one-man show at Arena Stage's Old Vat room. Wade brought "Banjo Dancing," songs and stories from America's folk culture, to Arena in 1981 and didn't stop performing that show until spring of 1989. Now his new show of folk songs and stories, "On the Way Home," is packing them in.

The embassies also offer their share of entertainment, low cost if not free. The **Embassy of France** (4101 Reservoir Rd. NW) has operas, plays, films, and concerts in its 265-seat theater. The new **Embassy of Canada** (501 Pennsylvania Ave. NW) has one-actor shows in its new theater, while the **embassies of West Germany, Switzerland**, the **Netherlands**, and **Britain** have shows on irregular schedules. For information about their activities, call the cultural affairs office at each embassy.

The clubs in the Washington area are concentrated in several areas: Georgetown along M Street and Wisconsin Avenue; Alexandria on and just off King Street; and Adams-Morgan on 18th Street and Columbia Road NW. For music and dancing, try Blues Alley (the rear of 1073 Wisconsin Ave. NW, Georgetown), which attracts some top stars, or the tap dancing—on the bar, yet—of pianist Johne Forgés at Cafe Lautrec (2431 18th St. NW, Adams-Morgan), the bluegrass and folk sounds at the Birchmere (3901 Mount Vernon Ave., Alexandria), or the off-beat dinner theater and cabaret at d.c. space (443 7th Ave. NW).

Other popular clubs include Mr. Henry's (1836 Columbia Rd. NW, Adams-Morgan) for jazz and R&B; One Step Down (2517 Pennsylvania Ave. NW) for jazz jams; 219 Basin Street Lounge (219 King St., Alexandria) for Dixieland and jazz; the nearby Wharf (119 King St., Alexandria) for pop and R&B; or Anton's 1201 Club (1201 Pennsylvania Ave. NW), a supper club with headliners of yore.

For dancing, you have several choices. If your favorite song predates World War II, try the Kennedy-Warren Ballroom (3133 Connecticut Ave. NW), where Richard Bray and his big band play on Friday nights, or the Spanish Ballroom at Glen Echo Park (MacArthur Boulevard, in the Maryland suburb of Glen Echo), where Bray's band plays on Saturday night from spring to autumn. For those who remember the Beatles, Déjà Vu (2119 M St. NW) plays hits that made the sixties famous. And the Kilimanjaro (1724 California Ave. NW, Adams-Morgan) has the best African-Caribbean sounds.

For quieter moments, try the Fairfax Bar in the Ritz-Carlton Hotel, which helped make Michael Feinstein a national star. Feinstein now plays for presidents and queens, but the entertainment in the bar is always first-class. The view from the open-air Sky Terrace at the Hotel Washington (15th and Pennsylvania Ave. NW) is stunning: a perch overlooking the White House and the monuments on the Mall.

Getting around to see all of this can be very easy. Take the **Metro**, the subway which is fairly cheap and is convenient to all the sights in town and the side trips to Bethesda and Alexandria. Fares range from eighty cents and up, depending on the length of travel and the time of your trip. Pick up a map of the system at any Metro station; you'll need it. Forget the buses.

If the Mall is your main target, save your time and feet by taking a Tourmobile. Buy your pass from the driver or from kiosks located on the Mall. Passes are nine dollars and allow unlimited reboarding. You can save by buying a pass after 4 P.M., when it's seven dollars and good the next day.

You can drive to Alexandria or Bethesda. Parking is limited at times, but not impossible.

❦ FOR MORE INFORMATION

Baltimore, Philadelphia, Richmond, and Washington are all easily reached by Amtrak. If you can, take the train. Call 800/USA-RAIL. For more information about these cities, write, call or visit:

- ❦ *Baltimore* The Office of Promotion and Tourism, 34 Market Place, Suite 310, Baltimore, MD 21202. 301/752-8632. For a recording of current events, call 301/837-4636.

- ❦ *Philadelphia* Philadelphia Convention and Visitors' Bureau, 1525 John F. Kennedy Boulevard, Philadelphia, PA 19102. 215/568-6599.

- ❦ *Richmond* Convention and Visitors' Bureau, 300 East Main Street, Richmond, VA 23219. 804/782-2777.

- ❦ *Washington* The Washington Convention and Visitors' Association, 1525 Eye Street NW, Suite 250, Washington, DC 20005. 202/789-7000. For daily events call 202/737-8866. For information about **Alexandria**, contact the Alexandria Tourist Council, 221 King Street, Alexandria, VA 22314. 703/549-0205.

Important Times and Numbers

In Baltimore:

- ❦ Baltimore Museum of Art 33rd and North Charles streets. Open 10-4 Tuesday-Saturday, 11-6 weekends. 301/396-7100.

- ❦ National Aquarium Pier 3, Pratt Street. Open daily 10-5, Friday 10-8. 800/448-9009.

- ❦ Walters Art Gallery 600 North Charles Street. Open 11-5 Tuesday-Sunday. 301/547-9000.

In Philadelphia:

✹ Independence National Historical Park, 3rd and Chestnut streets. Most attractions open daily 9–5. 215/597-8974.

✹ Morris Arboretum, Hillcrest Avenue between Stenton and Germantown avenues. Open daily 10–5, Thursdays 10–8. 215/242-3399.

✹ Mummers' Museum, 2nd Street and Washington Avenue. Open 9:30–5 Tuesday–Saturday, noon–5 Sunday. 215/336-3050.

✹ Norman Rockwell Museum, 601 Walnut Street. Open daily 10–4. 215/922-4345.

✹ Pennsylvania Horticultural Society, 325 Walnut Street. Open weekdays 9–5. 215/625-8250.

✹ Philadelphia Art Alliance, 251 South 18th Street. Open 10:30–5 Monday, Friday, and Saturday, 10:30–9 Tuesday–Thursday. 215/545-4302.

✹ Philadelphia Museum of Art, 26th Street and Benjamin Franklin Parkway. Open 10–5 Tuesday–Sunday, with free admission 10–1 Sunday. 215/763-8100.

✹ Rodin Museum, 22nd Street and Benjamin Franklin Parkway. Open 10–5 Tuesday–Sunday. 215/787-5476.

✹ University Museum of Archeology and Anthropology, 33rd and Spruce streets. Open 10–4:30 Tuesday–Saturday, 1–5 Sunday. 215/989-4000.

In Richmond:

✹ Agecroft Hall, 4305 Sulgrave Road. Open 10–4 Tuesday–Friday, 2–5 weekends. 804/353-4241.

✹ Maymont, Hampton and Pennsylvania streets. Open daily 10–7. 804/358-7166.

✹ Museum and White House of the Confederacy, 12th and Clay streets. Open 10–5 Monday–Saturday, 1–5 Sunday, 804/649-1861.

✹ Valentine Museum, 1015 Clay Street. Open 10–5 Monday–Saturday, 1–5 Sunday. 804/649-0711.

✹ Virginia House, 4301 Sulgrave Road. Open daily by appointment only. 804/353-4251.

✹ Virginia Museum of Fine Arts, Grove Avenue and North Boulevard. Open 11–5 Tuesday, Wednesday, Friday, and Saturday; 11–10 Thursday; 1–5 Sunday. 804/257-0844.

✹ Wilton, South Wilton Road. Open 10–4:30 Tuesday–Saturday, 2:30–4:30 Sunday. 804/282-5936.

In Washington:

🐝 Arena Stage, 6th Street and Maine Avenue SW. 202/488-3300.

🐝 Corcoran Gallery of Art, 17th Street and New York Avenue NW. Open 10–4:30 Tuesday–Sunday, until 9 Thursday. 202/638-3211.

🐝 Dumbarton Oaks, 1703 32nd Street. NW. Open 2–5 Tuesday–Sunday; gardens open 2–6 daily April through October. 202/342-3200.

🐝 Folger Shakespeare Library, 201 East Capitol Street. Open 10–4 Monday–Saturday. 202/544-7077.

🐝 Ford's Theater, 511 10th Street NW. Renovated museum reopens in spring, 1990. Regular hours 9–5 daily. 202/347-4833.

🐝 Freer Gallery of Art, 12th Street and Jefferson Drive SW. Open daily 10–5:30. 202/357-2700.

🐝 Hillwood, 4155 Linnean Avenue NW. Guided tours on Monday and Wednesday–Saturday at 9, 10:30, noon, and 1:30. Gardens open same days 10:30–4. 202/686-5807.

🐝 Hirshhorn Museum and Sculpture Garden, 8th Street and Independence Avenue SW. Open daily 10–5:30. 202/357-2700.

🐝 Kennedy Center, New Hampshire Avenue at Rock Creek Parkway. Tours daily 10–1. 202/254-3600.

🐝 National Museum of African Art, 950 Independence Avenue SW. Open 1–5 weekdays, noon–5 weekends. 202/357-2700.

🐝 National Gallery of Art, 4th Street and Constitution Avenue NW. Open 10–5 Monday–Saturday, noon–9 Sunday. 202/737-4215.

🐝 National Museum of American Art and the National Portrait Gallery, 7th and G streets NW. Open daily 10–5:30. 202/357-2700.

🐝 National Museum of Women in the Arts, 1250 New York Avenue NW. Open 10–5 Tuesday–Saturday, noon–5 Sunday. 202/783-5000.

🐝 National Theater, 1321 E Street NW. 202/628-6161.

🐝 Phillips Collection, 1600 21st Street NW. Open 10–5 Tuesday–Saturday. Concerts at 5 on Sundays September through May. 202/387-2151.

🐝 Renwick Gallery, 17th Street and Pennsylvania Avenue NW. Open daily 10–5:30. 202/357-2700.

🐝 Arthur M. Sackler Gallery, 1050 Independence Avenue SW. Open daily 10–5:30. 202/357-2700.

🐝 Supreme Court, Maryland Avenue and East Capitol Street. Open 9–4:30 weekdays. 202/479-3030.

❦ United States Capitol, east end of Mall. Open daily 9–4:30.

❦ Free tours conducted every half hour. Passes required to sit in gallery. Get them from your Congressional representative. 202/224-3121.

❦ White House, 1600 Pennsylvania Avenue NW. Open for tours 10–noon Tuesday–Saturday, but line up by 8. Your senator or representative can get you a pass to save you waiting in line, but you get the same brief tour. 202/456-2323.

Annual Events

Baltimore

❦ Wintermarket. The Atlantic Crafts Council crafts fair, Convention Center. Mid-February.

❦ Maryland House and Garden Pilgrimage. Tour more than 100 homes and gardens. Late April.

❦ Flower Market. Festival on Mount Vernon Place. Early May.

❦ Harbor Expo. Boat parades, music, windsurfing, and small-sailboat contests. Inner Harbor. Mid-June.

❦ Showcase of Nations Festival. Summer-long celebration of food, music, crafts, and culture of different nationalities. Festival Hall. June–September.

❦ Harborlights Music Festival. Jazz, pop, classical, and country concerts on Pier 6 in the Inner Harbor. Late June–August.

Philadelphia

❦ Mummers' Parade. A carnival of costumes and marchers on New Year's Day on Broad Street.

❦ Flower Show. One of the better such shows in the country. March.

❦ Philadelphia Open House. Tours of more than 100 homes in different neighborhoods. Early May.

❦ Freedom Week. Recreation of the events leading to the Declaration of Independence. Late June to July 4.

❦ International American Music Festival. Repertory of opera, comedy, cabaret, revues, and children's programs. September and October.

❦ Fairmont Park Historic Tours. See eighteenth-century decorations in old mansions. First weekend in December.

Richmond

❦ Historic Garden Week. The folks in Richmond take their garden tours very seriously. Late April.

❦ Old Timey Fourth of July. A Victorian Fourth in Maymont Park.

❦ International Festival of Music. Free and pay concerts featuring some of the top names in entertainment. June-August.

❦ Christmas Open House. Tours some of the historic homes in the Fan District. December.

Washington

❦ Every weekend, Washington visitors can attend free concerts, films, and exhibitions. For specific events taking place when you visit, pick up the Friday *Washington Post*. The "Weekend" section, a Friday tabloid supplement, lists activities, concerts, and nightlife around town.

❦ Inauguration and Inaugural Parade. It only happens every four years, but don't miss it in 1993.

❦ Cherry Blossom Festival. A two-week gala of music, food, parades, cruises, and more. And perhaps even the beautiful cherry blossoms. Late March/early April.

❦ Georgetown House and Garden Tours. Separate tours of some of the finest in this historic neighborhood. April.

❦ July 4th. Bigger and better every year on the Mall.

❦ The Kennedy Center's Christmas Festival. A month of free concerts, drama, entertainment, and other activities. Early December through the Viennese Ball in the Grand Foyer on New Year's Eve.

❦ Pageant of Peace. The National Christmas Tree and other trees representing every state and territory are lit on the Ellipse, just south of the White House. Entertainment every evening. From around December 20 to New Year's.

❦ HOTELS AND RESTAURANTS

If money is an important consideration, the major hotel chains—the Hyatts, Hiltons, Sheratons—offer some wonderful deals on rooms for the weekend. These packages often include a cocktail, a dinner, or brunch. Call their national toll-free numbers for more information.

Here are our favorite hotels and restaurants, but first an explanation of how we break down our cost categories:

For one night in an inn or hotel for two:

Inexpensive   Under $75
Moderate $75 to $125
Expensive   More than $125

For dinner for two (wine and drinks not included):

Inexpensive   Less than $25
Moderate $25 to $60
Expensive   More than $60

Baltimore

Admiral Fell Inn This beautiful inn just across from where the tugboats tie up in Fell's Point has thirty-seven rooms and one suite, all elegantly decorated. Moderate/expensive. 888 South Broadway, Baltimore, MD 21231. 301/522-7377 or 800/292-4667.

Betsy's Bed & Breakfast This 130-year-old townhouse, filled with antiques and contemporary furnishings, offers three spacious rooms. Inexpensive. Write c/o Amanda's Reservation Service, 1428 Park Avenue, Baltimore, MD 21217. 301/225-0001.

Inner Harbor Bed & Breakfast This mariner's house on Federal Hill was built when George Washington was president. Try to reserve the room with the sundeck overlooking the harbor. The three guest rooms are spacious and comfortable. Inexpensive/expensive. 112 East Montgomery Street, Baltimore, MD 21230. 301/528-8692.

Shirley-Madison Inn This Victorian and Edwardian masterpiece is elegant, with all seventeen rooms and the public areas furnished with meticulous care and marvelous taste. Inexpensive/moderate. 205 West Madison Street, Baltimore, MD 21201. 301/728-6550.

Society Hill Hotels There are actually three hotels—West Biddle, Government House, and Hopkins—incorporating fifty-nine rooms and ten suites. The differences: West Biddle is small and has a popular jazz piano bar in the basement. Government House has nice but not great rooms overlooking the city. Hopkins has suites for lovers of art deco as well as Victoriana. We like the last. Moderate/expensive. Write the Society Hill Hotels at West Biddle, 58 West Biddle Street, Baltimore, MD 21202 (301/837-3630); at the Hopkins, 3404 St. Paul Street, Baltimore, MD 21218 (301/325-8600); at Government House, 1125 North Calvert Street, Baltimore, MD 21205 (301/752-7722).

For fine dining in Baltimore:

Admiral Fell Inn Restaurant serves fine steaks, seafood, and a surprise—fondues. Moderate. 888 South Broadway. 301/522-7377.

Brass Elephant serves Northern Italian fare. Stick to the veal. Moderate. 824 North Charles Street. 301/547-8480.

Cafe Des Artistes is a French place that uses the original art on the walls to accent the fine lamb, veal, and seafood dishes from the kitchen. Moderate. 1501 Sulgrave Avenue. 301/664-2200.

Danny's sounds like a sports bar or perhaps an Irish pub, but this Danny's is known for its continental menu. Stick to the steak and crabs. Expensive. 1201 North Charles Street. 301/539-1393.

De Mimmo is an intimate and superb seafood restaurant in Little Italy with a little piano music as an appetizer. Moderate. 217 South High Street. 301/727-6876.

Gianni's has some of the finest pasta and seafood dishes in town. Try the mussels or the sautéed seafood. Moderate. 201 East Pratt Street. 301/837-1130.

Haussner's is a German-American restaurant known as much for its often odd collection of art as for its fine food. Great atmosphere, good food. 3244 Eastern Avenue. 301/327-8365.

Philadelphia

Atop the Bellevue The grand old lady of Broad Street is reborn, with a hotel that occupies the top seven floors of this historic building. The settings are luxurious, the rooms are marvelous, and the cost is expensive. Save it for a special occasion. 1415 Chancellor Court (Broad and Walnut streets), Philadelphia, PA 19102. 215/893-1776 or 800/229-0939.

Delancey Place This 130-year-old house near Rittenhouse Square offers two rooms and one suite, each furnished with Victorian antiques. A pleasant patio and garden can help you unwind after a day of touring. Moderate/expensive. Write c/o Bed & Breakfast of Philadelphia, P.O. Box 630, Chester Springs, PA 19425. 215/827-9650.

Newmarket This 180-year-old townhouse just off the historic waterfront offers but one guest room (great for privacy) and a lovely walled garden. Inexpensive. Write c/o Bed & Breakfast of Philadelphia, P.O. Box 630, Chester Springs, PA 19425. 215/827-9650.

Pelham Inn This forty-two-room English manor is in the countryside just outside of the city proper. The house is a marvel, well worth a visit, and the five guest rooms are spacious and filled with period pieces. Inexpensive. 30 Pelham Road, Philadelphia, PA 19119. 215/844-3727.

Sheraton Society Hill One of the few national chain hotels to make this book, this new hotel has a number of things going for it. It has a great location just a block off the waterfront and historic district, the rooms are lovely, and the public areas are gorgeous. Moderate/expensive, but ask for weekend packages. 1 Dock Street, Philadelphia, PA 19106. 215/238-6000 or 800/325-3535.

Society Hill Hotel Don't let the downstairs bar turn you away. This twelve-room inn, owned by the group that runs the inns of the same name in Baltimore, is a lovely mixture of elegant Edwardian and the bizarre. Some of the rooms are strange, with the bath separating the sleeping and sitting areas, but—hey! Loosen up and have fun. Great location near the historic district and the waterfront. Moderate. 301 Chestnut Street, Philadelphia, PA 19106. 215/925-1919.

Tradewinds The four terriers are friendly, but they live here, and if you want to stay you just have to accept them. This two-centuries-old townhouse near Philadelphia's historic district has two antique-filled guest rooms. Inexpensive. Write c/o Bed & Breakfast of Philadelphia, P.O. Box 6730, Chester Springs, PA 19425. 215/827-9650.

For fine dining in Philadelphia:

Alouette presents continental cuisine with French accents and oriental flair. Be adventurous here! 334 Bainbridge Street. 215/629-1126.

Astral Plane mixes a creative menu with the decor of an upper-class flea market. Moderate. 1706 Lombard Street. 215/546-6230.

Old Original Bookbinder's has been serving fish for 124 years at this location. Try the snapper soup, the sole, and swordfish. Moderate/expensive. 215 South 15th Street. 215/545-1137.

City Tavern's waiters and waitresses, costumed in colonial garb, serve traditional dishes from the colonial era: beef pie, baked crab, and roast duck. The food is good and the atmosphere is better. Moderate. 2nd and Walnut streets. 215/923-6059.

Ecco is a small restaurant that serves some of the finest continental fare in town. Stick to the seafood. Moderate. 1700 Lombard Street. 215/735-8070.

Friday, Saturday and Sunday sounds like some fern bar that caters to singles. It is really a cozy townhouse that serves an eclectic menu. Moderate. 215/546-4232.

Knave of Hearts is made for romance: candles, a garden, and a decor that is very funky. Keep that thought in mind while you study the creative menu. Moderate. 230 South Street. 215/922-3956.

La Camargue is known for its seafood and lamb served in a country inn atmosphere. Expensive. 119 Walnut Street. 215/922-3148.

La Truffe is romantic, the perfect place for a special dinner, with gilded mirrors, fresh flowers, and candlelight. The nouvelle cuisine isn't bad, either. Moderate. 10 South Front Street. 215/925-5062.

Lautrec serves excellent French cuisine. Try the boneless duck breast or the baby lamb. Expensive. 408 South 2nd Street. 215/923-6660.

Le Bec Fin is the finest restaurant in Philly, known around the nation for its superb French cuisine. Expensive. 1523 Walnut Street. 215/567-1000.

Richmond

The Berkeley Hotel This new, fifty-five-room inn is located in the center of Shockoe Slip's historic area of shops, restaurants, and galleries. The rooms, some with patios, are spacious and furnished with lovely pieces. Moderate. 12th and Cary streets, P.O. Box 1259, Richmond, VA 23219. 804/780-1300.

Carrington Row Inn This inn in Richmond's historic Church Hill neighborhood has four guest rooms furnished with antiques and reproductions. Inexpensive. 2330 East Broad Street, Richmond, VA 23223. 804/343-7005.

Catlin-Abbott House Built in 1845 by a slave, this elegant Greek revival townhouse has five rooms and two suites furnished with Federal antiques, canopied beds, and oriental rugs. The rooms are inexpensive, the suites are expensive. 2304 East Broad Street, Richmond, VA 23223. 804/780-3746.

Commonwealth Park Suites Hotel This forty-nine-suite hotel has won the Mobil five-star rating, and well it should. It mixes European style with elegant furnishings. Expensive. 9th and Bank streets, P.O. Box 455, Richmond, VA 23202. 804/343-7300. Outside Virginia, 800/343-7302.

Linden Row This block of seven Greek revival townhouses was built in the 1840s and carefully restored in 1988, with many of the original architectural details saved. The seventy-three rooms are spacious and furnished with beautiful antique reproductions. Moderate/expensive. 1st and Franklin streets, Richmond, VA 23219. 804/783-7000 or 800/533-INNS.

Monument Avenue Houses Four rooms are available in two Monument Avenue homes: three in the Federal House and one in the Classical House. All are comfortable and furnished with style and taste. Moderate. Write c/o Bensonhouse, 2036 Monument Avenue, Richmond, VA 23220. 804/648-7560.

The Jefferson Sheraton Hotel Once the grand dame of Richmond, this elegant hotel has been refurbished with care and a ton of money.

This 274-room white-brick hotel has a huge round stained-glass skylight above the statue of Jefferson and an ornate Palm Court Lobby that leads to a grand marble staircase some say was the model for the one made famous in the movie "Gone With the Wind." It is a storybook hotel, one worth visiting even if you cannot stay. Franklin and Adams streets, Richmond, VA 23220. 804/788-8000 or 800/325-3535.

For fine dining in Richmond:

Flying Cloud serves fine seafood in a nautical setting. Moderate. 2004 Dabney Road. 804/355-6412.

La Petite France is known for its French cuisine. Moderate. 2912 Maywill Street. 804/353-8729.

Lemaire, the elegant restaurant in the Jefferson Sheraton, serves continental cuisine accented with some old Virginia standbys. Expensive. Franklin and Adams streets. 804/788/8000.

Sam Miller's Warehouse is a fun place. Stick to the steaks. Moderate. 1210 East Cary Street. 804/643-1301.

Smokey Pig is a restaurant very different from the others on these pages. It's a great lunch place going to or coming from Richmond. It is not romantic, but it does have a wonderful motif: pigs, in posters, in ceramics, and in photographs. This one is for fun and superb barbecue. Don't miss the hush puppies, both the regular pups and the apple puppies. Cheap. On U.S. 1 in Ashland, fifteen miles north of the city. 804/798-4590.

Tobacco Company is one of those restaurants stuck in a renovated old building. In many cases the location is better than the food. Not so here. Stick to the steaks and fresh fish. Moderate. 1201 East Cary Street. 804/782-9431.

Washington

The Four Seasons This hotel is a bit too modern for our tastes, but it has a great location on the edge of Georgetown, a wonderful restaurant, a lovely indoor garden, and a setting overlooking the C&O Canal. Expensive. 2800 Pennsylvania Avenue NW, Washington, DC 20007. 202/342-0444.

Hay-Adams This 143-room hotel is more like an elegant club. The wood-paneled lobby, the tasteful but restrained decor, the subdued noise level in the public areas all combine to make this a special place. The hotel is on Lafayette Park across from the White House. Ask for a room on the south side of the building. Expensive. 1 Lafayette Square, Washington, DC 20006. 202/638-6600 or 800/424-5054.

The Jefferson Another elegant, club-like hotel popular with the moneyed and politically connected set. The 102 rooms are furnished with taste. Radio personality Larry King broadcasts his show from this hotel on the first Friday of the month. Expensive. 1200 16th Street NW, Washington, DC 20036. 202/347-2200.

Kalorama Guest Houses The six turn-of-the-century homes that make up these guest houses offer fifty rooms in two locations, one on elegant Cathedral Avenue near the National Zoo and the other in Adams-Morgan. The rooms are tasteful, decorated with some antique pieces. Moderate. 2700 Cathedral Avenue NW, Washington, DC 20008. 202/328-0860. 1854 Mintwood Place NW, Washington, DC 20009. 202/667-6369.

Morrison-Clark Inn This newly renovated Civil War–era inn offers fifty-four rooms and suites in the original structure and a new addition. Try to get one of the twelve rooms in the original building; they are furnished with Victorian antiques. Expensive. 11th Street and Massachusetts Avenue NW, Washington, DC 20001. 202/898-1200 or 800/332-7898.

Morrison House This forty-five room hotel in Alexandria just may be the finest hotel in the Washington area. Elegant appointments, tasteful furnishings, and perfect service are the hallmarks here. Don't miss the Chardon d'Or restaurant. Expensive. 116 South Alfred Street, Alexandria, VA 22314. 703/838-8000; outside Virginia 800/267-0800.

The Ritz-Carlton Another club for the wealthy and powerful, this one with 230 rooms on Embassy Row. The location is superb, the hotel is beautiful, and the rooms are luxurious. Expensive. 2100 Massachusetts Avenue NW, Washington, DC 20008. 202/293-2100.

Sheraton-Carlton This beautiful sixty-three-year-old hotel has been restored to its original glamor. The location, two blocks north of the White House, is great, the rooms are wonderful, and the lobby is opulent. Expensive. 923 16th Street NW, Washington, DC 20009. 202/638-2626.

Tabard Inn This funky inn has an identity crisis. It calls itself the Tabard Inn, the Hotel Tabard and the Hotel Tabard Inn. No matter. The rooms here are comfortable, but the main attractions are the romantic lounge, restaurant, and garden. Moderate. 1739 N Street NW, Washington, DC 20036. 202/785-1277.

Willard Inter-Continental The history of this hotel would fill a book. Charles Dickens, the Marquis de Lafayette, Dwight David Eisenhower (and every president before him back to Franklin Pierce), Jenny Lind, kings, queens, eighteen heads of state, and countless other household names have stayed here. The recently reopened hotel is lavish. If you can, try to get a honeymoon suite in the corner towers. The oval windows have a view of the Washington and Jefferson monuments, a beautiful sight at night. Expensive. 1401 Pennsylvania Avenue NW, Washington, DC 20004. 202/628-9100 and 800/327-0200.

For fine dining in Washington:

Aux Beaux Champs was a great surprise to us. We never expect much in a hotel dining room, but Aux Beaux Champs is stunning. Don't miss the marinated tenderloin of lamb appetizer, the veal, or duck. If you are adventurous, try the chef's surprise—even the waiters can't tell you what it is. Expensive. In the Four Seasons Hotel, 200 Pennsylvania Avenue NW. 202/342-0810.

Belmont Kitchen is a creative American restaurant in eclectic Adams-Morgan. Elegant decor, wonderful grilled seafood and fowl. Moderate. 2400 18th Street NW. 202/667-1200.

City Cafe looks more like a gallery of art deco and art nouveau than a restaurant. The food is as beautiful and as good as the surroundings. Try the hamburger, the salads, and anything grilled. Moderate. 2213 M Street NW. 202/797-4860.

Dar es Salam is a beautiful Moroccan restaurant serving exciting food in rooms decorated with marvelous woodwork, carved plaster ceilings and mosaic tiles. Try the *diffas*, the seven-course feast. A Moroccan murder mystery is held every Friday and there is belly dancing every Saturday. Expensive. 3056 M Street NW. 202/342-1925.

Iron Gate Inn is a charming place for a quick bite or afternoon drink, but only if the weather allows you to sit outside in the grape arbor patio. That's the best part; the Middle Eastern food is only so-so. Inexpensive. 1734 N Street NW. 202/737-1370.

Jockey Club's dark-wood-and-leather dining room is the spot for power breakfasts, lunches, and dinners. Try the veal, crab cakes, and fish, and do not miss the fresh-fruit desserts. Expensive. In the Ritz-Carlton Hotel, 2100 Massachusetts Avenue NW. 202/659-8000.

Le Chardon d'Or is the elegant and intimate dining room at the Morrison Hotel in Alexandria. The food is superb, creative beyond imagination. Try the grilled tuna; the breast of duck tarragon; or the salad of grilled scallops with saffron, tomato, and basil. And whatever else you order, don't miss the desserts.

Le Lion d'Or is small, but this French restaurant may be the best in town. Try the lobster soufflé or the sautéed pigeon. 1150 Connecticut Avenue NW. 202/296-7972.

Meskerem's Ethiopian food is always surprising. The mounds of what look like puréed meats or vegetables can be delicately spiced or fiery hot. Try the *wats* if you like hot and spicy fare. The dishes are eaten with the spongy bread called *enjera*. Inexpensive. 2434 18th Street NW. 202/462-4100.

The Occidental is the two-level resurrected version of the classic power dining spot. The upstairs room serves elegant meals that are wonderful, but head downstairs to the grill, where the appetizers alone—don't miss the onion crisps, the veal sausage, and the fried mozzarella—can make a meal. Moderate downstairs, expensive upstairs. 1465 Pennsylvania Avenue NW. 202/783-1475.

Old Angler's Inn is a funky old house out MacArthur Boulevard just across the road from the C&O Canal. The outdoor patio is a great place to nuzzle in nice weather, and the inside is a mix of mirrors and mismatched tastes. The food is just so-so, but the location, particularly on a warm summer's evening, makes it irresistible. Moderate. 10801 MacArthur Boulevard, Potomac, MD. 301/365-2425.

Old Ebbitt Grill is a branch of Clyde's, the casual but trendy restaurant that helped change the face of Georgetown nightlife in the early 1960s. This new branch bears the name of an old Washington landmark that fell victim to the wrecking ball, but it shares the menu and style of Clyde's. Grilled meats and fish are the stars. Moderate. 675 15th Street NW. 202/347-4800.

Rio Grande's Tex-Mex is packing them in at this sparse restaurant in Bethesda. Almost everything is good, but the portions are so large that it is easy to over-order. Go easy. Moderate. 4919 Fairmont Avenue, Bethesda, MD. 301/656-2981.

The 1789 is a beautiful restaurant created out of a series of small rooms in a townhouse in Georgetown. For years, diners came for the romantic atmosphere and not the food. Now they have the best of both worlds: the kitchen, under new ownership, is turning out some excellent seafood and fowl dishes. Don't miss the desserts! Expensive. 1226 36th Street NW. 202/337-2955.

Tabard Inn is the place you take someone very special. The lounge of red velvet Victorian sofas is nice for a drink before or after, and don't miss eating in the garden if the weather is nice. Stick with the grilled meats and fish and the salads. If you have room, the desserts are wonderful. Moderate. 1739 N Street NW. 202/785-1277.

219 serves some of the finest cajun dishes—blackened steaks, spicy shrimp, and fish—in the Washington area. Expensive. 219 King Street, Alexandria, VA. 703/836-2834.

Vincenzo is an Italian seafood restaurant that has won acclaim for its ravioli stuffed with fish, fish stews, and grilled fish. Expensive. 1606 20th Street NW. 202/667-0047.

Chapter Eight

A Change of Pace

Romance often gets lost in our world of constant change and fast-paced lifestyles. Before our lives became intertwined with such acronyms as MTV, VCR, ATM, and VISA, life was simpler, slower, and there was time to learn about one another.

Like you, we cannot turn back the clock, but there are places we like to visit where our surroundings are from another time, where the pace is slow enough to allow us to savor our relationship while we enjoy our surroundings.

In the Mid-Atlantic region, you can immerse yourselves in the colonial era, enjoy a Fourth of July in a beautiful village that could have sprung from the easel of Norman Rockwell, spend a weekend on a farm or ranch, or visit a small island community that remains isolated from mainstream America.

Our favorites:

❦ THE COLONIAL LIFE

We have two memories of visits to Colonial Williamsburg that remain crystal clear to this day.

❦ One summer day we arose early and walked the streets of this living museum of early Americana. It was a quiet hour, with none of the usual intrusions—cars, traffic lights, bustling commuters—of twentieth-century America. In the center of Colonial Williamsburg, a few people dressed in period costumes walked leisurely along the unpaved Duke of Gloucester Street; a team of horses clip-clopped as they pulled a carriage filled with other early-risers; and in the mist-shrouded fields nearby, the animals grazed quietly. This world seemed more peaceful than ours, and much more attractive.

❦ During the Christmas season one year, we strolled through the town, looking into the candle-lit historic homes and visiting the taverns and other public buildings. The beautifully decorated wreaths and trees and the occasional groups of carollers filled our evening with the joy of the season. Colonial Williamsburg's spell made us feel like we were part of a Christmas card that had come alive.

There is magic in the streets of Colonial Williamsburg, a one-mile-long, five-block-wide restored historic area that has recaptured the simple beauty of the town as it was three centuries ago, when it was the capital of the vast, wealthy colony known as Virginia.

The first permanent English settlement in the New World was founded in 1607 a few miles away on the north bank of a broad river. Both the river and the new colony took their names from the English king, James I.

Jamestown was an economic outpost, funded and founded by the Virginia Company of London to plunder the resources of the New World. The first colonists were a luckless lot. Their dreams of building an economic empire on glass-making, silkworm culture, and gold were just that—dreams. Disease, starvation, rebellions, Indian attacks, and fires took a heavy toll of these brave settlers.

The colony survived and flourished because it managed to cultivate a weed King James I called "lothsome to the eye, hatefull to the nose, harmefull to the braine, and dangerous to the lungs." Despite that royal admonition, the English lit up and enjoyed a smoke of that weed—tobacco.

Its economic future assured, or so it seemed at the time, the colonists built a statehouse and made Jamestown the capital of the vast Virginia Colony. In 1698, after the statehouse was destroyed by fire for a fourth time, the capital was moved to nearby Middle Plantation, an inland outpost built to defend against Indian attacks.

There, on the peninsula between the site where the first representatives of the king founded a colony and the future site of a battle that would shatter all ties to the crown, the new capital was born and christened in honor of the king of England, William III. The small capital quickly became the center of commerce and political activity in the richest colony in the new land called America.

History walked these streets. George Washington and Thomas Jefferson supped and socialized in the Raleigh Tavern. Patrick Henry shouted his defiance of the crown in its capitol. After the calls for independence were replaced by the deeds of revolt, the battles raged for five years up and down the coast before the final act in Yorktown, a few miles east on the York River, where General Cornwallis surrendered his forces as a British band played "The World Turned Upside Down."

The irony for Williamsburg is that the very revolution it nurtured in its government halls and taverns proved its undoing: In 1780, the government was moved to Richmond for safety from British attacks, never to return. For 150 years, Williamsburg slowly withered, its historic homes and sites falling prey to time.

The resurrection of Williamsburg began in 1926, when John D. Rockefeller, Jr. became a convert to the vision of a minister named W.A.R. Goodwin, who dreamed of a Williamsburg whose historic buildings, colonial homes, and gardens would be restored to their original majesty; where visitors could see the trades and crafts of that era practiced once again; and where scholars and archeologists could research colonial life. All Goodwin's vision needed was money. Rockefeller and his family made the dream reality.

More than a half-century later, **Colonial Williamsburg** is a masterpiece, a living museum where visitors can feel, touch, taste, and experience the wonders of the past.

There are more than eighty restored buildings and gardens in the historic area offering visitors a glimpse into the life of the colonists. The attractions of Colonial Williamsburg go beyond restored homes and majestic government halls. The life of the colonial residents is recreated every day by craftsmen, guides, musicians, artisans, and actors.

Some of the major sites include the **Governor's Palace**, where the House of Burgesses and the courts met; the **James Anderson House Archeological Exhibit**, which traces the restoration of Williamsburg; the **Abby Aldrich Rockefeller Folk Art Center**, perhaps the best collection of American folk art in the nation; **Bassett Hall**, the restored eighteenth-century house once home to the Rockefellers; the **Dewitt Wallace Decorative Arts Gallery**, a showcase of 8,000 decorative wonders from the seventeenth to early nineteenth centuries; **Raleigh Tavern** and **Christina Campbell's Tavern**, historic dining spots where Washington and his contemporaries relaxed; and **Carter's Grove**, a magnificent Georgian mansion and plantation built in 1755 on the banks of the James River just east of Colonial Williamsburg.

There is more to see than old buildings and formal gardens. Entertainment, educational events, parades, demonstrations, and concerts fill each day and evening. Special programs range from gardens and antiques to music and history (see Chapter 4, "Murder, Music, and More").

The most popular season in Williamsburg is the Christmas holidays, when concerts, bonfires, special dinners, and other activities bring the colonial yule to life. This also is the most difficult period in which to get accommodations at the elegant Williamsburg Inn or in one of the historic old homes or taverns. Make your plans very early in the year if you wish to visit during the last half of December.

There are enough sights and activities in and around Colonial Williamsburg to keep visitors busy for a week or more. In Norfolk, about forty minutes away, is the magnificent **Chrysler Museum**, where eight new galleries exhibit art treasures from the past 5,000 years. The focus at Chrysler is glass, ancient works from Egypt, and the modern artworks of designers like Tiffany.

Just a few minutes' drive from Williamsburg are **Jamestown**, the site of the first colony; **Yorktown**, where Cornwallis surrendered and independence was won; and the stately colonial plantations that line both sides of the James River.

Jamestown's importance in this nation's history cannot be measured by the meager ruins left today. The National Park Service operates the park, which has a visitors' center with films, exhibits, gift shop, a reconstructed colonial glass kiln where demonstrations of glass blowing are presented, and the modest ruins of the original town. We were struck by the location of the first English colony, an inhospitable spit of land flanked by swamps, surely a site that contributed to the woes of the first settlers.

Nearby, the **Jamestown Festival Park** is the re-creation of the colonists' first settlement. This park looks commercial at first glance, so we were surprised to find that the exhibits were interesting, informative, and well worth a visit. Costumed guides discuss the exhibits and demonstrate seventeenth-century crafts and activities; thatch huts and buildings give an idea of how spartan the colonists' lives were.

In Yorktown, the National Park Service's **Yorktown Battlefield** has a visitors' center with films, exhibits, and an overlook of the famed battlefield. The tour roads and paths take visitors along the battlefield trails trod by Washington and Cornwallis. There are numerous colonial-era buildings in town, some of which existed during those momentous days. The **Yorktown Victory Center** depicts the events leading up to the Revolution and offers exhibits on life in the colonies.

Jamestown and Yorktown are solid attractions, combining the professional exhibits usually found in National Park Service historic sites with the more entertaining local museum parks.

The final attractions in the Williamsburg area are the James River plantations, historic sites worth a separate visit if you cannot find the time while visiting Colonial Williamsburg.

These mansions were the first great houses built in the New World by the wealthier colonists; they have roots deep in the nation's history. Washington and Jefferson visited them, three presidents owned two of the main houses, and several were occupied by Union forces in the siege of Richmond.

Any tour of them should start on Route 5 in Williamsburg. Drive west until you come to **Sherwood Forest**, the longest frame house in America and one of only two homes in the nation owned by two presidents (the Adams house in Quincy, Massachusetts, is the other).

The first section of the house was built in the early 1700s, although the early ownership is unknown. William Henry Harrison, the ninth president of the United States, owned the house from 1789 to 1796. The property was known by several names and held by numerous owners, many of whom added wings; by 1846 the house had been widened to 300 feet. By that time it was renamed Sherwood Forest by its owner, John Tyler, a politician who fancied himself a political outlaw.

Tyler was elected vice president in 1840 on a ticket with Harrison. Harrison, however, caught pneumonia during his frigid inauguration ceremonies and died a month later. Tyler succeeded him and served out the term.

The plantation has stayed in the family since then and survived even the occupation by Union forces during the Civil War (saber slashes and burn scars from their visit are visible). Sherwood Forest's grounds are open daily. The house is open to visitors and groups by appointment.

Sherwood Forest is owned today by Harrison Tyler, grandson of President John Tyler and a descendant of William Henry Harrison. Harrison Tyler is only in his 50s, and that, as you can see, is another story. Ask when you visit.

West of Sherwood Forest on Route 5 are a number of other plantations, all with stories that could fill a book. Briefly, though, do visit **Belle Air**, a seventeenth-century house open by appointment; **Evelynton**, which has been in the Ruffin family since 1847, although the Geor-

❧ Westover, one of the majestic colonial plantations on the James River near Colonial Williamsburg. *Photo by Barbara Radin-Fox.*

gian Revival main house is only a half-century old (the original house was destroyed in 1862 during a battle between forces led by J.E.B. Stuart and James Longstreet); **Westover**, the finest Georgian mansion in the nation, open only during Garden Week in April; **Berkeley Plantation**, site of a thanksgiving feast a year *before* the pilgrims even arrived in Massachusetts and a house that was inherited by Benjamin Harrison, whose son and future short-lived president—William Henry—was born there; and **Shirley Plantation**, which has been home to ten generations of the Carter family. All of these plantations on Route 5 are well marked, much better than those on the south shore of the James River.

On the other side of the river (take Route 31 to the ferry near Jamestown) are more plantations, a bit less elegant but no less historic.

From the ferry landing on the south bank of the James, take Route 31 to **Smith's Fort**, site of the original fort built by Captain John Smith. The land belonged to Indian chief Powhatan, who gave it to John Rolfe as a wedding present when Rolfe married the chief's daughter, Pocahontas. From Route 31, go to Route 10, turn east to Route 612 and drive to **Chippokes**, a working plantation since 1621. The buildings are open for tours in the summer. Back on Route 10 west of Route 612, is **Bacon's Castle**, a Jacobean structure named for Nathaniel Bacon, who didn't live there but did hide out in the castle after he led an abortive revolt against the colonial government in 1676. (He and his followers tried to overthrow the colonial government because they felt it wasn't aggressive enough in dealing with Indian attacks on the frontier, which at that time was Richmond.) Next, drive west on Route 10 to Route 611 to **Brandon**, a beautiful plantation house designed by Jefferson. It is open during Garden Week in April and by appointment. Finally, continue west on Route 10 to Flowerdew Hundred Road and turn north to the **Flowerdew Hundred**, a plantation with a large working archeological dig that has uncovered thousands of artifacts dating back to 9,000 B.C.

Taking the Tour

Visitors to Colonial Williamsburg will need a ticket to enter many of the attractions. The tickets are sold at the Visitors' Center at the Colonial Parkway and Route 132, and at the ticket booth at North Henry and Duke of Gloucester streets.

There are three types of tickets. The Patriot's Pass is $25 and admits the bearer to all major exhibits, museums, buildings in Colonial Williamsburg, and the one-hour Patriot's Tour. The pass is good for one year. The Royal Governor's pass admits the bearer to all exhibits, museums, and buildings except Carter's Grove. It is $21 and is good for four days. The basic admission ticket is $17 and allows the bearer into twelve exhibits in Colonial Williamsburg, but not to the Governor's Palace, the Dewitt Wallace Gallery, Carter's Grove, or the one-hour Patriot's Tour.

The Jamestown and Yorktown parks and many of the James River mansions charge a modest admission fee.

Numbers and Addresses

❦ Colonial Williamsburg—P.O. Box C, Williamsburg, VA 23167. 804/229-1000.

❦ Williamsburg Chamber of Commerce—They can provide more travel and tourism information. 901 Richmond Road, Williamsburg, VA 23185. 804/229-6511.

❦ Jamestown-Yorktown Foundation (Colonial National Historic Park)—P.O. Box 1976, Yorktown, VA 23690. 804/887-1776.

❦ Jamestown Festival Park—On Route 31 on the bank of the James River. 804/229-1607.

The plantations on the north side of the James River, from west to east:

❦ Shirley Plantation—On Route 5 west of Route 156. Open daily. 804/792-2385

❦ Berkeley Plantation—On Route 5. Open daily. 804/829-6018.

❦ Westover—On Route 5. Grounds and gardens open year-round, but the fabulous mansion is open only during Historic Garden Week in late April. (No phone.)

❦ Evelynton—On Route 5. Open daily. 804/829-5075.

❦ Belle Air Plantation—On Route 5. Open by appointment. 804/829-2431.

❦ Sherwood Forest—On Route 5. Grounds always open, mansion open only by appointment. 804/829-5377.

On the south side of the James River (take the Route 31 ferry across):

❦ Smith's Fort—On Route 31. Open daily April through September. 804/294-3872.

❦ Chippokes—On Route 612 just north of Route 10. Open Wednesday through Sunday from Memorial Day to Labor Day. 804/294-3625.

❦ Bacon's Castle—On Route 10 west of Route 612. Open every day but Monday. 804/357-5976.

❦ Brandon—Six miles north of Route 10 on Route 611. Grounds open all year, mansion open during Historic Garden Week in late April and by appointment. 804/866-8616.

❦ Flowerdew Hundred—On Route 10 near Hopewell. Open daily from April through November. 804/541-8897.

❦ The Chrysler Museum—Olney Road and Mowbray Arch, Norfolk. Open daily except Monday. 804/622-1211.

Inns and Restaurants

Here are our favorites in Williamsburg, but first an explanation of how we break down our cost categories:

One night in an inn for two (often but not always including breakfast):

Inexpensive Under $75
Moderate $75 to $125
Expensive More than $125

For dinner for two (wine and drinks not included):

Inexpensive Less than $25
Moderate $25 to $60
Expensive More than $60

The Williamsburg Inn This five-star resort is one of the finest in the nation, and is discussed in more detail in Chapter 5, "The Grand Resorts." To get into the colonial spirit, stay at one of the eighty-five rooms in the restored taverns and houses in the historic area that are managed by the inn. The rooms are furnished in eighteenth-century style and are within walking distance of all the major sites in the restored area. The best of these are the **Raleigh Tavern, Peter Hay's Kitchen**, and the **Orlando Jones House**, all cozy retreats made for romance. Weekend package rates start at $169 per person and include two nights' lodging, a brunch, and a dinner in a tavern. Make your reservations as far in advance as you can. Call 800/HISTORY.

North Bend This 250-acre plantation was occupied by General Sheridan's Union troops in 1864. The desk used by him still sits in the front room of the two-story Greek Revival home whose current owner is the great-great-grandson of Edmund Ruffin, the man who fired the first shot of the Civil War. The three rooms are furnished with antiques and family heirlooms. Inexpensive; breakfast included. On Route 619 one mile north of Route 5 near Charles City. 804/829-5176 after 5:30 P.M. weekdays.

Piney Grove This bed and breakfast is on Southall's Plantation, a historic landmark whose original log portion dates back to 1800. The rooms are located in the main house and in the Ladysmith House on the plantation. Other buildings on the grounds are a smokehouse, a wellhouse, offices, and farm buildings. A garden and pool are available for relaxation. The rooms are furnished with antiques and many have cast-iron stoves. Moderate; breakfast included. The plantation is 20 miles west of Richmond. From Route 5, turn north on Route 623 and continue on it after it becomes Route 615. Piney Grove is on the right. Route 1, Box 148, Charles City, VA 23030-9735. 804/829-2480.

Sheldon's Ordinary This copy of an eighteenth-century tavern has one suite furnished with colonial touches. Inexpensive. Write c/o Bensonhouse, 2036 Monument Avenue, Richmond, VA 23220. 804/648-7560.

War Hill This pleasant home has more than thirty acres of grounds and is within a few minutes' drive of the historic area. There are two guest rooms, both furnished with antiques and family pieces. Inexpensive. Write c/o Bensonhouse, 2036 Monument Avenue, Richmond, VA 23220. 804/648-7560.

❦ The Orlando Jones House, one of the restored colonial homes in Colonial Williamsburg in which guests can stay. *Photo by Barbara Radin-Fox.*

Williamsburg Cottage This private, two-story cottage has its own herb garden, a rope swing, colonial furnishings, and a location within walking distance of the historic area. Moderate. Write c/o Bensonhouse, 2036 Monument Avenue, Richmond, VA 23220. 804/648-7560.

For dining, try the colonial taverns—**Christina Campbell's Tavern, Josiah Chowning's Tavern**, the **King's Arm Tavern**, and the newly opened **Shields Tavern**. The furnishings are colonial and the menus re-creations of colonial fare, with such regional dishes as Virginia ham, Brunswick stew, and filet mignon stuffed with oysters. Expensive but worth it, for an evening in these taverns recaptures the feel of the period. After dinner, guests are entertained by "gambols": eighteenth-century music, games, and diversion. All four are in the historic district; the number for all four is 804/229-2141.

The **Williamsburg Inn** offers elegant continental cuisine and dinner dancing. Expensive. 804/229-2141.

The Trellis is a trendy restaurant that offers new American cuisine, but dinner is better than lunch. 403 Duke of Gloucester Street on Market Square. Moderate. 804/229-8610.

The **Lafayette** serves continental fare that we still can recall vividly from a visit in the early 1980s. Expensive. 1203 Richmond Road. 804/229-3811.

Le Yaca, an elegant French restaurant, has won some acclaim. Expensive. 915 Pocahontas Trail in the Kingsmill Shops (U.S. 60E). 804/220-3616.

Sidetrip

Busch Gardens/The Old Country is just east of Williamsburg on U.S. 60. This European theme park has more than forty major rides and continuous entertainment, including some top pop and country stars during the summer season. It is open March to October. Admission is about $20 and includes all rides and most entertainment, but not the big names. 804/253-3350.

❦ PEACEFUL ISLAND

Tangier Island, a one-mile by three-mile strip of land in the Chesapeake Bay, can challenge Williamsburg for its colonial heritage. Captain John Smith visited in 1608, but it wasn't until 1686 that the first English colonists—John Crockett, his eight sons, and their families—arrived. Life there was peaceful until the War of 1812, when Tangier was turned into a fortress by British troops preparing their assault on Fort McHenry in Baltimore. The graves of the soldiers and the remnants of their fortifications are under water now, evidence of the constant erosion that dooms this isolated island.

Tangier is lost in time—and it is wonderful. You reach the island by taking a short ferry ride from Crisfield, Maryland, or Reedville, Virginia. Touring Tangier is done by foot or by bike. Keep that in mind if you are considering a visit.

Today there are 850 residents on Tangier. Their way of life is very American, but one that recalls the Eisenhower years, when all America (at least as depicted on television) was clean, church-going, hard-working, and courteous.

Most Tangier residents are proud of their heritage and agreeable to talking about the past and their ancestors. Take time to stroll the streets and observe the townfolk and the homes, all looking like they had sprung from the cover of some *Saturday Evening Post* of the 1940s or 1950s.

The three boatyards and marinas are worth visiting, for they are not the stuff of the fancy weekend sailor. The boaters and mariners here work the bay for a living, not for weekend pleasures.

You can visit Tangier for a few hours or spend a night in one of the few guest houses on the island. The accommodations are not the fanciest, but the slow rhythms of the land, the beautiful bay wildlife, and the stunning sunsets make this island worth a visit.

Getting There

There are two boats that go from the Eastern Shore of Maryland and the western shore of Virginia to Tangier Island. The *Steven Thomas* departs from Crisfield, Md., daily at 12:30 P.M. and returns at 3:45. Round-trip fare is $14. 301/968-2338 or 804/891-2240. The *Chesapeake Breeze* departs from Reedville, Va, at 10 A.M. daily and returns at 3:45. The roundtrip fare is $16. 804/333-4656.

Inns and Restaurant

Chesapeake House This inn isn't elegant, but there isn't much to choose from on the island. There are eight guest rooms. The rates are $25 per person. Reservations a must. Main Street. 804/891-2331.

The Sunset Inn There are six guest rooms in this inn, the only guest house on the island with air-conditioning. Rates are $20 and include a continental breakfast. Reservations a must. West Ridge Street. 804/891-2535.

For dining, whether or not you are staying there, try the **Chesapeake House**, where fritters, fish, and fries are worth a stop. Main Street. Inexpensive/moderate. 804/891-2331.

🐚 AN OLD-FASHIONED FOURTH

Lititz, Pennsylvania, is a small Lancaster County town where traditions are important. Moravian immigrants founded the town in 1756, naming it after the castle of the first Protestant king in Europe, King Podiebrad of Bohemia. For a century the Moravian church owned all the land in town and allowed people only of that faith to build there. That policy changed in 1856, and the church began selling land to members of other faiths, a move that helped the community grow and attracted some industry.

Today Lititz has about 7,000 residents and all the trappings of the American dream: clean streets; a large number of 200-year-old homes and other grand old buildings still in use; and a main square anchored by a park, quaint inn, two stately banks, a fountain, and the impressive Moravian church.

The seventeen-and-a-half acre park near the town square once was part of the church, and was used for social functions, including concerts, as far back as 1778. In 1822—when there were only twenty-four states —Lititz began celebrating the Fourth of July, a practice it has continued annually with only three major changes: in 1843 residents added the Fairyland of Candles, in 1846 they added fireworks, and in 1942 they added a Queen of the Candles pageant. And that year—1942—seems to be where Lititz and the Fourth of July celebration got stuck in time.

We stumbled across this festival by accident one recent Fourth, and were pleasantly surprised to find a celebration quite unlike those where lasers, massive fireworks displays, and loud rock bands are the norm.

In Lititz, the celebration on the Fourth (or on the Saturday nearest it) begins after lunch—plenty of time to allow you to spend the morning strolling the streets or visiting the **Sturgis Pretzel Factory** on East Main Street, where you can learn how to twist a soft pretzel. Or at the **Wilbur Chocolate Factory** just north of the park, where guides will show you how chocolate is made.

At 1 P.M., music and dancing begin in the band shell in the park, with groups playing rock, Dixieland, and swing music, and mimes and magicians conjuring up some laughs. The entertainment is great fun, but it is just a build-up for the main events.

At sunset, a local high school senior is chosen Queen of the Candles in a beauty and talent pageant that seems out of place in today's world. The queen then uses a candle to ignite the torches held by a troop of Boy Scouts, who fan throughout the park to light the 7,000 candles lining the narrow creek and placed in designs such as an American flag, a swan, and stars.

When all the candles are burning it is an amazing sight, one that draws oohhs and aahhs and cheers from the gathered crowd. It is a beautiful ceremony, simple but moving.

The evening is topped off with a fireworks ceremony, not as grand, perhaps, as those in Washington, Philadelphia, or New York. This one, though, meant more to us than those megashows. Then again, that's no surprise. In Lititz, you see, they *remember* why they are celebrating the Fourth of July. After all, they have been doing it the same way for more than a century.

Inns and Restaurants

Cameron Estate Inn Only a few minutes from the Mt. Hope Winery, this spacious eighteen-room inn is surrounded by farmland laced with trout streams and hiking trails. All but two of the rooms have private baths; all are filled with antiques and reproductions. The dining room's menu of American and continental cuisine has won acclaim. Inexpensive/moderate. RD #1, Box 305, Mount Joy, PA 17552. 717/653-1773.

Donegal Mills Plantation There are seventeen rooms in this eighteenth-century mansion, all furnished with period antiques. Adjacent to the inn is a restaurant in an old mill and a semi-restored village that is a tourist attraction. Moderate. Trout Run Road, P.O. Box 204, Mount Joy, PA 17552. 717/653-2168.

General Sutter Inn This twelve-room inn is on the square in Lititz. The inn is a quaint place, something you might find as the setting for a Victorian novel; the lobby is filled with exotic birds in cages and the main decorating theme in the rooms is wicker. Still, it is a fine place, with a nice dining room and garden plaza. Inexpensive. 14 East Main Street, Lititz, PA 17543. 717/626-2115.

For fine dining in the Amish country:

The **General Sutter Inn** serves surprisingly good American fare, but take time, if weather permits, to have a cocktail on the garden patio that overlooks the town square. Moderate. 14 E. Main Street, Lititz, PA. 717/626-2115.

Groff's Farm is a restaurant in an old stone farmhouse that serves authentic Pennsylvania Dutch fare, including some of Betty Groff's own creations, such as chicken Stoltzfus (chunks of chicken in a cream sauce on a bed of light pastry) and black raspberry tarts. Reservations required for dinner. Moderate. Pinkerton Road, Mount Joy, PA. 717/653-2048.

🐞 BACK ON THE FARM

One year, when we wanted to go away for the weekend after Thanksgiving, we decided to stay on a farm in Bucks County, figuring that it would be a change of pace that fit into the spirit of the holiday season.

The farm we chose was **Maplewood Farm**, a small estate with a fine old plastered fieldstone farmhouse with five beautiful guest rooms. The farmhouse, built in 1823, is a wonderful inn, but the real attractions were found in the barn and field in back.

There we got to meet the sheep, named Peaches, Cream, Olivia, and Freckie; a flock of unnamed chickens; countless barnyard cats; and a pair of frisky dogs. The sheep, dogs, and cats were fun, but the chickens provided the real down-to-earth farm experience.

Each morning eggs were gathered for breakfast and guests were encouraged to come along and help. This prospect—amateur hour in the barn—attracted the sheep, which strolled into the barn to watch the follies. We managed to get a few eggs from the wary hens, but our nine-year-old son was torn between trying this new experience and his true feelings: deep egg hatred.

The stay at Maplewood was special for our family, one that our nine-year-old considered a great change from the usual hotels with cable TV and video game rooms.

There are other farms in the Mid-Atlantic where you can stay and help out with the chores or just relax and enjoy the scenery. Here is a country sampler:

Maryland

Beaver Creek This 100-acre farm is home to peacocks, horses, goats, ducks, and chickens. There are six guest rooms in the 180-year-old stone farmhouse, all furnished with antiques and oriental rugs. Inexpensive; breakfast and afternoon tea and wine included. The farm is near Hagerstown in western Maryland, but write c/o The Traveler in Maryland, P.O. Box 2277, Annapolis, MD 21404. 301/269-6232.

The best romantic restaurant near Beaver Creek is in Mercersburg, Pennsylvania, about a thirty-minute drive north. There, in the fabulous **Mercersburg Inn**, a Swiss chef prepares some stunning dishes. Moderate. 405 South Main Street, Mercersburg, PA. 717/328-5231.

Pennsylvania

Barley Sheaf Farm This thirty-acre farm in the heart of Bucks County raises sheep and chickens and keeps bees. The house was once owned by playwright George Kaufman. Part of the main house predates the Revolution. There are six rooms, most with four-poster beds. Try the Strawberry Room, which has French doors that open to a view of the farmland. The breakfasts are filling (and the honey is from the hives). Moderate; breakfast included. P.O. Box 10, Holicong, PA 18928. 215/794-5104.

Brenneman Farm Bed & Breakfast This working dairy and tobacco farm offers five guest rooms in a 140-year-old log farmhouse. All the rooms are furnished with simple country furniture. Inexpensive; continental breakfast included. RD 1, Box 310, Donegal Springs Road, Mount Joy, PA 17552. 717/653-4213.

Maplewood Farm The plastered fieldstone farmhouse was built in 1826 and is furnished with simple country furniture and crafts. There are five rooms here, but the one you want is the suite, a two-level room on the top floor of the house. Afternoon tea, cookies, and brownies are surpassed only by the heavenly breakfast. Moderate; breakfast and afternoon tea and cookies included. P.O. Box 239, 5090 Durham Road, Gardenville, PA 18926. 215/766-0477.

Meadow Spring Farm This 240-acre dairy farm is the very picture of country life: hundreds of Holstein cows, scores of pigs, a flock of chickens, and lots of cats and dogs. Toss in a 150-year-old white brick farmhouse and a red barn with a silo and you pretty near have the essence of farm life. The four guest rooms here are filled with antiques that have been handed down in the family. For your weekend, ask for the room with the canopied bed or the one with the sleigh bed and fireplace. Inexpensive; breakfast included. 201 East Street Road, Kennett Square, PA 19348. 215/444-3903.

Nolt Farm This 100-acre Mennonite family farm raises corn, wheat, and cattle. The farmhouse dates from the early 1800s and offers four guest rooms, all simply furnished. Breakfasts are hearty, as is the welcome from Amos and Grace Nolt. Inexpensive; breakfast included. S. Jacob Street, Mount Joy, PA 17552. 717/653-4192.

Pleasant Grove Farm This dairy farm in the Amish country near Lancaster has four guest rooms in a farmhouse that dates back to the early nineteenth century. All are furnished nicely with country furniture and other pieces. Inexpensive; breakfast included. RD 1, Box 132, Peach Bottom, PA 17563. 717/548-3100.

Sweetwater Farm The original part of the Georgian farmhouse on this farm predates the American Revolution by forty years. It is a beautiful red-brick home, almost a mansion, and contains some elegant touches: delicate moldings, wonderful original woodwork, and a magnificent three-level staircase. Chickens, corn, and sheep are raised on the farm. There are nine rooms, many with working fireplaces. If it's available, reserve the master bedroom with the four-poster canopy bed. Moderate/expensive; breakfast and afternoon tea included. P.O. Box 86, Sweetwater Road, Glen Mills, PA 19342. 215/459-4711.

Whitehall Inn This is a Bucks County horse farm with the additional amenities of a rose garden, pool, and tennis courts. The large eighteenth-century farmhouse is located on thirteen acres. There are six guest rooms furnished with antiques and family pieces. Moderate/expensive; breakfast and afternoon tea included. RD 2, Box 250, Pineville Road, New Hope, PA 18938. 215/598-7945.

For dining in the Amish country, see the restaurants listed in this chapter under "An Old-Fashioned Fourth." For more choices, see the listings in Chapter 6, "Wine Country."

Our favorite Bucks County dining spots:

La Bonne Auberge is set in a two-century-old farmhouse and serves some fine French fare. If the weather is nice, reserve a table in the garden room. Expensive. Village 2, New Hope, PA. 215/862-2462.

The Carversville Inn is in a 180-year-old house. The menu is European and new American, with more formal dishes on the weekends. For relaxation try the pub-like bar. Moderate/expensive. Carversville and Aquetong roads, Carversville, PA. 215/297-0900.

Colligan's Stockton Inn has been a popular dining spot for some years—since 1832, to be exact. The cuisine is international and the air festive (there's a jazz pianist on many weekends). Moderate. Route 28, Stockton, NJ. 609/397-1250.

The best part about the **Cuttalossa Inn** is the park-like setting, perfect for a romantic dinner. The menu is American. Stick to the beef. Moderate. River Road, Lumberville, PA. 215/297-5082.

Odette's serves some fine American nouveau dishes in a park-like setting overlooking the Delaware River. Expensive. South River Road, New Hope, PA. 215/862-2432.

The Wycombe Inn menu is varied, but the setting is the great attraction: a charming Victorian with an indoor garden. Expensive. Mill Creek Road, Wycombe, PA. 215/598-7000. Call for directions.

Virginia

Caledonia Farm This fifty-two-acre Blue Ridge Mountain farm raises Angus cattle. The Federalist stone manor house was started in 1812 and expanded by later owners. There are three guest rooms, two in the main house and a suite in the former summer kitchen. All are furnished plainly. Moderate; breakfast included. Six-course dinners can be arranged. Route 1, Box 2080, Flint Hill, VA 22627. 703/675-3693.

Ingleside This large (1,250 acres) cattle farm is made for the outdoor enthusiast. Miles of hiking trails, the nearby Blue Ridge Mountains, and tennis courts await to get you off the porch and into some form of exercise. There is only one guest room in the 150-year-old red brick farmhouse, perfect if you are seeking some privacy. Inexpensive; breakfast included. Write c/o Guesthouses, P.O. Box 57, Charlottesville, VA 22905. 804/979-7264 weekdays noon to 5.

L'Auberge Provencale This 600-acre farm raises cattle, soybeans, and corn. The farmhouse here was built in 1753, and the estate is better known as a restaurant serving cuisine from the Provençal region of France than as a farm/inn. There are six guest rooms (four in a nearby guest house), all furnished with Victorian and French antiques. Moderate; lavish breakfast included. P.O. Box 119, White Post, VA 22663. 703/837-1375.

Shenandoah Valley Farm and Inn This 155-acre farm ten miles east of Harrisonburg raises exotic herbs and trees and Black Angus cattle. There are seven rooms furnished with early American antiques. Inexpensive; breakfast included. Route 1, Box 142, McGaheysville, VA 22840. 703/289-5402.

For dining, the standout choice, if you can get in, is the **Inn at Little Washington**, perhaps the finest inn/restaurant in the nation. The fixed-price menu has made the inn the best dining spot in the Washington (both the nation's capital and the small village of the same name in which the inn is located) area. The fare is French, prepared with some surprising local touches. Expensive and well worth it. Middle and Main streets, P.O. Box 300, Washington, VA 22747. 703/675-3800.

At **The Ashby Inn** seafood is the specialty. Sautéed scallops and shrimp have won acclaim at this Shenandoah Valley inn and restaurant. There are four dining rooms, ranging from a rustic pub to a formal room. Willard Scott, our favorite on NBC's "Today" show, raves about this restaurant. There are six guest rooms in the inn, furnished, as are the dining areas, with early American pieces. Rooms moderate; meals expensive. Routes 701 and 759, Paris, VA. 703/592-3900.

L'Auberge Provencale is described above; try it if you are staying there or at Caledonia Farm. Willard Scott, who has a farm nearby, also praises the food here.

The **1763 Inn** has three beautiful dining rooms, one with a fireplace and another overlooking a pond. The surprise is that the fare is German. Stick to that. The Bavarian Farmer's Platter, a feast of bratwurst, pork chop, and *kassler ripchen* (smoked pork loin) is wonderful, as is the goulash. Avoid the seafood. Rooms and dinners expensive. U.S. 50 between Upperville and Paris, VA. 703/478-1383.

For Ingleside farm guests, see the many choices in the Charlottesville area in Chapter 6, "Wine Country."

West Virginia

Hickory Hill This 2,000-acre farm has been in the family for more than two centuries. The 1809 Georgian farmhouse sits on a bluff overlooking the fields of corn and cattle and the south branch of the Potomac River that cuts through the property. Horseback rides can be arranged. Inexpensive; breakfast included. Route 1, Box 355, Moorefield, WV 26136. 304/538-2511.

Prospect Hill The main house on this 255-acre fruit-tree farm is too magnificent to be called a farmhouse. It is a spacious Georgian mansion built between 1795 and 1804 and furnished with antiques, oriental rugs, and Chinese and Indian art. There are two large guest rooms furnished with colonial pieces. Moderate; breakfast and tea included. P.O. Box 135, Gerrardstown, WV 25470. 304/229-3346.

Stonebrake Cottage This cute three-bedroom cottage is on a small farm just outside Shepherdstown. The bedrooms are furnished with simple country furniture, but the real draw here is the peaceful setting on an isolated country lane. There are ten acres of pasture and forest to roam and there is a pond, but the cows have reserved it. Moderate; breakfast supplies included. P.O. Box 1612, Shepherd Grade Road, Shepherdstown, WV 25443. 304/876-6607.

Fine, romantic dining spots are hard to find in these two areas of West Virginia. Hickory Hill guests should ask for guidance about restaurants in Moorefield. The ones we found are okay for lunch but mediocre for dinner. Prospect Hill guests should drive to Shepherdstown, a distance of twenty-two miles, where they will find:

The Bavarian Inn, a four-star inn on the bluffs over the Potomac River. This rustic stone restaurant serves German/American cuisine. Moderate. In Shepherdstown on Route 480 just south of the Potomac River. 804/876-2551.

The **Yellow Brick Bank Restaurant** is actually in a red brick building that was once a bank (the walk-in vault is used as the wine cellar). The fare here is American nouveau, and in recent years its acclaim has lured Nancy Reagan, George Will, and other luminaries from the capital. The owners recently opened another restaurant in New England, a move we hope will not distract them from their caring touch at this restaurant. Stick to the massive prime ribs and veal dishes. Moderate. German and Prince streets, Shepherdstown, WV. 304/876-2208.

Chapter Nine

Mountain Manors

Have you ever paused long enough to watch the setting sun turn mountain ridges into shades of purple and gold? Or gazed in wonder as huge birds—hawks, or perhaps even eagles—soared silently in circles over endless forest? Or taken a walk into unspoiled woods seeking undiscovered wonders?

The mountains and forests of the Mid-Atlantic lure us at those times when we need quieter pleasures. In this seven-state area are four very special mountain resorts and more than thirty charming inns and elegant, small hotels. All are located in some of the most beautiful mountain country we have seen in the East.

The four resorts—Grove Park Inn, Mountain Lake Hotel, Hound Ears Club and Wintergreen—are places where we have enjoyed the beauty of our surroundings as well as seemingly endless sports and entertainment.

Grove Park Inn

The resort in the Blue Ridge Mountains just outside of Asheville, North Carolina, has been luring travelers for more than seventy-five years. The stone and red-tile hotel, located on the slope of Sunset Mountain between the forest and the golf course, has 510 guest rooms.

This elegant resort was built when grandeur was expressed with big entrances and large lobbies. Grove Park's lobby is a huge stone room flanked by two grand stone fireplaces. This feeling of grandeur and spaciousness extends throughout the hotel. Everything at Grove Park, from the public areas to the guest rooms, is spacious, well-furnished, and situated to give visitors a view of the mountain and valley.

There are five restaurants at Grove Park, and the open-air terrace is a perfect spot for a meal or a drink while watching the setting sun.

For recreation, there is an eighteen-hole golf course; tennis courts; indoor and outdoor swimming pools; and a sports complex with indoor tennis, racquetball, squash, a complete exercise and aerobics room, and weights stations.

If you want to tour the forests, a horse-drawn carriage will take you on a romantic ride through the dark woods and past the ruins of several old stone buildings on the resort.

Every February the inn hosts a Valentine's Weekend and Sweetheart Ball. Other theme weekends include an arts, crafts, and antiques festival; a jazz festival; a Christmas celebration that fills the entire month of December; and a New Year's party.

🐾 **The Grove Park Inn** There are package plans for tennis and golf, but the one you want is called Romance for Two, which offers two nights' lodging, champagne, flowers, chocolates, use of the Nautilus center and pool, and a tour of the nearby Biltmore Estate for $269 per couple. Normal rates are $100 to $155 per person. 290 Macon Avenue, Asheville, NC 28804. 800/438-5800; in North Carolina call 800/222-9793.

Hound Ears Club

This elegant lodge in the Blue Ridge Mountains just north of Asheville, North Carolina, is like a private club. The difference is that we— and you—are welcome to visit.

Hound Ears, its name taken from an unusual rock formation on the ridge behind the lodge, is small, with only twenty-seven rooms in the chalet-style hotel. Other rooms are available in the many chalets and condominiums on the golf course nearby.

The pace is casual here, well suited to a setting that almost compels you to stop and enjoy the scenery. But in the woods, fields, and hills around the lodge are numerous opportunities for fun, including golf, horseback riding, tennis, hiking, skiing, and swimming.

Indoors, the rooms are tastefully furnished, much like one would

🐾 The Grove Park Inn is a majestic stone resort set high in the mountains in North Carolina. *Photo courtesy of the Grove Park Inn.*

expect in a small, fashionable resort. The dining room here is an additional delight, famed for the quality of its food, and the downstairs club is a relaxing place to end a day with dancing and music.

Nearby, in the resort town of Blowing Rock, are antique shops, a craft center, and a small railroad to take you on a scenic tour of the mountains.

🐾 **Hound Ears Club** The rates at this wonderful resort start at $94 per person and include two meals a day. Golf, tennis, and skiing fees are additional. P.O. Box 188, Blowing Rock, NC 28605. 704/963-4321.

Mountain Lake Hotel

Remember "Dirty Dancing"? Well, this mountaintop resort in southern Virginia was the setting of the steamy movie starring Jennifer Grey and Patrick Swayze about the coming of age of a young woman at a mythical Catskills resort.

All the scenes in the move save two—Johnny's cabin and the closing ballroom scene—were shot at Mountain Lake, a bit of Hollywood that has left its mark on the famous old resort.

The movie is shown at least once every day, and "Dirty Dancing" weekends with the music and dances of the early 1960s are held often during the year.

The focus on the movie is fine, but it overlooks the attractions of Mountain Lake: a half-century-old stately stone hotel on Salt Pond Mountain 3,800 feet above sea level. Around the hotel are log cabins, newer lodges, and a half-mile-long lake surrounded by twenty-foot-tall rhododendrons. Recreation facilities include boating, fishing, tennis, golf, hiking, swimming, lawn games, board and table games, nightly entertainment, and a spirit of fun.

Our room here was in the Chestnut Lodge, a new two-story building in the woods near the main hotel. It was tastefully furnished and certainly spacious: two large beds and a sitting area with a fireplace and a screened porch overlooking the woods and lake.

The rooms in the main hotel are not as spacious as those in the lodge, but they are fine accommodations. The public areas—dining room, veranda, and nightclub—are charming, with an atmosphere of casual elegance.

A separate activities barn houses table games, a large-screen TV (there are no televisions in the rooms), a snack bar, and a large hall used for special events such as a weekly steak cookout on the adjacent terrace.

Finally, if you have an irresistible urge to say you shared a bed with Swayze or Grey, you can. Swayze slept in Room 232 and Grey in 218 while they were filming at the resort.

❦ **Mountain Lake Hotel** Rates range from $116 to $150 a couple, two meals included. Mountain Lake, VA 24136. 800/346-3334.

Wintergreen

There are 11,000 acres to this resort that hugs the Blue Ridge Parkway in the mountains east of Charlottesville, Virginia. Better yet, more than half of this resort remains virgin wilderness, never farmed or occupied by settlers because it was too steep.

Wintergreen has created a resort of homes, townhouses, and condominiums that blends into the environment. That is mainly due to the resort's managers, who have a naturalist on the staff to advise them on development and to create programs and trips that help educate as well as entertain residents and visitors.

The programs focus on such subjects as wild flowers, the forest animals, the geology of the mountains, the stars in the clear skies over-head, a highly acclaimed wildflower symposium every May, and jeep safaris that explore the undeveloped 6,700 acres of Wintergreen.

This commitment to nature, rare in a resort, won Wintergreen the National Environmental Award from the American Hotel and Motel Association.

Wintergreen has two golf courses, one on the mountain top and the other down on the valley floor. In the summer there is a fourteen-degree difference in temperature between the Devils Knob course, the highest in Virginia, and Stoney Creek, the new course at Wintergreen that is 1,400 feet lower in elevation.

The golf courses are popular feeding areas for the many herds of deer that make Wintergreen their home.

Other recreational facilities include ten ski slopes; twenty-two tennis courts; one wonderful indoor pool and five outdoor pools; a sixteen-acre lake for swimming, boating and fishing; stables and riding trails; hiking paths; and the Wintergarden spa and exercise facility.

The lodging is in condominium apartments, townhouses, homes, a twelve-room country inn called Trillium House and the larger Mountain Inn at the shopping and restaurant complex. The condos we have stayed in were on the slopes, offering breathtaking views of the mountain ranges and luxurious accommodations.

One of the big surprises at Wintergreen is the quality of the food. The Trillium House, the Garden Terrace, and the Copper Mine Restaurant serve some surprisingly high-quality dinners. And the Rodes Farm Inn, a small restaurant down in Wintergreen's valley, serves country-style food like Grandmother used to make.

🐭 **Wintergreen** There are a number of packages that include tennis fees, golf green fees, ski lift tickets, and more. The basic rates range from $129 per person for a studio to $156 for a one-bedroom apartment. Wintergreen, VA 22958. 800/325-2200.

🐭 MOUNTAIN INNS AND RESTAURANTS

The Mid-Atlantic has many small inns and hotels in its mountains. The main attraction here is the scenery and the outdoor activities—hiking, rafting, and fishing. Fine dining is a bit more difficult to find without a long drive. We have included recommendations for restaurants either on the premises or nearby.

Here are our favorites, but first an explanation of how we break down our cost categories:

One night in an inn for two (often but not always including breakfast):

Inexpensive Under $75
Moderate $75 to $125
Expensive More than $125

For dinner for two (wine and drinks not included):

Inexpensive Less than $25
Moderate $25 to $60
Expensive More than $60

For inns on a Modified American Plan (breakfast and dinner included) or American Plan (all meals included), the cost categories are per person per night.

Maryland

Bluebird on the Mountain This hideaway is located on South Mountain in the Catoctin chain just south of the Pennsylvania state line. There are four luxurious rooms, one with a fireplace and two with Jacuzzis. Nearby activities include hiking, fishing, and swimming in Catoctin Mountain Park, and antiquing and shopping in Hagerstown and Frederick. For dining, see the Frederick section in Chapter 6, "Wine Country."

Rates are moderate and include a continental breakfast. 14700 Eyler Avenue, Cascade, MD 21719. 301/241-4161.

The Casselman Inn For more than 160 years this small building has been an inn on what was the nation's first road, now the historic National Pike, or U.S. 40. There are five rooms in the Federal-style brick hotel and forty more in a new, adjacent motel. Make certain your room is in the old building. The inn is close to the four-season recreation areas around Deep Creek Lake in Maryland and the Laurel Highlands of Pennsylvania.

The hotel restaurant features inexpensive Mennonite dishes. Room rates are also inexpensive. P.O. Box 299, Grantsville, MD 21536. 301/895-5055.

The Castle at Mount Savage This is one of those places that you find but you never *ever* tell anyone else about. This twenty-eight room castle has been a bar, brothel, casino, and elegant mansion during more than a century of life. Today it is an elegant mountaintop inn surrounded by an eighteen-foot stone wall. The six guest rooms are furnished ex-

quisitely with antiques from the seventeenth and nineteenth c
and large beds adorned with fine, old linens and mounds of fea.
pillows. The closet holds his and her robes and the dresser has a decanter
of sherry or cognac. Outside, the rolling Allegheny Mountains stretch
endlessly. Visitors may walk through the nearby state forests or browse
through the antique stores spotting the countryside.

For dinner try the **Bistro**, a moderately-priced French restaurant in
Cumberland (37 North Centre Street, 301/777-8462). The Castle's rates
are moderate, and include breakfast and high tea. P.O. Box 578, Mount
Savage, MD 21545. 301/759-5946.

North Carolina

Cataloochee Ranch High in the Great Smoky Mountains in western
North Carolina, this inn has thirty-five rooms in a renovated nineteenth-
century log and stone barn, the new Silverbell Lodge, and seven cabins.
The rooms are rustic, but very comfortably furnished. The ranch offers
horseback riding and tours of the wilderness, tennis, swimming, trout
fishing, and lawn games. Nearby recreation spots include Cherokee Indian
reservations, antiques, golf, ruby and sapphire mines, fishing, white-water
sports, swimming, and hiking into the surrounding mountains.

Rates are inexpensive and include lunch and dinner. The ranch is
closed in March, April, and November. Route 1, Box 500-B, Maggie
Valley, NC 28751. 704/926-1401.

Fryemont Inn This rustic wooden lodge near Great Smoky Mountains National Park has thirty-six rooms, all furnished simply but comfortably. The inn is a throwback to the time when resorts offered fine
accommodations, beautiful scenery, and the opportunity for outdoor
activity. That the inn does, without the trappings of glitter occasionally
found at some resorts. For active couples, white-water sports, hiking,
and fishing are nearby.

Meals are served country-style. Lunch and dinner are included in
the rates, which are moderate. P.O. Box 459, Bryson City, NC 28713.
704/488-2159.

Greystone Inn This luxurious inn in the mountains south of Asheville mixes the elegance of a small, fine hotel with the soft accents and
gracious hospitality of the South. There are twenty rooms in the main
house, a restored Swiss revival residence on the shores of Lake Toxaway,
and twelve more in Hillmont, a lakefront building next to the mansion.
All the rooms are spacious and meticulously furnished with antiques
and period reproductions. Many of the rooms have fireplaces and porches,
and all but one have Jacuzzis in the bathrooms. Nearby attractions in-

clude hiking, fishing, white-water sports, and small mountain resort towns with antique shops and some marvelous old buildings.

Rates are moderate and include breakfast and dinner. P.O. Box 6, Lake Toxaway, NC 28747. Call collect 704/966-4700; outside North Carolina call 800/824-5766.

Gideon Ridge Inn There are eight guest rooms in this stone house with a stunning view of the Blue Ridge Mountains. All the rooms are furnished with antiques. Nearby are hiking trails, ski resorts, fishing, and white-water sports. Dinner can be arranged at the inn by reservation, but you should try the nearby **Green Park Inn** in Blowing Rock. The restaurant serves a moderately priced continental menu and often has a band playing during dinner. It is two miles southeast of Blowing Rock on U.S. 321 (704/295-3141).

The Gideon Ridge Inn's rates are moderate. 6148 Gideon Ridge Road, Blowing Rock, NC 28605. 704/295-3644.

Meadowbrook Inn This is a wonderful hotel located amid gardens and next to a stream in the quaint town of Blowing Rock. There are forty-seven guest rooms in this hotel, all meticulously furnished with elegant antique reproductions. Some have whirlpool baths and fireplaces. The **Garden Restaurant** at the inn overlooks the gardens, a romantic backdrop for a memorable meal featuring American and regional favorites.

The inn is close to the antique shops of Blowing Rock, the outdoor recreation areas of the mountains, and such sports as skiing, golf, tennis, fishing, and more.

The dinner rates are moderate. The room rates vary widely, from inexpensive to expensive, depending on the room and the season. Main Street, Blowing Rock, NC 28605. 704/295-9341 or 800/456-5456.

Pennsylvania

Eagles Mere Inn Once upon a time, this mountain lake area was a Victorian resort attracting the rich and famous from the big cities. Today, this 121-year-old inn is an elegant witness to those days when the lake and the mountain breezes were the main attractions. There are fifteen rooms in this restored Victorian, all comfortably and tastefully furnished. Activities nearby include mountain hiking, swimming, boating, fishing, skiing, tennis, golf, and horseback riding. The famed Eagles Mere Toboggan Slide operates in the winter.

Rates are inexpensive and include breakfast and dinner. P.O. Box 356, Eagles Mere, PA 17731. 717/525-3273.

Glades Pike Inn For almost 150 years this cozy two-story red-brick building has attracted travelers in the Laurel Highlands. In 1987, new owners carefully restored the inn, preserving its hardwood floors and high ceilings while turning it into a comfortable bed and breakfast inn. The five rooms are furnished in a comfortable, contemporary manner. Three of the five rooms and the living room have fireplaces. Nearby attractions include the Laurel Highlands parks, cross-country and downhill skiing at Hidden Valley resort, hiking, fishing, golf, and antiquing. The Hidden Valley restaurants are your best bets for a fine dinner.

The inn's rates are moderate and include a breakfast and a weekend wine and cheese social.

The inn is on Route 31 six miles west of Somerset. RD 6, Box 250, Somerset, PA 15501. 814/443-4978.

Grant House Bed and Breakfast This restored Victorian is on the main street of the small town of Ligonier in the Laurel Highlands. The inn offers three rooms: one furnished with French Provincial antiques, another with Victorian antiques, and the third with country pieces including two four-poster beds. A patio next to an herb garden and a private back porch allow guests to relax outside. Nearby attractions include the sights and shops in Ligonier, and the golf, skiing, and other outdoor sports at Hidden Valley resort and the Laurel Highlands wilderness areas. For dinner, try the Hidden Valley restaurants.

Rates are moderate and include breakfast. 244 West Church Street, Ligonier, PA 15658. 412/238-5135.

Heritage Guest House This turn-of-the-century lodge is located in Dushore, a small village in the beautifully named Endless Mountains of north-central Pennsylvania. There are four rooms here, all furnished with fine antiques that can be purchased. Nearby attractions include state parks with skiing, fishing, hiking, and other forms of recreation.

Rates are inexpensive (actually, they are downright cheap) and include breakfast. Dinners can be arranged for an extra charge. Take advantage of their offer. RD 2, Box 52, Dushore, PA 18614. 717/928-7354.

Inn at Meadowbrook This Poconos inn has sixteen rooms, eleven in the 147-year-old manor house and five in the sixty-five-year-old Mill House. All are carefully and tastefully furnished, a perfect match with the buildings and grounds at this retreat. Recreation facilities include cross-country skiing, swimming, ice skating, fishing, hiking, or just relaxing and reading a book under the tall trees that shade the manor. For dinner, the Pine Knob Inn and Pump House Inn in nearby Canadensis serve excellent food at moderate to expensive prices.

The inn rates are inexpensive to moderate and include a continental breakfast. The mailing address is RD 7, Box 7651, East Stroudsburg, PA 18301. 717/629-0296. The actual address is Cherry Lane Road, Tannersville, PA.

Inn at Starlight Lake For more than eighty years travelers have enjoyed the mountain scenery at this resort in northeastern Pennsylvania. There are 900 acres of grounds and a beautiful lake here, offering a wonderland of sports and recreation in all seasons. There are twenty rooms in the main house and small cottages. Nearby activities include hiking, skiing, fishing, swimming, boating, and a regional theater.

The inn's restaurant serves superb continental cuisine. Breakfast and dinner are included in the rates, which are moderate. Box 27, Starlight, PA 18461. 717/798-2519.

Nethercott Inn This 1893 Victorian is located in the small village of Starrucca in the Endless Mountains of north-central Pennsylvania. There are seven rooms in this Victorian, all furnished with antiques. Nearby attractions include skiing, fishing, and hiking in the Endless Mountains and strolling through the streets and shops of the village.

For dinner try the Inn at Starlight Lake, only eight miles away. (See above.) Rates are cheap to inexpensive and include breakfast. P.O. Box 26, Main Street, Starrucca, PA 18462. 717/727-2211.

Overlook Inn This secluded inn is a retreat designed for guests who like sports. There are hiking and skiing trails, tennis courts, badminton, shuffleboard, and a pool on the inn's fifteen acres. Best of all, there is the quiet of the forest that surrounds this inn on a small wooded lane. There are twenty-one rooms at the inn: twelve in the main building, six in the lodge, and three in a carriage house. All are furnished with antiques and country items. Just a few minutes' drive away are ski resorts, rafting outfitters, antique shops, and scenic mountain drives. The dining room is known for the quality of its ambitious menu, featuring game and seafood.

Rates are expensive, and include breakfast and dinner. RD 1, Box 680A, Canadensis, PA 18325. 717/595-7519.

Pine Knob Inn This quiet, charming inn in the Pocono Mountains is a perfect place for quiet relaxation as well as a base for skiing, antiquing, and touring the mountain scenery. There are twenty rooms here, but those in the main inn are better than those in adjacent buildings. The inn is next to a quiet stream whose waters pass by the shuffleboard court and pool. If swimming is a bit chilly, try the tree-shaded tennis court, the surprisingly good art gallery in the barn, or just reading on the broad lawn. Nearby, the beautiful Poconos, ski resorts, raft outfitters, and some high-quality art and antique shops await your visit.

The dining room is the real surprise here, serving up sumptuous breakfasts and surprisingly fine dinners in a charming room. Rates are moderate and include breakfast and dinner. Route 447, Box 275C Canadensis, PA 18325. 717/595-2532.

Pump House Inn Known perhaps more for its food than for its six guest rooms, this inn just outside Canadensis in the Poconos is a perfect retreat. The rooms are comfortably furnished and the dining room is the centerpiece of the striking house. The cuisine served in the restaurant is provincial French, featuring lamb, beef, and fresh seafood. The adjoining pub, a room with a massive stone wall and a fireplace, is a quiet place for a pre- or after-dinner drink.

The room rates are moderate; dinner is expensive. Skytop Road, P.O. Box 430, Canadensis, PA 18325. 717/595-7501.

Sterling Inn This half-century old Poconos resort is on 105 acres of lovely grounds that are loaded with recreation facilities. These include hiking and nordic ski trails; tennis; a lake for swimming, boating and fishing; ice skating; sledding; and horse-drawn sleigh rides. There are sixty rooms in this resort decorated in a wide range of styles from Victorian to 1940s rustic. Near the inn are the Poconos ski resorts, antique shops, mountain scenery, and rafting outfitters.

All meals are included in the room rate, and the meals served at the Sterling Inn are excellent but not fancy. Rates are moderate. Liquor is not served. Box 2, South Sterling, PA 18460. 717/476-3311.

Wiffy Bog Farm The charmingly named century-old Victorian has seven rooms, all furnished with Victorian and Queen Anne antiques. The inn is located on eighty acres and offers hiking trails and trout fishing. Nearby, antique shops, downhill ski resorts, and hiking trails offer more diversions. For dinner, it's either a long drive to the Inn at Starlight Lake or the **Ryah House** in Scranton. The latter serves a standard American menu. The Ryah is at the Inn at Nicholas Village, 1101 Northern Boulevard, Clarks Summit, PA 18411. 717/587-1135.

Wiffy Bog's room rates are inexpensive and include breakfast during the ski season. Box 83, West Clifford RD 1, Uniondale, PA 18470. 717/222-9865.

Virginia

Conyers House There are nine guest rooms in this four-story farmhouse that sits at the foot of Walden Mountain, the peak made famous in the popular television series. The house was built around 1770, added to over the years and in time served as a store, post office, and toll house. In 1979 new owners refurbished the inn and furnished it with antique pieces from the family. Nearby attractions include numerous antique shops, hiking and climbing on Rag Mountain, and horseback riding. The inn can serve an elegant candlelight dinner by arrangement. Try the magnificent **Inn at Little Washington** a few minutes away if you can get reservations. It is expensive, but it is arguably the finest restaurant in the Mid-Atlantic.

Conyers House rates are moderate and include breakfast. 157 Slate Mills Road, Sperryville, VA 22740. 703/987-8025.

Graves Mountain Lodge Tucked away near the little village of Syria in the Blue Ridge Mountains near Shenandoah National Park, this rustic lodge has been attracting visitors since the days of the Depression. Then, economics forced the Graves family to help support their apple orchard business by taking in boarders. Today there are thirty-eight hotel rooms, eight cabins and seven rooms in the old farmhouse. The rooms are furnished with contemporary pieces, but the cabins and the rooms in the farmhouse are the most charming. For recreation, there are tennis courts; a trout pond and stream; nearby antique, craft, and pottery shops; and a swimming pool.

Rates are inexpensive to moderate and include all meals, a real bargain. The meals have won the praise of NBC television personality Willard Scott, who swears by them. Syria, VA 22743. 703/923-4231.

Inn at Gristmill Square Once, long ago, the little village of Warm Springs was a resort attracting the famous and wealthy of this and other nations. Today it is a sleepy village anchored by this quaint inn with fourteen rooms in five buildings. The decor is varied and can be either elegantly formal or simple country. In the complex of buildings is an antiques shop and a restaurant serving creative American cuisine at moderate prices. Nearby attractions include the thermal springs that lured Washington and other colonial leaders, and the sports facilities (tennis, golf, skiing) and nightly entertainment at The Homestead, our favorite grand resort, a few miles away in Hot Springs.

Inn rates are moderate and include a continental breakfast. Box 359, Warm Springs, VA 24484. 703/839-2231.

Inn at Narrow Passage This log inn on the Shenandoah River served as Stonewall Jackson's headquarters in the Civil War campaigns of 1862. There are a dozen rooms, all furnished in early American decor and some equipped with fireplaces. Nearby attractions include the mountains on both sides of the valley, skiing, Civil War battlefields, antique shops, interesting caverns, and hiking. For dinner, try the **Hotel Strasburg** in Strasburg or the **Ashby Inn** in Paris. Both serve fine food at moderate prices.

The inn rates are moderate. Woodstock, VA 22664. 703/459-8000.

Martha Washington Inn This southwestern Virginia inn was built around 1832 for a niece of Patrick Henry. Over the years the building was expanded and used as a girls' finishing school and a Civil War hospital. It languished for many years until 1984, when new owners spent millions to restore the inn to its original elegance. There are sixty-one guest rooms in the inn, some with fireplaces and Jacuzzis and all furnished with antiques. Nearby attractions include the scenic beauty of the Virginia Highlands, antique and craft shops, fishing, hiking, and drives along the Blue Ridge Parkway. The two restaurants at the inn are known for their continental and regional cuisine and their moderate prices.

Inn rates vary from moderate to very expensive, depending on the room. 150 West Main Street, Abingdon, VA 24210. 703/628-3161.

Meander Inn at Penny Lane Farm This farmhouse inn, situated on a hill next to a river with a beaver dam, has five guest rooms, all furnished with an eclectic mix of Victorian and other antique pieces. Inside attractions include a player piano, while outside are a hot tub on the deck, fields of hay, horseback riding trails (the innkeepers can get you a horse), the beaver dam, and the rolling hills made for hiking and exploring. Nearby, antiquing, fishing, and the wonderful Wintergreen golf and ski resort offer other diversions. For dining, try the Wintergreen's **Copper Mine Restaurant** or the **Rodes Farm Inn**. Both are moderately priced but serve wonderful meals.

The inn's rates are moderate and include breakfast. Box 443, Nellysford, VA 22958. 804/361-1121.

Sugar Tree Inn This inn is unusual, for it is located on thirty acres in the George Washington National Forest, a wilderness wonderland made for hiking, fishing, and exploring. The inn's seven rooms are furnished with antiques, but the real attractions are outdoors. You can canoe, hike, and fish within walking distance. For scenery-lovers, the adjacent Blue Ridge Parkway offers magnificent views, either by car or by foot on the maze of trails.

The restaurant serves country French cuisine at moderate prices. The inn is open May through October. Rates are moderate. Vesuvius, VA 24483. 703/377-2197.

Sycamore Hill House This inn sits atop fifty-two wooded acres on Menefee Mountain, just a few minutes from the Skyline Drive. The two suites are furnished with modern furniture, oriental rugs, and original art. Nearby attractions include fishing, hiking, antiquing, and craft shopping. In the best of all worlds, you would have dinner at the nearby Inn at Little Washington. It is American nouveau, expensive, and famous. Otherwise, try the Hotel Strasburg in Strasburg or the Ashby Inn in Paris. Both are a short drive away and serve fine food at moderate prices.

The inn rates are $85 and $125 and include breakfast. Route 1, Box 978, Washington, VA 22747. 703/675-3046.

Three Hills Inn This hilltop mansion was built in 1913 by novelist Mary Johnston, author of "To Have and To Hold." The three-story gray mansion overlooks the Valley of the Warm Springs, a perfect setting for sunset-lovers. There are nine rooms and suites with kitchenettes in the mansion; all are furnished with some remarkable antique pieces of different periods. The living room, foyer, and dining room are filled with wonderful antiques. (Don't miss the art-deco telephone stand by the front door.) The seven guest cottages on the estate offer more rustic accommodations, with simple furniture that complements the wood and stone cabins. Nearby attractions include antique shops, mountain scenery, and the numerous sports and entertainment facilities at the fabulous Homestead resort in Hot Springs a few miles away. You can dine at **The Homestead**, or at the inn on selected evenings during the fall. Prices of both places are moderate to expensive.

The inn rates are moderate, and include breakfast. P.O. Box 99, Warm Springs, VA 24484. 703/839-5381.

Trillium House This twelve-room inn is country-cute, a place that would be a real attraction even if it were not located inside the marvelous mountain resort called Wintergreen. The rooms are furnished with country furniture and crafts. The main attraction of the inn is the two-level entryway that leads to a sunroom and an upstairs library, perfect areas for afternoon socializing and relaxing. Nearby attractions include the tennis, golf, ski, and other facilities at Wintergreen. Dining at Trillium House is marvelous, though the menu is limited to one entrée at dinner. For other possibilities, cross the road to the restaurant at the **Wintergarden** spa, the indoor pool and sports facility at Wintergreen. The dining room there overlooks the Shenandoah Valley, a great place to watch the sun set. Prices at Trillium's restaurant are moderate. The Wintergreen restaurants range from moderate to expensive.

Trillium's room rates are inexpensive to expensive and include breakfast. P.O. Box 280, Nellysford, VA 22958. 804/325-9126.

Vine Cottage Inn This Victorian inn is nestled next to the Homestead, the magnificent resort in Hot Springs. The location is a superb place to enjoy many of the Homestead's facilities without paying the Homestead's daily rate. The fourteen rooms are furnished with antiques and works of art. Nearby attractions, in addition to the facilities at the Homestead, include state parks with lakes and hiking trails, a beautiful falls (take Route 220 south to Falling Springs and pull off for a view of the cascade), the thermal baths at Warm Springs a few miles away, and antique and craft shops in both Hot Springs and Warm Springs. The closest good restaurant is **Sam Snead's Tavern**, a Homestead-operated spot in town. It serves American fare at moderate prices. The other Homestead restaurants live up to their praise, and are expensive.

The inn's rates are inexpensive and include a continental breakfast. P.O. Box 918, Hot Springs, VA 24445. 703/839-2422.

West Virginia

Cheat Mountain Club More than 100 years ago this elegant lodge was used as a private hunting club. Today the stately log and stone building is an inn, offering some stunning mountain scenery and gracious accommodations. There are nine rooms in the club, all furnished with simple pieces. The main attraction here is outdoors in the surrounding Monongahela National Forest, thousands of acres of wilderness made for hiking, fishing, cross-country skiing, and climbing.

Lodging rates include all meals and are inexpensive. Durbin, WV 26264. 304/456-4627.

Cheat River Lodge This lodge is actually several rustic cabins located on the river in the Monongahela National Forest. The cabins are fairly isolated, spacious, and comfortable, with such amenities as hot tubs, wood stoves, and full kitchens. The forest offers a world of activities, including hiking, fishing, exploring, climbing, and hunting. Nearby Elkins offers a wonderful crafts and music festival every August. For dinner, try the **Cheat River Inn**, in the building where you checked in. It doesn't look like much, but in this case appearances are very deceiving: the food is super and moderately priced.

The lodge rates are expensive. Route 1, Box 116, Elkins, WV 26241. 304/636-2301.

General Lewis Inn This antique-filled inn in the mountain town of Lewisburg is also a museum of life a century ago. Games, tools, musical instruments, and other relics from the nineteenth century are displayed throughout the inn, a touch that adds an air of the past to this elegant hotel. Not all the historic pieces are just for display: the front desk, still in service, dates from 1760 and was used by Thomas Jefferson and Patrick Henry when they registered at the Sweet Chalybeate Springs Hotel, one of the extinct spas of the Virginias. The main hotel was built in 1929 as an addition to the original 1834 structure. There are twenty-seven rooms in the inn, all furnished with antiques and artifacts. Nearby attractions include antique shops in town, water sports and hiking in the Greenbrier Valley, and mountainous national forests. The elegant Greenbrier Resort is just a few minutes' drive away. For dinner stick to the inn, which is known for its regional cuisine served at moderate prices.

The inn rates are inexpensive. 301 East Washington Street, Lewisburg, WV 24901. 304/645-2600.

Hilltop House This hotel sits on a bluff overlooking the convergence of the Shenandoah and Potomac rivers in Harpers Ferry. The view is stunning. There are sixty-four rooms here, all plainly furnished. The dining room serves family-style meals at moderate prices. A few minutes away are antique shops, the Harpers Ferry Historic Park and district, white-water sports, and hiking.

The inn rates are moderate. P.O. Box 930, Harpers Ferry, WV 25425. 304/535-6321.

Chapter Ten

Adventure and Sports

*E*xcitement, anticipation, unexpected climbs and just-as-sudden
drops, heart-wrenching twists and turns, and, finally, fulfillment. This
sounds like a white-water raft ride—or a new romance.

We are not athletic, but some of our most memorable weekends
have occurred when we got our pulses racing with an exciting new
adventure. In recent years we have enjoyed horseback rides in the mountains, hang gliding on the Outer Banks, white-water rafting in West
Virginia, and more. What's great about these adventures is that you
don't have to be a physical-fitness fanatic to enjoy them. The sports and
activities we have taken part in are for the beginner as well as the expert.

Once, during a visit to Harpers Ferry, West Virginia, we broke away
from the crafts-and-antiques circuit to take a half-day raft ride on the
Shenandoah River. The river there is not threatening; the rapids are
rated I to III, depending on the river level. Those ratings are the low
end of a scale that goes up to VI, a level that indicates extremely dangerous white water.

The river valley at water level was a new world to us, one filled
with waterfowl, fish, river animals, historic ruins, and stunning landscapes.

We traveled with a guide and two other couples in a large rubber raft. The raft, shaped like an oval Cheerio with a rubberized fabric bottom, was flexible, and bucked at times like a horse.

All this combined to make the ride wet and wild, for the low sides of the raft often were swamped by some of the larger rapids. It was a great new thrill that made that weekend special.

Another memorable adventure we had was during a visit to the Outer Banks. One of the features of the North Carolina barrier islands is the sand dunes at Kitty Hawk, large expanses that attract kite-flyers of both types: those who stand on the ground and hold a string, and those who fly aloft with their kites.

We were always attracted by the beauty and grace of the kites, but repelled by the thought of actually *flying* while holding onto a kite.

On this weekend, Larry signed up for hang-gliding school. Barbara, recovering from an illness, decided to be the official photographer, cheerleader, and, if needed, next of kin.

Hang gliding, Larry learned, is easy to master. Basically, you hook yourself up to the kite, pick up the control bar, run into the wind, and then "fly" the kite back down the dune. The flights never went too far or soared too high, but boy! was it exhilarating!

If you can, we urge you to try both hang gliding and rafting. There are other adventures waiting in the Mid-Atlantic, and resorts where the more standard sports of golf and tennis are king. Here is our roundup:

❦ BALLOONING

Drifting silently above the landscape, perched in a basket hanging from a colorful balloon, couples can find beauty, peace, and romance. From a balloon, all the cares of the world seem far away.

The price of a romantic balloon ride can vary widely, but they generally start at about $100 per couple and depend on the day, time, and length of flight. The biggest factor is not the cost, but the weather. Hot-air balloons can go up only in calm weather.

Consider turning this adventure into something very special. Some ballooning firms offering champagne, landings for lunch or breakfast, sightseeing over estates not visible from the highways, and more. The costs of these special rides, of course, soar like, well, like a hot-air balloon.

❦ Adventures Aloft—Rockville, MD. 301/881-6262.

❦ Balloon Utopia—Allentown, PA. 215/719-9900.

🍎 Barnstormers Air Shows—Ashland, VA. 804/798-8830.

🍎 Blue Ridge Balloon Port—Culpeper, VA. 703/937-4386.

🍎 Boar's Head Inn—This Charlottesville, VA, resort offers morning balloon rides for about $80. 804/296-2181.

🍎 Bucks County Balloon Adventures—Quakertown, PA. 215/LETS-FLY.

🍎 Chesapeake Balloon Service—Baltimore County, MD. 301/667-6789.

🍎 Fantasy Flights—Montgomery County, MD. 301/966-7676.

🍎 Keystone State Balloon Tours—Pipersville (Bucks County), PA. 215/294-8034.

🍎 Lancaster Hot Air Balloons—Lancaster, PA. 717/733-7495.

🍎 Magical Mystery Flights, Inc.—Collingdale (West Chester area), PA. 215/237-9873.

🍎 HANG GLIDING

Hang gliding is thrilling and simple, a sport learned with about an hour of ground instruction before your first flight. The hang glider is nothing but a large kite designed to be launched into the air after a run of about ten steps into the wind. After you get airborne, you control the flight by moving a bar a few inches forward or back.

To enjoy this sport, go to Nags Head, N.C. There, across from the magnificent sand dunes at Jockeys Ridge State Park, you will find Kitty Hawk Kites. They offer three-hour lessons that will give you about ninety minutes of ground instruction and about six flights off the dunes. They train thousands every year. A beginner's lesson is about $50.

Hang gliding isn't dangerous and doesn't require any special skill except the ability to hold onto a control bar while keeping your feet together and pointed straight back. And it is great fun, something we will do again soon.

Kitty Hawk Kites is at Mile Post 13 on the Route 158 Bypass in Nags Head. Lessons are offered year-round, but reservations are suggested for the summer weekends. 919/441-4124.

🍎 SOARING

Have you ever envied the large birds that circle silently above the countryside? You can fly silently above the landscape in a two-person glider that is towed aloft by a power airplane, then freed to find its own way to the heavens. The cost can be high, too. The usual rate is $50 to $100 per person.

🐝 Bay Soaring—Woodbine, MD. 301/781-6095 or 800/248-7627.

🐝 Blue Ridge Soaring Society—Salem, in southwestern Virginia. 703/864-6403.

🐝 Brandywine Soaring Association—Wilmington, DE. 302/478-9293.

🐝 Kutztown Aviation Service—In Pennsylvania Dutch Country. 215/683-3821.

🐝 Mid-Atlantic Soaring Association—Frederick, MD. 301/473-8984.

🐝 Warrenton Soaring Center—In Virginia's Hunt Country. 703/347-0054.

🐝 Mountaineering Soaring Association—Charlestown, WV. 304/744-2846.

🐝 RAFTING

No experience is required for an adventure afloat. However, rafting novices should be careful to take trips on rapids rated I, II, or III. These are the milder forms of white water, rough enough to thrill but not tough enough to threaten you. Wear a life jacket and a helmet and dress to get wet.

If you are new to the sport, choose a half-day trip. You can always go again for a longer journey. Rates vary, of course, but expect to spend about $30 per person for a half-day trip that usually includes lunch. All-day trips are $50 and up.

White-water trips in the Mid-Atlantic are in the Poconos, western Maryland, West Virginia, or south-central Pennsylvania.

🐝 Appalachian Wildwaters, Inc.—They run some of the toughest rapids in the East. Choose your first trip carefully. Albright, WV. 304/329-1665 or 800/624-8060.

🐝 Canyon Cruise—Safe trips through Pennsylvania's Grand Canyon. Wellsboro, PA. 814/435-2969.

🐝 Cheat River Outfitters—The trips can get hairy. Choose wisely. Albright, WV. 304/329-2024.

🐝 Class IV River Runners, Inc.—For the advanced white-water enthusiast. Lansing, WV. 304/574-0704.

❦ Harpers Ferry River Riders—Knoxville, MD. 301/834-8051.

❦ Laurel Highlands River Tours—Raft trips in Pennsylvania, Maryland, and West Virginia. Ohiopyle, PA. 412/329-8531.

❦ Mountain River Tours Inc.—Day trips and overnight adventures. Hico, WV. 304/658-5266.

❦ North American River Runners—Hico, WV. 304/658-5276.

❦ Pocono Whitewater Rafting—Trips through the Lehigh River Gorge. Jim Thorpe, PA. 717/325-3656.

❦ River and Trail Outfitters—Knoxville, MD. 301/695-5177.

❦ White Water Adventures—Ohiopyle, PA. 800/WWA-RAFT outside Pennsylvania, 412/329-8850 in Pennsylvania (call collect).

❦ CANOEING AND KAYAKING

A calm paddle along the shores of a peaceful river can do wonders for the soul. Before you go, know what kind of water your guide will be leading you into, and wear a life jacket.

❦ Appalachian Wildwaters Inc.—Mild trips for beginners. Albright, WV. 304/329-1665 or 800/624-8060.

❦ Downriver Canoe Co.—Trips on the South Fork of the Shenandoah in Virginia. Bentonville, VA. 703/635-5526.

❦ Endless Mountains Canoe Outfitters—Trips on the Susquehanna River. Mehoopany, PA. 717/833-5938.

❦ Kittatinny Canoes—Trips on the Delaware River in the Poconos. Dingmans Ferry, PA. 717/828-2338.

❦ Nantahala Outdoor Center—Instructions for all levels of canoeists and kayakers. Bryson City, NC. 704/488-2175.

❦ Northbrook Canoe Company—Trips on the scenic Brandywine River. West Chester, PA. 215/793-2279.

❦ Point Pleasant Canoe—Trips on the Delaware River in Bucks County. Point Pleasant, PA. 215/297-8823.

❦ Shenandoah River Outfitters—Trips on a river that passes through some beautiful and historic country. Luray, VA. 703/743-4159.

❦ Tee Pee Canoe Rental—Guided trips on the Susquehanna River. Towanda, PA. 717/265-3309.

❦ Whitewater Challengers—Classes and trips for beginning and advanced canoeists and kayakers. White Haven, PA. 717/443-9532.

❦ Wilderness Canoe Trips—Canoeing on the Brandywine River. Wilmington, DE. 302/654-2227.

❦ HORSEBACK RIDING

The mountains of the Mid-Atlantic offer some stunning scenery from the gentle trails at these riding centers:

❦ Cataloochee Ranch—Rides into the Great Smoky Mountains National Park. Maggie Valley, NC. 704/926-1401.

❦ Coolfont Stables—Rides and lessons at this mountain resort. Berkeley Springs, WV. 304/258-4500.

❦ C&W Riding Stables—Trails in the Endless Mountains of Pennsylvania. Nicholson, PA. 717/942-6230.

❦ Double G Ranch—McHenry, MD. 301/387-5481.

❦ SAILING

You can take a romantic sailboat cruise by calling one of the yacht charter agencies. They can arrange for a boat of any length and a captain and crew to sail it for you. The cost depends on the size of the boat and the length of the cruise, but plan to spend at least $200 a day for boat and captain. We have had wonderful trips with the following: Adventures Float, whose offices are at 1415 ½ 21st Street NW, Apartment A, Washington, DC 20036, 202/452-9563; and North-East Wind Yacht Charter, 326 First Street, Annapolis, MD 21403, 301/267-6333.

For your own sailing adventure:

❦ The Mystic Clipper—A 125-foot-long schooner that makes one- and two-night cruises from the City Dock in Annapolis, Maryland, to St. Michaels or Tilghman Island. The cruises are only in May, June, September, and October. Reservations required for overnight trips. 800/243-0416.

❦ Eastern Bay Charters—Offers day sails aboard a forty-foot schooner that sails at 9 and 2. 301/745-2329.

Lessons run about $200 a student for two days of sailing. The best schools:

🦃 Annapolis Sailing School—Weekend courses for beginners and novices. 601 Sixth Street, Annapolis, MD. 800/638-9192.

🦃 Chesapeake Sailing School—Weekend courses for all skill levels. 7074 Bembe Beach Road, Annapolis, MD. 301/269-1594.

🦃 Womanship—Classes mostly for women but some weekend courses for couples. Their motto is: "We don't yell." 137 Conduit Street, Annapolis, MD. 301/267-6661.

🦃 GOLF AND TENNIS RESORTS

If rafting, ballooning, and sailing are more adventure than you can handle, pick up your clubs and rackets and head to these superb golf and tennis resorts. Before you go, read Chapter 5, "The Grand Resorts," and then ask these spas about tennis and golf packages:

🦃 Greenbrier—Three eighteen-hole golf courses and five indoor and fifteen outdoor tennis courts. White Sulphur Springs, WV. 304/536-1110 or 800/624-6070.

🦃 Grove Park Inn—Championship golf, seven lighted tennis courts, and three indoor courts. Asheville, NC. 704/252-2711.

🦃 Hidden Valley—Tennis and golf in a lovely mountain setting. Somerset, PA. 800/458-0175.

🦃 The Homestead—Three eighteen-hole championship courses and outdoor tennis courts. Hot Springs, VA. 703/839-5500 or 800/468-7747.

🦃 Hotel Hershey—Five championship courses, one nine-hole course, and tennis courts. Hershey, PA. 717/533-2171 or 800/533-3131.

🦃 Hound Ears Club—Championship golf course and tennis courts. Blowing Rock, NC. 704/963-4321.

🦃 The Tides Inn—Three eighteen-hole golf courses, one nine-hole par-3 course, and outdoor tennis courts. Irvington, VA. 804/438-5000 or 800/446-9981.

🦃 Williamsburg Inn—Tennis and nine- and eighteen-hole golf courses. Williamsburg, VA. 804/229-1000 or 800/HISTORY.

🦃 Wintergreen—Two eighteen-hole championship courses and numerous tennis courts. Wintergreen, VA. 804/325-200 or 800/325-2200.

🐝 SKIING

🐝 Hidden Valley—Downhill and cross-country in a lovely mountain setting. Somerset, PA. 800/458-0175.

🐝 The Homestead—Downhill skiing on the oldest slopes in the South. Hot Springs, VA. 703/839-5500 or 800/468-7747.

🐝 Hotel Hershey—Cross-country skiing on the grounds, downhill nearby. Hershey, PA. 717/533-2171 or 800/533-3131.

🐝 Hound Ears Club—Downhill skiing. Blowing Rock, NC. 704/963-4321.

🐝 Wintergreen—Great skiing! Wintergreen, VA. 804/325-200 or 800/325-2200.

Chapter Eleven

A Wealth of Festivals

When we go away for the weekend we try to save some time for one of the many fine festivals in the Mid-Atlantic that can add some spice to a getaway. You can tour historic homes and gardens, enjoy colorful music and dances that celebrate ethnic and regional heritages, browse through some terrific craft shows (the perfect place to pick up a few special gifts), or sample the regional cuisine.

The festival season usually runs from March to November, but an avid festival-goer can find a celebration every month of the year.

Our favorite festivals are listed here. Dates vary from year to year, so before you put a festival into your weekend plans check with the local chamber of commerce or visitors' center and ask for the schedules.

For the best in inns, hotels, and restaurants, look up the city or region you're visiting in the index in the back of the book.

❦ DELAWARE

For complete schedules and information: Delaware State Travel Service, 99 Kings Highway, Box 1401, Dover, DE 19901. 800/441-8846.

The best in festivals:

🐭 Odessa Spring Festival. Tour two historic homes and see Victorian furnishings. Early April. 302/378-4027.

🐭 A Day in Old New Castle. This Delaware Bay town of grand old homes, nice restaurants, and quaint shops opens its historic homes, gardens, and museums for tours. Late May. 302/328-2449.

🐭 Wilmington Garden Day. Tour grand homes and fine gardens on the first Saturday in May. 302/652-4088.

🐭 Indian Summer Festival. The last days of the beach season are celebrated in Rehoboth Beach with parades, music, antiques, and more. September and October. 302/227-2233.

🐭 MARYLAND

For current schedules and more information: Maryland Office of Tourist Development, 45 Calvert Street, Annapolis, MD 21401. 800/543-1036.
The best in festivals:

🐭 Atlantic Crafts Council Crafts Fair. More than 500 artisans display and sell their wares in one of the nation's finest (and best-attended) craft shows. The show, which fills two convention halls in downtown Baltimore, is in February around the Presidents' Holiday. 301/837-INFO.

🐭 Winterfest. Ski races, parades, and fireworks in mid-March in Oakland in western Maryland. 301/334-1948.

🐭 Maryland Day. A two-day festival to mark the birthday of the state. Crafts, music, entertainment, and more in St. Mary's City. Late March. 301/889-6060.

🐭 Maryland's House and Garden Pilgrimage. Tour historic homes, private homes, and lovely gardens at locations throughout the state. April and May. 301/821-6933.

🐭 Bay Bridge Walk. Hike over the span that crosses the Chesapeake Bay. The Sunday before the Memorial Day weekend. Annapolis. 301/563-7104.

🐭 Chestertown Tea Party Festival. Raft races, music, food, and a reenactment of the famed tax revolt in this Eastern Shore town. Late May. 301/778-0416.

🐭 Commissioning Week. Commencement week at the Naval Academy in Annapolis, with parades, concerts, an air show, and more. Late May. 301/267-3109.

❦ Historic Baltimore Day. Take a free ride on buses and trolleys to Baltimore's nineteen museums. Late May. 301/837-3262.

❦ Frederick Craft Fair. More than 500 artisans display and sell their works. Demonstrations, music, and food. Third weekend in May. 301/663-8703.

❦ Shenandoah Apple Blossom Festival. A lavish parade, music, food, crafts, and other celebrations of the apple. May. Winchester. 703/662-4118.

❦ National Pike Festival. The nation's longest festival—eighty-nine miles of activities—honors the historic National Pike (U.S. 40). Festivities include the Pioneer Wagon Train, historic sites, crafts, and food in numerous towns in Maryland and Pennsylvania. Third weekend in May. 301/777-5905.

❦ Sugar Loaf Mountain Crafts Festival. More than 300 artisans display and sell their wares in a weekend filled with crafts, music, and entertainment. May. Gaithersburg. 301/840-1400.

❦ Annapolis Arts Festival. Local and national artists exhibit their works on the City Dock. Mid-June. 301/268-TOUR.

❦ Baltimore Boat Show. This show is not as big as Annapolis' shows, but offers scores of sail and power boats and all the trinkets boaters love. June. 301/837-INFO.

❦ Leitersburg Peach Festival. This little town near the Pennsylvania border remains close to our hearts, for every August it hosts a wonderful festival celebrating the modest peach in homemade ice cream, freshly baked pies, cobblers, pie-eating contests, and more calorie-laden events. For dieters, they have music, crafts, and a bunch of guys pretending to be soldiers from another time. Forget them and order another helping of pie. Better yet, take some ice cream and a pie or two home with you. 301/791-3130.

❦ Maryland Renaissance Festival. Medieval games, music, entertainment, and jousting (the state sport). August–September. Crownsville. 301/267-6118.

❦ Maryland Seafood Festival. A celebration of the bay's watermen with music; lots of oysters, crabs, and fish; Skipjack races; and more. The weekend following Labor Day, in Sandy Point State Park, just north of Annapolis, on the bay. 301/268-TOUR.

❦ New Market Days. This historic old town brings back the past, with costumed guides, eighteenth-century crafts, and other entertainment. And it's a good town for antiquing. Late September. 301/831-06712 or 301/831-6464.

😈 Annapolis Boat Shows. Two consecutive weeks of boat shows in the first half of October, with sailboats in the first week and power boats the second. This really is an amazing show, whether you sail or not. 301/268-8828.

😈 Chesapeake Appreciation Day. A festival to honor the state oystermen with food, music, and Skipjack races. Late October in Sandy Point State Park, north of Annapolis on the bay. 301/268-TOUR.

😈 National Craft Fair. More than 400 artisans display and sell their wares in a weekend filled with music, food, and other entertainment. October. Gaithersburg. 301/840-1400.

😈 Catoctin Mountain Colorfest. Tour the autumn foliage, covered bridges, and quaint nearby towns. Then browse through the crafts of more than 300 artisans. October. Thurmont. 301/271-4432.

😈 Autumn Foliage Festival. Arts and crafts, concerts, music contests, parades, antiques, and more. October. Oakland. 301/334-1948.

😈 Waterfowl Festival. A wonderful celebration of ducks and geese in photographs, paintings, sculpture, and other media. Music, entertainment, duck-calling contests, and more. November. Easton. 301/822-4606.

😈 Annapolis Boat Parade. A remarkable, colorful parade of more than seventy gaily decorated boats through the harbor, City Dock, creeks, and river in this old port city. The Saturday evening before Christmas. 301/268-TOUR.

😈 NEW JERSEY

For current schedules and more information: State Division of Travel and Tourism, CN-286, Trenton, NJ 08625. 609/292-2470.
The best in festivals:

😈 Victorian Week. A celebration of Victoriana and tours of the historic and lovely inns in Cape May. February and March. 609/884-5508.

😈 Tulip Festival. Admire the more than 60,000 blooming tulips as Cape May celebrates spring with garden and house tours, music, and entertainers. Late April. 609/884-8504.

😈 Victorian Homes Tour. Tour twenty-five private homes in Cape May. Late June. 609/884-8628.

😈 Victorian Week. Tours, antiques, music, entertainment, and crafts in Cape May. October. 609/885-5508.

❦ Christmas in Cape May. A month-long celebration with music, tours, plays, antiques, and more. December. 609/884-5508.

❦ NORTH CAROLINA

For current schedules and more information: Travel and Tourism Division, 430 North Salisbury Street, Raleigh, NC 27611. 800/VISIT NC.
The best in festivals:

❦ World Gee Haw Whimmy Diddle Competition. This contest has to be heard to be believed. Second Friday and Saturday in May. Asheville. 704/298-7928.

❦ Gliding Spectacular. Hang-gliding contests for all skill levels. Even if you don't hang glide, the event is a colorful sight. Second weekend in May. Nags Head. 919/441-4124.

❦ Rogallo Kite Festival. Named after a NASA engineer who invented the hang glider, this festival attracts some of the most unusual and colorful kites in the nation. Nags Head. 919/441-4124.

❦ Southern Highland Handicraft Guild Fair. More than 100 southern artisans exhibit and demonstrate their crafts. Other attractions include food and entertainment. July and October. Asheville. 704/298-7928.

❦ Mountain Dance and Folk Festival. Lovers of fiddles, banjoes, and clog dancing shouldn't miss this festival on the first weekend in August. Asheville. 704/258-5200.

❦ Waterfowl Weekend. Waterfowl are celebrated in photographs, paintings, carvings, and other works of art. Late September. Nags Head. 919/261-2626.

❦ PENNSYLVANIA

For current schedules and more information: Pennsylvania Travel Bureau of Development, Department of Commerce, 416 Forum Building, Harrisburg, PA 17120. 800/VISIT PA.
The best in festivals:

❦ Philadelphia Mummers' Parade. Famous minstrels parade on Broad Street for eight hours on New Year's Day. 800/VISIT PA.

❦ Chocolate Festival. This festival celebrates the town's main product. February. Hershey. 717/534-3005 or 800/533-3131.

❦ Philadelphia Flower Show. One of the best of the spring festivals. Mid-March at the Civic Center. 215/568-6599.

❦ Phipps Conservatory Flower Show. Spring, fall, and Christmas shows. Schenley Park, Pittsburgh. 412/255-2375.

❦ Pennsylvania Crafts Fair. Crafts demonstrations and sales in the courtyard of the beautiful Brandywine River Museum from late April to early September. Chadds Ford. 215/388-7601.

❦ Bach Festival. An outstanding musical event performed by the Bach Choir and famous artists at Packer Memorial Church, Lehigh University, in mid-May. Bethlehem. 215/866-4382.

❦ Mary Packer Cummings Weekend. A celebration of the benefactress of the town of Jim Thorpe, at the Harry Packer Mansion. Arts, crafts, entertainment, and more. May. Jim Thorpe. 717/325-3229.

❦ Gettysburg Bluegrass Festival. Marathon of approximately eighteen bluegrass bands and stage shows. Workshops for amateurs. Early May. Gettysburg. 717/642-8749.

❦ Philadelphia Open House. Tours in various neighborhoods of more than 150 private homes, gardens, historic homes, and buildings. Many tours include lunch, candlelight dinners, or high teas. Early May. 215/928-1188 or 215/597-7919.

❦ Mercer Folk Fest. Artisans demonstrate eighteenth- and nineteenth-century crafts methods. Quilting bee, folk music, dancing, and performances by a colonial militia camped on the grounds. Mid-May. Doylestown. 215/345-0210.

❦ National Pike Festival. The nation's longest festival—eighty-nine miles of activities—honors the historic National Pike (U.S. 40). Festivities include the Pioneer Wagon Train, historic sites, crafts, and food at almost every town on the Pike in Pennsylvania and Maryland. Third weekend in May. 412/439-5610.

❦ Devon Horse Show. One of America's leading equestrian events. Country fair and antique carriage marathon. The ten-day show starts on Memorial Day. Devon. 215/964-0550.

❦ Brandywine River Museum Antique Show. The museum's galleries are transformed into lovely room settings by more than thirty Americana antique dealers. End of May. Chadds Ford. 215/388-7601.

🐝 Three Rivers Arts Festival. Music, theater, dance, mime performances, and a display of art at several locations in Pittsburgh, including Point State Park, where the Ohio, Monongahela, and Allegheny rivers converge. June. 412/261-7040.

🐝 Pocono Laurel Blossom Festival. The blossoming of Pennsylvania's state flower is celebrated with arts and crafts festivals, entertainment, and train rides. Mid-June. Jim Thorpe. 717/325-3673.

🐝 Old Bedford Village Craft Festival. A juried arts and crafts show in late June. Bedford. 412/623-1156.

🐝 Civil War Heritage Days. There are many events to see, including a re-creation of an army encampment, lectures by historians, a Civil War collectors show, a period concert, a festival, and a parade. Late June to early July. Gettysburg. 717/334-6274.

🐝 Pennsylvania Dutch Folk Festival. This festival of the culture, food, and pageantry of the Plain and Fancy Dutch has been going on for more than forty years. Late June to early July. Kutztown. 215/683-8707.

🐝 Pennsylvania Renaissance Faire. A festival of medieval games, music, foods, roaming groups of costumed actors, Shakespearean plays, a jousting tournament, and much more at Mt. Hope Estate and Winery. It runs from the first weekend in July to the first weekend in October. Mannheim. 717/665/7021.

🐝 Bedford Springs Festival for the Performing Arts. Excellent concerts, ballet, films, poetry, and art here from early July to mid-August, at a historic Victorian hotel. Bedford. 814/623-9001 after June 15.

🐝 Musikfest. A feast of music and food in a historic eighteenth century Moravian city. Classical, regional, and German music; shows; strolling musicians; and mimes. Late August. Bethlehem. 215/861-0678.

🐝 Ligonier Highland Games and Gathering of the Clans of Scotland. A Scottish fair held on Labor Day features sports, bagpipe bands, fiddling, dancing, spinning and weaving demonstrations, and a genealogy booth. Altoona. 412/238-3666.

🐝 "The Crossing". Reenactment of Washington's crossing of the Delaware River Christmas night in 1776. December 25. Washington Crossing Historical Park (Bucks County). 215/493-4076.

❦ VIRGINIA

For current schedules and more information: Virginia Division of Tourism, 202 North 9th Street, Suite 500, Richmond, VA 23219. 804/786-4484; and the Virginia Travel Council, 7415 Brook Road, P.O. Box 15067, Richmond, VA 23227. 804/266-0444.

The best in festivals:

❦ George Washington's Birthday Celebrations. Parades, plays, street actors, special ceremonies, and more in Alexandria and nearby Mount Vernon. February. 703/549-0205.

❦ Historic Garden Week. This statewide celebration includes tours of historic sites, homes, gardens, and more. Late April. 804/644-7776.

❦ Crozet Crafts Festival. A craft fair that is often overlooked, but it has some of the state's finest artisans. Great music and dancing, too! Early May. Crozet. 804/293-6789.

❦ Wildflower Symposium. A national gathering of wildflower lovers and experts at Wintergreen resort. May. 804/325-2200.

❦ Spring Sampler. Craft demonstrations, art exhibits, and folk music. Abingdon. Memorial Day weekend. 703/628-8141.

❦ Heritage Festival. More than 300 contestants, using everything from inner tubes on up, compete in the Great Rappahannock River Raft Race. Other activities include music, food, games, and crafts. July 4th weekend. Fredericksburg. 703/373-1776.

❦ Virginia's Scottish Games. Athletic contests, Highland music, dancing, food, and exhibits. Late July. Alexandria. 703/549-0205.

❦ Virginia Highland Festival. Handicrafts, plays, music, and house tours. Early August. Abingdon. 703/628-8141.

❦ Publick Times and Fair Days. A colonial fair and market with crafts, auctions, and a military encampment in Williamsburg. Labor Day weekend. 802/229-1000.

❦ Christmas in Williamsburg. A month-long celebration of the holidays with special exhibits, entertainment, and more in Colonial Williamsburg. Mid-December through early January. 804/229-1000.

❦ Scottish Christmas Walk. A celebration of Alexandria's Scottish origins. First weekend in December. 703/549-0205.

❦ Christmas Open House Tour. See some of the historic homes in Richmond's Fan District and Church Hill. December. 804/782-2777.

❦ WASHINGTON, DC

For complete schedules and information: Washington Convention and Visitors' Association, 1575 I Street NW, Suite 250, Washington, DC 20005. 202/789-7000.

The best in festivals:

❦ National Capital Cherry Blossom Festival. A week-long series of events that starts with the lighting of the 300-year-old Japanese stone lantern at the Tidal Basin and concludes with a three-hour parade. 202/789-7000.

❦ White House Spring Garden Tour. The grounds and gardens of the executive mansion are open for tours in mid-April. 202/456-7041.

❦ Georgetown House Tour. More than a dozen private residences are open for tours during this April tradition. 202/338-1796.

❦ Georgetown Garden Tour. Thirteen private gardens are open to tours in mid-April. 202/333-6896.

❦ Embassy Tours. Tour a half-dozen elegant embassies. April/May. 202/636-4225, ext. 223.

❦ Washington Craft Show. The Interior Department's fine celebration of arts and crafts. 202/789-7000.

❦ Festival of American Folklife. Sponsored by the Smithsonian Institution and the National Park Service, this is one of the finest folk celebrations in the country. June or July. 202/426-6700.

❦ Pageant of Peace. The National Christmas Tree and nightly entertainment on the Ellipse just across from the White House. Late December. 202/456-7041.

❦ Festival of Lights. A fairyland of lights, nightly carolling, and more at the Mormon Temple in Kensington, MD., just outside Washington. 301/587-0144.

(See Alexandria festival listings under the Virginia heading.)

❦ WEST VIRGINIA

For complete schedules and more information: Travel Development Program, Department of Commerce, State Capitol, 1900 Washington Street East, Charleston, WV 25305. 800/CALL WVA.

The best in festivals:

❦ House and Garden Tour. Visit some of the historic homes and gardens in Charles Town, Harpers Ferry, Martinsburg, and Shepherdstown. April. 304/876-2242.

❦ Mountain Heritage Arts and Crafts Festival. More than 200 artisans demonstrate their crafts and sell their works. Music, food, and other entertainment. Harpers Ferry. 304/725-2055.

❦ Augusta Heritage Arts Festival. A celebration of the arts and music of mountain people. Music, crafts, food, and storytellers. Mid-July to mid-August. Elkins. 304/636-1903.

Chapter Twelve

Travel Tips

Travel can be wonderful, exhilarating, and fun. It also can be difficult and tiring, even when everything goes as planned. There are shortcuts you can take and plans you can make to avoid these pitfalls and to ensure that your weekend is more romantic.

Add a Little Romance

With a little planning, you can surprise your traveling companion with some wonderfully romantic touches.

For example, you can call the innkeeper where you are staying and have some special flowers, chocolates, wine, or champagne delivered to your room. If the innkeeper cannot help make the arrangements, FTD florists can arrange for flower deliveries, and some national chocolatiers can ship a box to the innkeeper to be held for your arrival. Pack a bottle of wine or champagne in your case and just ask the innkeeper for a bucket, ice, and two glasses.

A smaller touch, but one that is no less romantic, is to bring along a special card that expresses your love. When you can, tuck it inside his or her night things or prop it on a pillow.

You also can pack a surprise for a mid-afternoon bite or a before-bed snack. Fill a cooler or picnic basket with a bottle of champagne, wine, or waters; some cheese; pâté; fruit; crackers; and perhaps something sweet: cookies or chocolates. Bring along appropriate glasses, napkins, and serving implements.

Always Make Reservations

The best restaurants and most romantic inns often turn away customers. Be sure the two of you are not disappointed by making your inn reservation as far ahead as possible. Dinner reservations, with few exceptions, can be made the week ahead.

The inns often require a minimum stay—two nights on most weekends, three nights on holiday weekends. If this doesn't suit your travel plans, go in the off-season, when you may be able to negotiate a stay of one night.

Better yet, take your "weekend" in the middle of the week if you can, when most inns and restaurants are not filled.

Packing

We should be the last couple to give advice on packing, for we always take more clothes than we require, yet manage to leave at home the one item—a shawl for chilly nights, a swimsuit for an unexpected pool—we really need.

The dress codes in almost all of the restaurants we have described here are not dressy, with the few exceptions of the resorts and the dining spots in the big cities. Casual elegance is the rule: jacket for a man, tie optional, and a dress or suit for a woman. The more rustic spots—mountain lodges, ranches, and farms—are totally casual. At the Greenbrier, the Homestead, and the Williamsburg Inn, black tie is optional.

Plan appropriately, and then go ahead and do what we do: overpack.

The Inn Life

Staying at an inn or bed and breakfast requires some adjustments. For example:

❦ Not every room in an inn or B&B has a private bathroom. If you must have one, make sure there is one in the room you reserve.

❦ While most inns offer plenty of privacy, they may have thin walls and floors that hamper your romantic mood. If silence is a must, consider the bigger inns or small hotels. This sound-sensitivity works the other way: leave your big stereo radios and tape decks at home. They will not be appreciated.

❦ Breakfasts at the inns range from simple continental snacks—roll or croissant, juice, and coffee—to diet-busting feasts. The bad news is that often the meal is served during only a short period in the morning. If you rise late or must leave early, inform the innkeeper so he or she can arrange something for you before or after the serving hour.

❦ If the inn has rooms in more than one building, ask for a room in the house in which the owner lives. Almost without exception, the rooms in that building are better than those in the other structures.

The scores of inns we have described here are special, and that means they often will not have a room for a last-minute traveler. So what can you do? Three things:

❦ Ask the innkeeper for a recommendation. This has resulted in our getting a room in an inn that is just as elegant as the one that turned us away.

❦ Ask the visitors' bureau for advice. Many keep track of where rooms are available during the busier periods. They can tell you which inns still have rooms. This saves time and long-distance calls.

❦ Call one of the inn associations, which usually represent inns of similar quality in a small region. These have helped us find many new inns. The associations to call:

Bed & Breakfast of Philadelphia Listings in the city and in Montgomery, Bucks, and Chester counties of Pennsylvania. P.O. Box 630, Chester Springs, PA 19425. 215/827-9650.

Bed and Breakfast of Delaware Listings in the state and nearby counties of Pennsylvania. 3650 Silverside Road, Wilmington, DE 19810. 302/479-9500.

Bed and Breakfast of New Jersey Listings in the state and through the country. 103 Godwin Avenue, Suite 132, Midland Park, NJ 07432. 201/444-7409.

Bensonhouse Listings in Richmond's historic district and Williamsburg. P.O. Box 15131, Richmond, VA 23227. 804/648-7560.

Blue Ridge Bed and Breakfast Farms and inns in the mountain region of Pennsylvania, Maryland, Virginia, and West Virginia. Rocks & Rills, Rt. 2, Box 3895, Berryville, VA 22611. 703/955-1246.

Great Inns of America Some of the finest inns we have visited, and all with equally good restaurants. P.O. Box 2003, Annapolis, MD 21404. 800/533-INNS.

Guesthouses Bed & Breakfast, Inc., of Charlottesville Listings in Jefferson's country. P.O. Box 5737, Charlottesville, VA 22905. 804/979-8327.

Guesthouses Accommodations in elegant homes and mansions in Pennsylvania and other areas of the Mid-Atlantic. They can even put you up on a yacht. RD 9, West Chester, PA 19380. 215/692-4575 noon to 4.

The Traveller in Maryland Accommodations in inns, homes, and on yachts throughout the state. P.O. Box 2277, Annapolis, MD 21404. 301/269-6232. (From Washington, DC, 261-2233.)

There's Something About a Train

Most of the trips outlined in this book are meant to be made by auto. However, we recommend that you take the train if you are traveling to the major cities or the Williamsburg, Homestead, or Greenbrier resorts.

The major cities can be a nightmare if you are not accustomed to heavy traffic and parking shortages. Why spoil your visit by spending much of your time in traffic or looking for a parking spot? The parking lots in Washington and Philadelphia can cost as much as $12 for one hour. That pays for a lot of cabs and subway fares.

In the resorts you have no need for a car. And the only time you would need a car during a visit to Williamsburg is if you also wanted to visit some of the plantations and other attractions outside the colonial district.

If you need a final argument, try this: trains are fun.

Amtrak's trains can take you to these destinations:

❦ Williamsburg—The **Colonial** travels from New York through Philadelphia, Baltimore, Washington, Richmond, and Williamsburg on its way to Virginia Beach.

❦ The Four Cities—The **Virginia** connects New York and Richmond, with stops in Baltimore, Washington, and Philadelphia.

❦ The Resorts—The **Cardinal** connects New York and Chicago. In between it stops in Philadelphia, Baltimore, Washington, Charlottesville, Covington (where the Homestead will pick you up), and White Sulphur Springs (across the street from the Greenbrier).

For more information about Amtrak schedules, tour and hotel packages, and fares, call 800/USA-RAIL.

Index

A

Academy House, 39
Academy of Music, 126
Adamstown, 9
Agecroft Hall, 128
Aldie, 10
Alexandria, Va., 133
American Playwrights' Theater, 133
American Zephyr Train, 74
Amish Country Central Market, 9
Amish Homestead, 8
Amish Country, 8
Amish Farm and House, 8
Amtrak, 204
Annapolis Marketplace, 35
Annapolis Yacht Club, 35
Annapolis, Md., 34
Annapolis City Dock, 35
Annapolis Government House, 36
Annenberg Center, 126
Arena Stage, 133
Arthur M. Sackler Gallery, 131
Arts, Crafts and Antiques Weekends,
 85

Ash Lawn-Highland, 11
Asheville, N.C., 13
Asheville Art Museum, 13
Assateague Island National Seashore,
 55

B

Ballooning, 184
Baltimore, Md., 122
 Federal Hill, 122
 Fell's Point, 122
 Little Italy, 122
 Mt. Vernon Place, 123
Baltimore Museum of Art, 122
Baltimore Convention Center and
 Festival Hall, 123
Banner Elk, N.C., 14
Barbara Fritchie House, 2
Barnaby House, 39
Barns-Brinton House, 7
Benjamin Stevens House, 40
Bethesda, Md., 133
Biltmore, 13
Blowing Rock, N.C., 14

Boone, N.C. 14
Brandywine River Museum, 7
Brandywine Battlefield Park, 7
Brandywine Valley, 5
Brunswick, Md., 3
Buck-Bacchus Store Museum, 37
Bucks County Peddler's Village, 4
Bucks County, 3
　Delaware Canal, 5
　Font Hill, 4
Bucks County Playhouse, 4
Bucks County Tourist Commission, 5
Bullitt House, 40
Busch Gardens, 158
Buxton Woods Nature Trail, 58

C

Canoeing and Kayaking, 187
Cape May Migratory Bird Refuge, 53
Cape May, N.J., 52
Cape Hatteras Lighthouse, 58
Cape Henlopen State Park, 55
Cape Hatteras National Seashore, 58
Cape May State Park, 53
Cape May-Lewes Ferry, 54
Cape May Welcome Center, 53
Capital Centre, 133
Carpenters' Hall, 125
Catoctin Mountain Park, Md., 3
Charlottesville, 10
Chase-Lloyd House, 36
Chesapeake Bay Maritime Museum,
　38
Chester County Historic Society, 7
Chestertown Chamber of Commerce,
　37
Chestertown Historical Society House,
　37,
Chestertown Customs House, 36
Chestertown, Md., 36
Chincoteague, Va., 55
　Toms Cove Visitor Center, 55
Christ Church Burial Ground, 125
Christmas Weekends, 77
Chrysler Museum, 151
Colburn Mineral Museum, 13
Cold Spring Village, 53

Colonial Williamsburg, 148
　Historic sites, 149
Corcoran Gallery of Art, 131
Crozet Arts & Crafts Festival, 11
Cunningham Falls State Park, Md., 3

D

Delaware River Valley, Pa., 3
Delaware Art Museum, 7
Delaware Seashore State Park, 55
Doylestown, Pa., 4
Drama Weekends, 78
Duck, N.C., 59
Dumbarton Oaks, 132

E

Eastern Neck Wildlife Refuge, Md., 37
Easton Waterfowl Festival, 40
Easton, Md., 40
Easton Historical Society of Talbot
　County, 40
Eleutherian Mills, 6
Embassies:
　Canada, 134
　France, 134
　Switzerland, 134
　The Netherlands, 134
　West Germany, 134
Emlen Physick Estate, 53
Emmitsburg, Md., 3
Ephrata Cloister, 9

F

Farms:
　Barley Sheaf Farm, 162
　Beaver Creek, 162
　Brenneman Farm Bed and Breakfast,
　　162
　Caledonia Farm, 164
　Hickory Hill, 166
　Ingleside, 164
　L'Auberge Provencale, 165
　Maplewood Farm, 161 and 163
　Meadow Spring Farm, 163
　Nolt Farm, 163
　Pleasant Grove Farm, 163

Prospect Hill, 166
Shenandoah Valley Farm and Inn, 165
Stonebrake Cottage, 166
Sweetwater Farm, 163
Whitehall Inn, 163
Festivals, 191
Folger Shakespeare Library, 131
Folger Theater, 133
Folk Art Center, 13
Food and Wine Weekends, 83
Ford's Theatre, 133
Foxley Hall, 40
Franklin Court, 125
Frederick Everedy Square and Shab Row, 2
Frederick Crafts Fair, 2
Frederick Visitor Information Center, 2
Frederick Schifferstadt Architectural Museum, 2
Frederick, Md., 2
Frederick County, Md., 2
Fredericksburg, Va., 12
Visitor's Center, 12
Freer Gallery of Art, 131

G

Garden Weekends, 79
Golf and Tennis Resorts, 189
Grymes Building, 40

H

Hagley Museum, 6
Hammond-Harwood House, 36
Hang Gliding, 185
Harborplace, 122
Hatteras, N.C., 58
Health & Fitness Weekends, 78
Higbee's Beach, 53
Hillsboro, 10
Hillwood, 131
Hirshhorn Museum and Sculpture Garden, 131
Historic Society of Frederick, 2
History Weekends, 86
Hopewell Village, 7
Horseback Riding, 188

Hotels, Inns and Resorts:
Abbey, 62
Admiral Fell Inn, 140
Annapolis Hilton, 44
Ark and Dove, 44
Ashby Inn, 29
Atlantic Hotel, 68 and 75
Atop the Bellevue, 141
Auburn Hill, 27
Bed and Board at Tran Crossing, 19 and 115
Bedford Springs Hotel, 84
Berkeley Hotel, 143
Berkley Center Country Inn, 68
Betsy's Bed and Breakfast, 140
Biking Inn-to-Inn, 80
Black Bass Hotel, 22
Bluebird on the Mountain, 172
Boar's Head Inn, 27, 97 and 113
Brampton, 46
Bright Morning, 80
Buttonwood Farm, 21
Cameron Estate Inn, 24, 117 and 161
Captain Mey's Inn, 62
Carrington Row Inn, 143
Casselman Inn, 172
Castle at Mt. Savage, 172
Cataloochee Ranch, 173
Catlin-Abbott House, 143
Chalfonte, 62, 72, 75, 83, 84, 85, 87
Chanceford Hall, 67
Channel Bass Inn, 67 and 83
Charles Inn, 44
Cheat Mountain Club, 181
Cheat River Lodge, 181
Chesapeake House, 159
Cole House, 46
Commonwealth Park Suites Hotel, 143
Conyers House, 177
Coolfont, 78
Corner Cupboard Inn, 65
Cornerstone, 21
David Finney Inn, 21
Delancey Place, 141
Donegal Mills Plantation, 24, 117 and 161
Duke of Windsor Inn, 62

Hotels, Inns and Resorts (*cont.*)
Eagles Mere Inn, 174
1876 House, 49
Esmerelda Inn, 31
Everymay-on-the-Delaware, 22
Fairville Inn, 21 and 117
Flint Street Inns, 31
Four Seasons, 144
Fryemont Inn, 173
General Sutter Inn, 24, 117 and 161
General Lewis Inn, 181
Gibson Hall Inn, 29 and 114
Gideon Ridge Inn, 174
Glades Pike Inn, 174
Gladstone Inn, 65
Golden Pheasant Inn, 23
Governor Calvert House, 44
Grant House Bed and Breakfast, 175
Graves Mountain Lodge, 178
Great Oak Manor, 46
Green Park Inn, 174
Greenbrier, 90
Greystone Inn, 173
Grove Park Inn, 31, 97 and 167
Guest Yachts, 82
Guesthouses & Boxwood Tours, 72,
    79, 81 and 86
Hambleton Inn, 48
Hamorton House, 21 and 117
Harry Packer Mansion, 73 and 77
Hay-Adams, 144
Heritage Guest House, 175
Hidden Valley, 99
High Meadows, 113
Hill's Inn, 46
Hilltop House, 182
Hollilief, 23
Homestead, 92
Hotel Du Pont, 21
Hotel Hershey, 98
Hound Ears Club, 31 and 168
Imperial Hotel, 46
Indian Rock Hill, 23
Inn at Buckeystown, 19 and 116
Inn at Fordhook Farm, 119
Inn at Gristmill Square, 178
Inn at Little Washington, 27 and 112
Inn at Meadowbrook (Pa.-, 176

Inn at Mitchell House, 82
Inn at Narrow Passage, 178
Inn at Perry Cabin, 48
Inn at Phillips Mill, 23 and 119
Inn at Starlight Lake, 176
Inner Harbor Bed and Breakfast, 140
Jefferson Sheraton Hotel, 143
Jefferson, 145
John S. McDaniel House, 49
Jordan Hollow Farm, 81
Joseph Ambler Inn, 23
Kalorama Guest Houses, 145
Kemp House Inn, 48
Kenmore Inn, 30
Kent Manor Inn, 46
L'Auberge Provencale, 29
Lantern Inn, 46
Laurel Brigade Inn, 2 and 114
Linden Row Hotel, 143
Little Traveler Inn, 67
Log House at Battle Hill, 21 and 118
Logan, 23
Lord Proprietors' Inn, 87
Mainstay Inn, 62
Martha Washington Inn, 178
Maryland Inn, 44
Mayhurst Inn, 27
McGrath House, 30
Meadowbrook Inn (N.C.), 174
Meander Inn at Penny Lane Farm,
    179
Mercersburg Inn, 24
Mill House, 26
Mill House, 118
Miss Molly's, 67
Monument Avenue Houses, 143
Morrison House, 145
Morrison-Clark Inn, 145
Mountain Lake Hotel, 169
Nethercott Inn, 176
New Market, 141
Nicola, 27
North Bend, 156
Old Reynolds Mansion, 31
Orkney Springs, 85
Orlando Jones House, 156
Outer Banks Bed and Breakfast, 68
Overlook Inn, 176

Parsonage Inn, 48
Pelham Inn, 141
Peter Hays Kitchen, 156
Pickering Bend, 21
Pine Knob Inn, 176
Pineapple Hill, 23 and 119
Piney Grove, 156
Pleasant Inn, 65
Poor Richard's Inn, 62
Prospect Hill, 28
Pump House Inn, 177
Queen Victoria, 62 and 77
Radcliffe Cross, 47
Ragged Garden Inn, 31
Raleigh Tavern, 156
Red Rocker Inn, 31
Red Fox Inn, 29 and 114
Reynolds Tavern, 44
Richard Johnson Inn, 30
Ritz-Carlton, 145
River House, 78
Robert Johnson House, 44
Robert Morris Inn, 49
Rolph's Wharf, 47
Rose Hill Farm, 79
Roundtop, 26
Sanderling Inn, 69
Scarborough Inn, 69
1740 House, 119
Seventh Sister Guest House, 64
Sheldon's Ordinary, 156
Sheraton Society Hill, 142
Sheraton-Carlton, 145
Shirley-Madison Inn, 140
Silver Thatch Inn, 28 and 113
Snow Hill Inn, 68
Society Hill Hotels (Baltimore), 73
    and 140
Society Hill Hotel (Philadelphia), 142
St. Michaels Inn, 48
Statehouse Inn, 44
Sterling Inn, 81 and 177
Strawberry Inn, 20 and 116
Sugartree Inn, 179
Summer House, 20 and 116
Sunset Inn, 159
Sweetwater Farms, 118
Sycamore Hill House, 179

Tabard Inn, 145
Tattersall Inn, 23
Tembo Guest House, 65
Three Hills Inn, 180
Tides Inn, 100
Tidewater Inn, 50
Towers, 65, 74 and 84
Tradewinds, 142
Trillium House, 180
Turning Point Inn, 20 and 116
200 South Street, 28, 74 and 113
Victorian Rose, 64
Vine Cottage Inn, 180
War Hill, 156
Wedgwood Inn, 87 and 120
White Swan Tavern, 47
Widow Brown's Inn, 23
Wiffy Bog Farm, 177
Wilberham Mansion, 64
Willard-Intercontinental, 145
Williamsburg Inn, 79, 85, 86, 95 and
    156
Williamsburg Cottage, 157
Windsor Inn, 29 and 114
Wintergreen, 101 and 170
Witmer's Tavern, 26
Year of the Horse Inn, 67
Hugh Mercer Apothecary Shop, 12
Hunt Country, Va., 10
Hunt Country Stables Tour, 10
Hynson-Ringgold House, 36

I

Independence National Historic Park,
    125
Independence Hall, 125
Inn-Keeping Seminars, 87
Inns, see Hotels, Inns and Resorts

J

Jamestown, 151
Jamestown Festival Park, 151
Jefferson's Country, 10
Jockey's Ridge State Park, 57
John Chad House, 7
Joseph Meyerhoff Symphony Hall, 123

K

Kennedy Center, 133
Kitty Hawk, N.C., 59
Kutztown Antique & Collectors
    Outdoor Extravaganza, 9

L

Lambertville Porkyard, 4
Lambertville, N.J., 4
Leeming's Run Botanical Gardens, 53
Leesburg, 10
Liberty Bell Pavilion, 125
Lincoln, 10
Lititz, Pa., 159
Longwood Gardens, 6
Lyric Opera House, 123

M

Manteo, N.C., 59
Maymont, 128
McGuffey Arts Center, 11
Mercer Museum, 4
Michener Art Center, 5
Mid-Atlantic Center for the Arts, 52
Middleburg, Va., 10
Monticello, 11
Montpelier, 11
Moravian Pottery and Tile Works, 4
Morris Arboretum, 126
Morris Mechanic Theater, 123
Morven Park, 10
Mt. Vernon, 133
Mummers Museum, 125
Murder Mysteries, 71
Museum and White House of the
    Confederacy, 128
Museum of Glass, 53
Music Weekends, 84
Mystic Clipper, 83

N

Nags Head, N.C., 59
National Museum of Women in the
    Arts, 131
National Portrait Gallery, 131
National Museum of American Art, 131
National Museum of African Art, 131
National Gallery of Art, 131
National Aquarium, 122
National Theatre, 133
Naval Historic Museum, 35
Naval Academy, 35
Nemours Mansion and Gardens, 6
New Castle, Del., 7
New Market, Md., 3
New Hope, Pa., 3
Newtown, Pa., 5
Norman Rockwell Museum, 125

O

Ocracoke, N.C., 57
Old Slave Block, 12
On the Water Weekends, 82
Outer Banks, N.C., 57
Oxford Museum, 39
Oxford Customs House, 39
Oxford, Md., 39
Oxford-Bellevue Ferry, 39

P

Peabody Conservatory of Music, 123
Pennsbury Manor, Pa., 5
Pennsylvania Horticultural Society, 126
Pennsylvania Dutch Convention and
    Visitors Bureau, Amish Country
Philadelphia Art Alliance, 125
Philadelphia Museum of Art, 125
Philadelphia, Pa., 124
  Congress Hall, 125
  Old City Hall, 125
  Rittenhouse Square, 126
  Rodin Museum, 125
  Society Hall, 125
  South Street, 126
  The Bourse, 126
  University Museum of Archeology
    and Anthropology, 126
Phillips Collection, 132
Piedmont Vineyards and Winery, 108
  Willowcroft Farm Vineyards,
Plantations, 108
  Elk Run Vineyards, 109
  Loew Vineyards, 109

Plantations along the James River, 152–154

R

Rafting, 186
Reading Terminal Market, 126
Rehoboth Art League, 54
Rehoboth Beach, Del., 54
Remington Farms, Md., 37
Renwick Gallery, 131
Resorts, see Hotels, Inns and Resorts
Restaurants:
Accomac Inn, 26
Admiral Fell Inn, 140
Alexander's, 64
Alouette, 142
Ashby Inn, 30, 165 and 178
Astral Plane, 142
Atlantic Hotel, 68
Aux Beaux Champs, 146
Back Porch (Ocracoke), 69
Back Porch Cafe (Rehoboth Beach), 66
Bavarian Inn, 166
Bayberry Inn, 64
Beachway, 68
Belmont Kitchen, 146
Bistro, 173
Black Bass Hotel, 120
Blue Moon, 66
Brass Elephant, 141
Buckley's Tavern, 119
Bull Alley, 28
Bushwaller's, 20 and 116
C&O Restaurant, 28 and 114
Cafe Normandie, 44
Cafe des Artistes, 141
Café René, 69
Camel's Hump, 66
Cameron Estate Inn, 26 and 118
Carrol's Creek Cafe, 44
Carversville Inn, 164
Centre Bridge Inn, 23 and 120
Chadds Ford Inn, 119
Chambers, 50
Channel Bass Inn, 68
Chart House, 44

Cheat River Inn, 181
Chesapeake House, 159
Chez la Mer, 66
Chimney's Tavern, 31
Christina Campbell's Tavern, 157
City Tavern, 142
City Cafe, 146
Colligan's Stockton Inn, 164
Copper Mine, 102 and 179
Country House at Kimberton, 22
Crate Cafe, 45
Cuttalossa Inn, 164
Danny's, 141
Dar es Salam, 146
David Finney Inn, 22
DeMimmo, 141
Di Francesco's, 20 and 117
Dilworthtown Inn, 119
Dover West, 50
Ecco, 142
Fin, Fur, Feather Inn, 47
Flying Cloud, 144
Friday, Saturday and Sunday, 142
Froggy Dog, 69
Garden Terrace, 102
Garden, 174
General Sutter Inn, 26, 118 and 161
Gianni's, 141
Golden Pheasant Inn, 23 and 120
Green Park Inn, 32
Griffins, 45
Groff's Farm, 26, 118 and 161
Grove Park Inn, 32
Hampton House, 45
Harbor Lights, 66
Harry Browne's Restaurant, 45
Hausner's, 141
Hemingway's, 47
Homestead, 180
Hotel Du Pont, 22
Hotel Strasburg, 178
Hound Ears Club, 32
Imperial Hotel, 47
Inn at Buckeystown, 20 and 116
Inn at Historic Yellow Springs, 22
Inn at Little Washington, 165
Inn at Oley, 26
Inn at Perry Cabin, 49

Restaurants (*cont.*)
Inn at Phillips Mill, 23 and 120
Irish Eyes, 66
Iron Gate Inn, 146
Ivy Inn, 28 and 115
Jason's, 45
Jockey Club, 146
Josiah Chowning's Tavern, 157
Kenmore Inn, 31
Kent Manor Inn, 47
King's Arm Tavern, 157
Kitty Knight House, 48
Knave of Hearts, 142
L'Auberge Provencale, 30 and 165
La Bonne Auberge, 164
La Camargue, 142
La Gallerie, 28 and 115
La Petite Auberge (Va.), 31
La Petite France, 144
La Toque, 64
La Truffe, 143
La Petite Auberge (Pa.), 26
Lafayette, 158
Lautrec, 143
Le Snail, 29 and 115
Le Yaca, 158
Le Chardon d'Or, 146
Le Lion d'Or, 146
Le Bec Fin, 143
Lemaire, 144
Lemon Tree Inn, 26 and 118
Longfellows, 49
Mad Batter, 65
Marmaduke's Pub, 45
Martingham Harbourtowne Inn, 49
McGarvey's Saloon, 45
Mercersburg Inn, 27 and 162
Meskerem's, 146
Middletown Tavern, 45
Miller's Waterfront Restaurant, 70
Mitchie Tavern, 28 and 115
Mosby's Tavern, 30 and 115
New River Inn, 32
O'Leary's Seafood, 45
Odet's, 164
Old Mill, 28 and 115
Old Mudd Tavern, 31
Old Ebbitt Grill, 147

Old Angler's Inn, 147
Old Wharf Inn, 48
Old Original Bookbinder's, 142
Peach Blossom, 50
Pier Street, 49
Ragged Garden Inn, 32
Red Fox Tavern, 30 and 115
Reynolds Tavern, 45
Rio Grande, 147
River Inn, 48
Robert Morris Inn, 49
Rock Hall Inn, 48
Rodes Farm Inn, 102 and 179
Ryah House, 177
Sam Snead's Tavern, 180
Sam Miller's Warehouse, 144
Sanderling Inn, 70
1763 Inn, 30 and 165
1789, 147
Shields Taverns, 157
Sign of the Sorrel Horse, 24 and 120
Silk Purse, 22
Silver Thatch Inn, 29 and 115
Smokey Pig, 144
Smythe's Cottage, 31
St. Michaels Inn, 49
Sydney's Side Street and Blues Place, 66
Tabard Inn, 147
The Occidental, 147
The Narrows, 48
Tidewater Inn, 50
Tilghman Inn, 49
Tobacco Company, 144
Towne Hall, 22
Treaty of Paris, 45
Trellis, 157
Trillium House, 102
Turning Point Inn, 20 and 116
219, 147
Upper Black Eddy Inn, 24
Vicker's Tavern, 24
Vincenzo, 147
Voilá, 20
Walking Treaty Inn, 24
Washington Inn, 65
Washington Street Pub, 50
Weeping Radish, 70

Williamsburg Inn, 157
Windsor House, 30 and 115
Wycombe Inn, 164
Yellow Brick Bank, 166
Richmond, Va., 125
Shockoe Slip, 128
Main Street Station, 128
Rising Sun Tavern, 12
Roanoke Island, N.C., 59
Rock Hall, Md., 37
Rockwood Museum, 7
Ruckersville Antiques, 11

S

Sailing Schools, 41, 188
Sailing (cruise ships), 188
Ski Resorts, 190
Soaring, 185
Source Theater, 133
Sports Weekends, 80
St. Mary's Square Museum, 38
St. Michaels, Md., 37
St. Peter's Village, Pa., 7
Studio Theater, 133
Sugarloaf Mountain, Md., 3
Swiss Pines Park, 7

T

Talbot Country Women's Club, 40
Talbot County Courthouse, 40
Tangier Island, Va., 158
Ferries, 159
The Grapevine House, 39
The Forrest Theater, 127
The Oatlands, 10
Third Haven Friends Meeting House, 40
Thomas Perrin House, 40
Tilghman, Md., 39
Todd House, 125
Tomb of the Unknown Soldier of the American Revolution, 125

U

University of Virginia, 11
Upperville, 10

V

Valentine Museum, 127
Victoriana Weekends, 75
Vineyards, 107, 110
Vineyards, 107
Dominion Wine Cellars, 107
Meredyth Vineyards, 107
Peace Valley Winery, 110
Virginia House, 128
Virginia Museum of Fine Arts, 127

W

Walnut Street Theater, 127
Walters Art Gallery, 122
Warner Wildflower Sanctuary, 40
Washington, D.C., 130
Adams Morgan, 132
Capitol Hill, 132
Georgetown, 132
Old Post Office, 132
Union Station, 122
Washington Square, 125
Waterford, 10
West Chester, Pa., 7
Wheaton Village, 53
William Paca House, 36
Wilmington & Western Railroad, 8
Wilton, 128
Wineries:
In Maryland—
Berrywine Plantations, 108
Catoctin Vineyards, 108
Elk Run Vineyards, 109
Loew Vineyards, 109
In Pennsylvania:
Allegro Vineyards, 109
Buckingham Valley Vineyards, 110
Bucks County Vineyards, 109
Chaddsford Winery, 109
Mt. Hope Winery & Estate, 109
Peace Valley Winery, 110
In Virginia:
Barboursville Plantation, 106
Dominion Wine Cellars, 107
Meredyth Vineyards, 107
Montdomaine Cellars, 106
Oakencroft Vineyards, 105

Wineries (*cont.*)
  Piedmont Vineyards and Winery, 108
  Prince Michel, 107
  Willowcroft Farm Vineyards, 108
Winterthur, 6
Wolf Trap Farm Park, 133

Y

Yorktown Victory Center, 152
Yorktown Battlefield, 151
Yorktown, 151